JIMMY BOYLE

A SENSE OF FREEDOM

THE BEST SELLING CLASSIC OF GANGS, PRISON AND REDEMPTION

EBURY
PRESS

1 3 5 7 9 10 8 6 4 2

Ebury Press, an imprint of Ebury Publishing
20 Vauxhall Bridge Road
London SW1V 2SA

Ebury Press is part of the Penguin Random House group of companies
whose addresses can be found at global.penguinrandomhouse.com

Penguin
Random House
UK

This edition published by Ebury Press in 2016
First published in the 1977 by Canongate Publishing Ltd and Pan Books Ltd

www.eburypublishing.co.uk

A CIP catalogue record for this book is available from the British Library

ISBN 9781785033032

Typeset in India by Thomson Digital Pvt Ltd, Noida, Delhi

Printed and bound in Great Britain by Clays Ltd, St Ives PLC

Foreword

By Irvine Welsh

A *Sense of Freedom* was published back in the heady seventies. Now, that decade is seen to represent the last days of the crumbling, optimistic post-war consensus, where an aspiration to democracy and universalism over elitist privilege still abounded. It was the last time our society held dear a belief that positively altering the environment within which an individual operated would lead to desirable changes in the behaviour of the person concerned.

This book, the story of Jimmy Boyle's transformation from violent gangster and convict to acclaimed artist, caused a big stir in Scotland and beyond on its original publication. Some of it was positive, some of it not so much. Jimmy became a leading light in Barlinnie Prison's Special Unit, a political football of a rehabilitation project, which set out to help some of Scotland's most violent prisoners find a route back into mainstream society. Jimmy, and one or two others, stood out from the pack with their articulate understanding of the process they were going through and their willingness to engage in it fully, and also in their fight to shape it so they could own it, in order that the change (as it must for any individual) could take place on their own terms.

Much of the negative reaction to the book, and the Special Unit itself, was centred on a very immature understanding of this process. A lot of the hostility was directed against Jimmy personally, for committing perhaps his biggest crime in the eyes of society: that of being working class but also charismatic and articulate. In some ways this reaction exposed Scotland as a timid, vicious parochial backwater, this sponsored by the sheepishness of a political and administrative class who very much took their cues from the most reactionary elements of their ruling counterparts in the UK.

So there was a lot of very silly talk from people who ought to have known better and some who probably did but still felt compelled to execute their roles as mouthpieces for the ring-pieces. Therefore much of the tabloid-led "debate" centred on how working-class kids wanted to be Jimmy Boyle, the gangster. Consequently, there was very little discussion on how others (like myself) were inspired by his journey into becoming artists. For an angry but creative soul growing up in a working-class environment, role models are essential, and during my youth Jimmy was a ubiquitous cultural figure. When I was a kid, nobody from my street and scheme, to my knowledge, had written a book or made an acclaimed piece of art. Yet there was scant discussion on how inspirational it was for someone like myself, as a somewhat lost youth (basically, like all of them), to see a person from a background I could identify with, doing just this. And far more than that, somebody who had been effectively buried by the system, fashioning the tools of their own resurrection through their art.

My Muirhouse of the seventies was quite a bit different to Jimmy's Gorbals in the sixties. It was a peripheral housing scheme on the outskirts of town, designed to facilitate the displacement of people from those tenement inner-city areas, in my case Leith, through what was called "the slum clearance" programme. Whereas Jimmy's generation of youth had to endure lively, bustling slums and obvious teeming squalor, so close to the tempting riches of the city centre and the "snobbier" areas, mine battled with boredom in soulless concrete outposts, then devoid of the social facilities essential to communities. In such circumstances, the streets, and the influence of peer groups, were always around to provide the kind of excitement that poorly paid low-status employment couldn't hope to match.

But what was also around in those days, and has since gone, is the escape hatch of education. Yet, while you had the one-pound evening classes and free university education, with full grants for working-class students, the cultural barriers to the taking of this route were still considerable. This was what "snobby" people did. *They* made art. *They* wrote books. That wasn't for the likes of *us*. Then along comes Jimmy Boyle, Gorbals gang leader and Britain's most violent and notorious prisoner, with his art and his book *A Sense of Freedom*. It was a cultural game changer. Permission granted.

On his release, Jimmy still had his battles to fight, and they ensured that he'd remain at the forefront of popular consciousness in Scottish society. Though grateful to those who put themselves out to assist him, he was wisely reluctant to get involved with cynical authorities in an establishment that would alternately denigrate and then tout him as a poster boy for rehabilitation, as the changing winds of political opportunism dictated.

Instead, he wisely concentrated on consolidating and expanding the reputation he had established in prison as an internationally renowned sculptor, and giving back to deprived youth by working with passion and diligence on Edinburgh's innovative Gateway project, which he'd helped found. This drug counselling and rehabilitation organisation was way ahead of its time, using the staples of art and music to help troubled kids understand themselves and the world they lived in.

It was, and probably remains, very difficult for the less progressive elements in Scottish society to embrace Jimmy Boyle. His refocusing of his energies into art and trying to encourage others to do the same was often calculatingly and malignly marginalised by the press, with a constant regurgitation of lurid stories of his past. People believed in the accuracy and objectivity of the press much more back then. Now, in the social media era, most of those stories would be ridiculed as that of Glasgow drunks half-remembering – or concocting – a Boyle anecdote for a few pints dispensed from the account of the tabloid hack. It's not as if if Jimmy Boyle lacked candour about his violent past: it's all in this book. But underlying this spiteful desire to see him fail sat a malign ideology: if such a high-profile "rehabilitated" individual fell by the wayside, then this established that there was no point wasting time and money on diverting resources into these practices. Just make prison about punishment and containment: lock them up and forget them, and when they come out and reoffend, do it again.

The more I learned in life, the more I found out that Jimmy's journey, if highly dramatic and extreme, was actually very far from unique. I've personally met so many people down the years who, constrained by poverty, violence, depression, physical and sexual abuse, and in particular, drug addiction, have fashioned their own personal escape routes through art. One friend from my teens was never out of jail until, like Jimmy Boyle, he discovered sculpture, as well as painting and music. I have a good friend whom I first met in prison when I was doing a reading there. He had never read a novel before but loved my debut book, *Trainspotting*. The next time I saw him was in a Waterstones bookstore. He told me he had started an Access course at university, in order to gain entrance to a degree programme where he planned to study for an arts and social sciences degree. We've stayed in touch down the years through the various stages on his journey to where he is now: a professor of English Literature. When researching my novel, *Crime*, I met a woman who had been a prostitute and drug addict, and is now regarded as an international authority on working with sexual abuse survivors. I'm now working with a guy from my old stamping ground of Muirhouse, who was once a chronic heroin addict, but liberated himself from this through discovering his talent as a filmmaker. But these are the exceptions rather than the rule: individuals fortunate enough to have strong support networks, and/or in spite of all the adversity in front of them, an indomitable sense of self. For most people in disadvantaged situations, this is not the typical experience. With our prisons now bursting at the seams, despite the brave efforts of many staff (and I've seen these at first hand), containment is the main name of the game with rehabilitation pretty much an afterthought.

As a species we are increasingly struggling to survive in the environment we've created. Our behaviour is a product of that struggle. The obvious answer is to divert our resources into improving our environments and therefore broadening our choices. This message, in the age of austerity, is now more subversive than ever, but even more crucial. Jimmy Boyle's story in *A Sense of Freedom* will hopefully encourage a new generation of working-class kids to put art before criminality: the complete reverse of economic policy in the UK, which does the opposite by concentrating on channelling wealth to the already rich.

Since Jimmy published *A Sense of Freedom*, the post-war gains of the working class have all but been eradicated. Full employment, comprehensive education, fees and grants paid by the state have gone, the NHS is following, replaced by elitism and privilege, and with austerity economics designed to lower pay and conditions to Third World levels permanently in place. In this current neoliberal order, working-class kids no longer view education as a legitimate means of social mobility. Ironically, the more enterprising ones often see the route out through drug dealing and other criminal activities, heralding a return to the post-war deprivation and limited options that spawned Jimmy's own gangsterism. In this era, a failing capitalism means that the option of work for young working-class (and now also middle-class) people has been essentially replaced by the choice of creative expression versus the drug trade. In a sane world this should be no choice at all. However, our economy and society are set up around the maintenance of entrenched privilege at all costs, rather than equity and sanity. And, as they say in America: "bitch gotta eat".

Jimmy Boyle's own personal journey is long complete. He's now been an artist much longer than he's been a convict or a gangster, and these days his ferocity is channelled into his intellectual and creative pursuits. To this end, he is indistinguishable from any other successful artist from a working-class background. A practitioner of the admirable philosophy of "living well is the best revenge", he now enjoys an elegant and luxurious lifestyle in the south of France and Morocco. A great treat in going to the Cannes Film Festival is that I get to hang out with this cultured, bookish man who loves good food and wine, movies, politics and conversation. It's a life far removed not just from the impoverished circumstances he grew up in, but also, ironically, from the grubby bedsit jakeyism of many of the redundant tabloid sleazebags who once hounded him.

As a piece of writing, the book is a remarkable document, in that it captures the excitement and awe of a man growing up in public. It has all the dynamism of the outsider's critique, with the self-educated writer's penchant for the adjective-laden dramatic line, delivered with a natural raconteur's caustic wit. The most difficult autobiographical line is walked in this book: it has the gift of being highly personal, yet also able to stand outside the subject matter of the self and look inwards with a forensic clarity. To get to that point, the writer has to journey to desperate places and fight those no-holds-barred battles with their greatest opponents, all those sabotaging, redundant voices of former selves. *A Sense of Freedom* often reads like a novel, stylistically influenced by Dostoyevsky's *Crime and Punishment*; it is a book that resonantly chimes with Jimmy's sensibilities as he starts to try and make sense of his life.

A Sense of Freedom lays down a challenge to individuals in disadvantaged and perilous circumstances: channel your energy into pursuits that will break your chains rather than simply forge new ones. It's a challenge that is as liberating and inspiring as ever. Its message to a society that is now more economically and socially broken than at any time since the war, and which faces the impending detonation of fiscal, demographic and environmental time bombs, is an even more provocative one. It asks us to acknowledge that this zoo, which we're building around ourselves, no longer meets our needs as members of this species. Instead of turning it into a monstrous prison, we should be making it into a massive playground.

Irvine Welsh
2016

Introduction and Dedication

Writing this book has been a difficult and very painful experience as it has meant not only opening my own thoughts and experiences to the reader, but revealing a private and personal part of my family life. This includes my mother, children, brothers and other relatives, all of whom are hard working, decent people, and most of whom have never had any trouble with the police. These are what I would call the invisible victims of the offender and the offence.

The issues raised in the book are not peculiar to the city of Glasgow, but are part of a very serious worldwide pattern that is escalating to an alarming degree. From a personal viewpoint, the salient and most alarming factor is that the age of the person involving him or herself in crime is getting younger and the offence more serious.

I entered this world with the innocence of every child; had dreams of being a fireman, train driver, superman, along with the fantasies that are part of childhood. What went wrong? I do hope that laying open my thoughts and experiences as I felt them at the time will make a positive contribution to a better understanding of the problem. Personal experience has led me to believe that the pattern of my own life in crime is analogous to the vast majority involved in it.

In anticipating any criticism and debate that may arise as a result of the contents of this book, I would like to make it clear that my position is such, unlike that of other authors, that I won't be able to take part in them, though I would dearly love to. It is not meant as a deliberate or calculated indictment on any particular section of society; that would be too simplistic a view. It would be nearer the truth to say that the book is an indictment on the whole of society, and I have no hesitation in placing myself amongst that number.

In writing the book in a manner that expresses all the hatred and rage that I felt at the time of the experiences, especially the latter part, I have been told that I lose the sympathy of the reader and that this isn't wise for someone who is still owned by the State and dependent on the authorities for a parole date. The book is a genuine attempt to warn young people that there is nothing glamorous about getting involved in crime and violence. I feel that the only way any real progress can be made in this direction is through having a better understanding of it and the only way this will be achieved is by putting our cards on the table, and this I've tried hard to do. I don't feel that sympathy or popularity contests have anything to do with it.

It is appropriate that the proceeds from this book should go to the issue that it is highlighting. I have asked that my royalties should be used to set up a trust fund to help kids in the socially deprived areas in the west of Scotland. So anyone who buys this book will be making a contribution.

There are a number of people that I owe my survival to, and many that have reached out and touched me. I won't name them as they know who they are. It is to them that I am tempted to dedicate this book, but won't. Instead, I dedicate it to my two children, not only because I am their father, but more importantly, because they are symbols of the future. A future that is in *our* hands.

Jimmy Boyle
Special Unit, Barlinnie
1976

PART ONE

PART ONE

1

I don't think it's good enough for me to say that I was born in the Gorbals, in May 1944, and leave it at that. Perhaps it's all I can say, but who am I? I don't really know who I am. The one thing I am certain of is the womb I came from. And if it were possible for one to choose the womb that one was conceived in, then this is the one I'd have chosen. My mother, Bessie, was in many ways too good for this world, and the more I got to know the world the more I believed this.

When I was born my mother already had two sons, Tommy and Pat – aged four and eight respectively. My father's name was Tommy. From birth to the age of five my memories are vague snatches of a complete family living in a room-and-kitchen in an old Gorbals tenement building. Throughout this period certain memories remained with me that were connected with the physical and spiritual feeling of the house, such as the big coal fire that was always burning in the kitchen, which was a very small room though it managed to hold the table where everyone ate; the cooker, some furniture, and my parents' bed which sat in a recess. The kitchen was where most things were done, and everyone would sit around the fireplace talking. The fireplace played a principal role in our home as it did in most homes in the district. My father would stand in front of it with his hands behind his back, and this is one of the few memories I have of him. On a Saturday night my mother would get the tin bath out from under the bed and fill it with water to bathe all three of us, one after the other. This was a time I always disliked. Saturday was also the night that my parents' friends and relatives would come up to our house with "carry-outs" to drink and have a party.

We would be put to bed in the small room while the adults sang songs and danced, but once they started getting mellow with the booze we would get out of bed and mix with them, asking them for money while they were in this happy frame of mind. Parties and people being what they are they would either finish in a fight, or with everyone embracing each other.

The room of our house was where we three boys slept. There was a fireplace in the room but it was rarely used as we couldn't afford it; there were also other pieces of furniture, including a large wardrobe that held the whole family's clothes. Our bed was in a recess with Pat and Tommy sleeping at the top of it and me at their feet to give us more room. I think sleeping with Pat was a good preparation for the tough life ahead because he was the worst sleeper in the world. All through the night he would nip me with his fingers if I moved near his part of the bed, and he would do this instinctively at the slightest infringement onto his area. Other times he would kick, and being the youngest, I had to accept it, though at the time I always resented it and wanted a bed of my own.

Sunday morning was always the essence of family life in our house as Mother would get us all up and made ready for chapel, which was at the corner of our road, Sandyfaulds Street. Mother took us all down, giving us a ha'penny each for the collection plate. Leaving chapel was a great occasion as everyone used to eye everyone else up to see what they were wearing, and to see who was there. If anyone had a new suit or new clothes of some kind then they always wore them to chapel. People stopped and talked in the street after mass to gossip, and there was a very close community feeling at such times. From there, Pat, my eldest brother, was sent to the nearby newsagents to buy the Sunday newspapers – no *News of the World* permitted. Mother, Tommy and I returned to the house where she began the breakfast. The Sunday breakfast surpassed all others, as it was ham, eggs, black pudding and potato scones. This was a ritual repeated throughout the district in most homes on a Sunday morning. While Mother was preparing this

Tommy would be breaking sticks for the fire, while I was grudgingly getting coal from the bunker, which meant that I had to wash my hands for the second time that morning. By the time the fire got going, breakfast would be ready so we would all sit around the table and wire in. I can't remember my father sitting down with us but somehow I imagine he got his breakfast in bed as my mother seemed that sort of woman. Immediately after the meal Mother would clean up and prepare for the Sunday dinner, which usually took her the rest of the morning and afternoon, while we kids went down the streets to play.

The Gorbals was full of old tenement buildings three storeys high, each floor containing three houses. Two of the houses were one-room-and-kitchen, the other in the centre was a single end (one room). The toilet was on the stairway, shared by the three families on each landing. The door of these toilets usually had no locks, which meant that the user had to sit on the seat with one hand holding the door so that none of the neighbours would come rushing to use it only to find someone sitting there – a common occurrence. The toilets were always in a terrible state, which meant that during the daylight hours one could sit doing the toilet with a view onto the backcourts and see what was going on there. This was okay so long as the wind wasn't blowing.

The backcourts and streets were our playgrounds, the backcourts in particular playing a significant part in the Gorbals sub-culture. In these backs there were old washhouses – brick shelters – which, like most things in the district, had fallen into disrepair and were no longer used for the purpose for which they were built. However, they did make ideal gang huts. The backs had at one time been sectioned off, so much space to so many houses, but the metal railings and stone dykes that had acted as partitions were now either completely obliterated, or had large gaps torn in them so that the inhabitants could use the gaps as a passageway. This meant that there were two routes to a destination: through the backs, or by the street. People in a hurry took the back way as it was quicker, but it was more dangerous, and I don't mean in a criminal sense but in an environmental one, as the back-courts always had large puddles of black muddy water that one would have to navigate. There would always be one adventurer who would create a passage over the large puddle for those using this route. Improvisation was at its best then, as bricks from the nearby torn dykes would be dotted across the muddy water so that the traveller could step from brick to brick and make a safe journey. With practice one became adept at this and in fact the backcourt route became a busy thoroughfare. The middens were another characteristic of these backs. They were brick shelters with four bins for the householders to put rubbish in. These middens were nicknamed "midgies". There was a distinction between the midgies in our own backs to the ones in the "toffy" backs which we called "lucky didgies". The reason they acquired this name was due to a Gorbals "industry" of searching middens in the middle-class areas for anything they threw out that could be used or sold.

Middle- or upper-class people were "toffs" and sometimes disposed of articles that were of good quality, with damaged parts that were repairable, children's toys in particular. Groups of us, usually with the arse torn out of our trousers, snot running from our noses and filthy, would head for Queens Park, a "toffy" district, to rake the lucky didgies. These people were so toffy that they had even locked doors in their closes to prevent strangers getting into their backcourts! When a group of us went out midgie raking there was always an agreement to share any "lucks" found. We would overcome the locks on the close doors by going up the stairs to the first landing, opening the window, climbing out and dropping the fifteen feet or so to the ground. From there we would climb the iron railing or stone dyke to the neighbouring midgie, and repeat this till we struck gold or were chased by the householders, who were disgusted to find scruffs such as us polluting their midgies. It was amazing what we found: toys the like of which we had never seen. Anything which could be used was like gold to us, although we never restricted ourselves just to toys. But I am digressing from our backs in the Gorbals.

While "Ma" was making the Sunday dinner all the kids would be playing in the backs and there were various favourite games. Up to the age of five, my pals and I would get lumps of wood and sail them in the muddy puddles and play at boats, using stones to throw at each other's boats if the game happened to be war-ships. We would also get spoons and dig holes in the ground, not building castles or anything in particular but just digging hole after hole, and I guess this was why the backs were all muddy and full of puddles.

One kid from the next close to me added to the attraction of digging holes as he would swallow all the worms we found. When he was around we would all dig like little Navvies and give them to him. All of us would gather round as he would drag it out and make it a big deal before taking the worm in his mouth and chewing it up. He had a very bad burn mark on his face which was a source of ridicule, and he was rejected by most of us until we discovered his appetite for worms. When it got back to his mother she would be on the lookout, and catching sight of her son surrounded by us all looking, open-mouthed, while he dropped a big "blood-sucker" into his mouth, she would scream at the top of her voice and come charging downstairs, but by that time we would have made off. The kids in my brother Tommy's age group would always be lighting fires in the backs at night. Everyone would go off to collect fuel for the fire, finding toilet-doors or floor-boards from empty houses. On the whole the kids immediately older than us would reject us as they felt they were men, though in reality they were aged eight to ten.

The midgies held one of the other favourite pastimes of the dark, and that was rat-catching. The Gorbals was full of rats and they were a feature of the place and could be seen often on the stairways as one went up to the house at night. They were in many of the houses, but the backcourts were full of them and in particular the midgies. The first rule of rat-catching was, if you wore long trousers, to tuck the bottoms into your socks in case the scampering rats ran up your trouser-leg, as there were lots of rumours of this having happened. It would start with a couple of kids going to the midgie where rats would be foraging amongst the rubbish for food. One kid would pull the bin out and this would panic the rats into rushing out. The rest of us would be waiting to hit them with whatever weapon we happened to have, or with our boots. As the group went from midgie to midgie we grew in number, which meant that before long a large group of kids was going from back to back, some carrying dead rats on the ends of sticks. There were times when this group would have a maximum crowd and that was when a mongrel dog called Laddie was with them. This dog was a sort of legend in the Gorbals and in fact went on to win Corporation medals for the number of rats it had killed. No one really owned it and it used to wander the district. It had a place of pride amongst the locals, yet most of them were scared to let it lick them because of the rats it had killed. When Laddie was out rat-catching it was a pleasure to see him in action. He would catch one rat, throw it in the air snapping its neck and, without stopping to see if it was dead, run and kill the next. We would go into all the midgies and old washhouses but the supply of rats was inexhaustible and the ones that the kids killed had no effect whatsoever in improving the situation. The rats were just like everyone else, fighting for survival. It was a common sight to see big cats, sitting on hot ashes that had been thrown out, while rats, some as big as the cats, moved around the cats almost as though they didn't exist. As one used the back route at night-time the squeak of fighting rats was a familiar sound.

Another backcourt game was dyke jumping. This was a game where kids would jump over a large gap, from one part of the dyke to another, the height from the ground being considerable. It was a prestige game and in many ways very dangerous; inevitably there were a lot of accidents, sometimes resulting in broken limbs, but this game was usually reserved for the older kids of about nine or ten. Most streets had a good jumper so there was plenty of competition between kids.

There was also the "Bogie", which was a plank of wood with two halves of a roller skate nailed to each end and a wooden apple box nailed on top which we leaned on so that we could push it up and down the street. Usually one "Bogie" was owned by a handful of kids, so it was a case of shots each. The streets were always busy with a multitude of kids playing street-games, and we would play until the early hours of the morning. The Gorbals streets had their own warm blend of character that was very comforting to the locals. In most cases the conditions were that of gross deprivation with buildings that were crumbling around them, but in a funny sort of way the closeness of the community compensated for the material deficiencies. The women of the district would either lean out of their windows or, if the weather was good, take chairs down to the streets to sit and gossip about anything and anyone. I remember when I was about four my ma called me over to a group of neighbours sitting and standing around the close-front saying, "Let Cathy hear you speak proper", and I, all blushing and trying to hide behind my ma, would finally be persuaded to say "My name is James", and they would all have a good laugh. Everyone was very familiar with each other and we kids were out and in each other's houses as though they were our own. There was a tremendous community spirit about the Gorbals people and this extended to all things fortunate and unfortunate that occurred in our lives.

Although the architectural structure of the old buildings may have encouraged a sort of closeness, I think the dominant factor for this unity was that everyone was in the same boat, and didn't have two pennies to rub together. The physical surroundings were bad, but that wasn't the fault of the inhabitants. Each householder did their bit to keep the place as clean as possible, taking turns to clean the stairs and if someone was sick then a neighbour would always do the sick person's turn. The houses were as clean as circumstances would allow. If someone in the street died, the neighbours would go round the street houses collecting money in a bedsheet to help the family meet the costs of the burial. Though people couldn't afford much they would usually try to contribute something. From the extreme circumstance of a death to the simple need of borrowing a cup of sugar, help was always at hand.

Sandyfaulds Street was a strange one as two cultures thrived within the one place. All the buildings were identical, but of the fifty or so close-mouths, three were different because the people in them were "toffs", and in a way there was a resentment even amongst the kids from our closes against those who stayed in them, to such an extent that we wouldn't even rake their midgies for "lucks". The exterior of their part of the building was no different from that of ours. The difference lay in the interior, as their windows were always beautiful with a fresh appearance about them, nice curtains, coloured glass, bright paint making the houses look very warm and cosy, like palaces. The close-mouth was always clean, with white chalk running up the sides and it smelled of fancy disinfectant when washed. It was really a sharp contrast from the houses in the rest of the street, though they weren't rich enough to have doors on their closes to prevent strangers getting into their back courts. The kids in these three closes kept together when playing and none of them ever played with us in the poorer closes. However, this didn't bother us as our parents called them "half-boiled toffs", and when clustered around the closes at night our mothers used to gossip about them, mimic their proper accents and laugh at them. None of the mothers from the toffs' closes ever stood around gossiping late into the night nor, for that matter, did they lean out of their windows to talk to each other; there seemed to be a hollowness about them. Their kids were always clean as new pennies with their hair combed neatly and their nice clothes, with stockings pulled up to the knees, a clear sign of a toff. Most of them were in the Boy Scouts or the Cubs and wore the uniforms. Even at this early age I remember feeling inferior to the lot that stayed in those closes, as though there was this strange feeling that they never really belonged in the district in the first place, and in fact most of them were waiting on the first chance to move out to a better area.

Another street game was catching "Hudgies". This meant jumping on to the tail of cars and lorries as they slowed to turn the corner and jumping off as they slowed down again to turn the corner at the top of the street. Those of us who were too young for this would hang on to the back of the much slower horses-and-carts that were on their way to the nearby stable. This was really great fun though usually the driver would get off and chase us up the road, if he was sober. If we were hungry I would go into the back and shout up to the kitchen window, asking my ma for a piece'n-jam (sandwich with jam in it) and if any of my pals were with me then they got one too. This shouting for a piece was a common occurrence throughout Glasgow. The same applied to meal times, if I happened to be playing with one of my pals and his mother shouted him into the house for his meal then usually I would be shouted in too. This happened with most families unless things were so bad that the food just wasn't there. There were various ways we kids would make cash, and one was to go for messages to the shops for neighbours for a few pence, or a couple of empty bottles that could be traded for cash. There were certain neighbours that were favourites to go messages for, simply because they gave the really good "bungs". Another way of making cash was to go round the doors in the nearby streets asking for empty beer bottles. The best day for this was a Monday, after the regular weekend parties. We would get tu'pence on the return of each bottle so it was profitable, particularly if the boozing had been heavy. The times when the competition was thickest were at the Glasgow Fair, and the New Year. Then we would take bags or large sacks and go round the doors filling them up as early as possible before the others got there. Some of the publicans put a special stamp on the labels of their beer bottles and would only take their own back, so there were all sorts of moves afoot to tear the labels where the stamp should have been or improvisations to fake a stamp.

Hallowe'en was another favourite time as we would all get done up, the favourite make-up being soot from the chimney, and hundreds of little Al Jolsons would be seen going around. We would turn our jackets inside out or put our shirts on back to front and crash into pubs to sing for money. The older kids would get us younger ones to do it, take the cash and get us some sweets. At this early age we were almost professional beggars: we would stop strangers in the street, act very distressed, and say we had lost our car-fare home. More often than not they would give it to us, though some people would offer to take us home and that was a sign for taking off. Most of us had relatives who were very fond of us – a favourite aunt or uncle – who would give us a few pence when we went to their houses. Usually they stayed at the other end of the district or out of it altogether, so we didn't go up too often or a good thing would be spoiled.

When I was four my ma had another baby, a boy, and he was named Harry. I can't remember it too clearly but do recall being told, no doubt after constant enquiry, that he was found in a cabbage patch and that was the only explanation I was given as to how he came to be in the house. At the age of five I started school at St Francis' infants' school that was in our street, attached to the chapel. There are only a few memories of this, one being my first day when all of us kids were crying our eyes out and refusing to let our mothers leave. Most of my pals were in the same class though some of them went to the nearby Protestant school. But even all these familiar faces didn't stop us crying on that first day.

It was shortly after this that disaster struck our family and changed the whole pattern of our family lives, as we had known it. My father died in his late thirties. I've tried hard to remember him and shall describe the memories I have. He would stand in front of our kitchen fire with his back to it, and on one of these occasions I was in the tin bath in front of the fire on a Saturday night, and can vividly remember him kissing my ma. On another occasion I remember owning a massive racing car that he got me, but for some reason it was taken away and I was told it was away to the garage for repairs. That was the last I saw of it. Once he took my brother, Pat, into the room and leathered his arse with a slipper after catching him skipping into the Paragon picture house without paying. When he came out, leaving Pat in the room screaming, he told us we would get the same if we did anything wrong like that. I can always remember being taken to the motor cycle speedway racing by him and being bought a rosette – for some reason or other I connect this with Hampden football park. Just shortly before he died I came out of the infants' school at three o'clock and caught a hudgie on the back of a passing horse and cart. I was clinging to it quite happily as it headed in the direction of my close when I was kicked on the backside. It was my father who was with some pals and as I ran away they all laughed.

I can vividly recall waking up one morning and finding this man lying beside me covered in bandages like a mummy, with bloodstains seeping through the dressings. To this day I don't know if it was my father or one of his pals, but one thing I do know is that something terrible had happened the previous night with my father and his pal getting badly injured. I can remember on another occasion my father struggling violently to reach up to a shelf in the small lobby to get a parcel, but being restrained by others in the house, and somehow a vague recollection connects this parcel to a gun. These are the total memories I have of my father, though I did hear plenty about him in later years as he was much talked about and respected by the older men in the district and even the present day guys who knew him have a good word for him.

Usually in a criminal environment there are the cliques who are the good thieves and those who are the "heavies", the fighters. But in my father's time there was a particular clique who were thieves and heavies, and my father was one of these. They were good money getters, and in particular, safe-blowers. This was known in the district and respected in its own way. One memory that I have is getting a biscuit tin of "smash" – silver coins, florins, and half-crowns – from my father and his pals. The few of us shared it amongst ourselves. It probably came from a robbery that was particularly fruitful so that after sharing the paper money they would give the smash to the kids of the house they were in to divide amongst themselves. The incident when the injured man was in a mummified condition in our bed was, in fact, a notorious incident in the district that led to a series of shootings. A rival gang had waylaid my father and one of his pals in a dark, quiet lane in the next street to ours. They really worked them over and as a result they were taken to hospital, but on regaining consciousness they immediately signed themselves out, hence me finding one of them in our bed. The reason why this is all so vague is that the old folks didn't talk to us kids about such things, one only knew what one overheard or saw with one's own eyes.

I was kept off school the day my father was buried and a neighbour's son from my class at school was also kept off to keep me company. I distinctly remember kneeling at the coffin to say some prayers before he was taken away, and laughing with my pal simply because I didn't know what it was all about. Had I known what was ahead for me I'd have cried my heart out. I remember returning to school with my pal next day and telling the kids in my class that we had smuggled ourselves into the boot of the hearse and had gone to my father's burial. The truth was that I was never allowed to go to the graveyard, but somehow this fantasy stayed very strong within me and remains vividly clear to this day.

After my father died our lifestyle didn't immediately change much. All my father's friends came to see my ma and helped her in any way possible, but as time went on they got fewer and fewer, though many kept in touch. Those very close to Ma were my Aunt Peggy, my ma's sister, and my ma's pal, whom we called Aunt Maggie. It became apparent to Ma that she would have to get a job to keep the house and four boys going. This meant a change in our routines. She got a job cleaning tram cars, which meant that Pat, my eldest brother, took over the house-cleaning and chores, and Tommy gave him a hand. My job was to look after Harry, who was at Nursery by this time, so I had to collect him from there every day. Before we got used to this Ma had to give up the tram cleaning, and took a part-time job till eventually she worked from 5.30 a.m. till 8 a.m., which meant she was home to get us out to school, and from there go to a big house and clean it out. Lastly she went to a Jew's house from 4 p.m. till 9 p.m. to do cleaning, and help look after a senile old guy in the house while the rest of the family were at their businesses.

With Ma away most of the time we soon took to the streets and lived there all the time. I would collect Harry from the Nursery and supposedly take him home but we would wander all over the place or go to our Aunt Peggy's – she was very much a second Ma – and get something to eat. Sometimes we would go home but if we had been raking midgies, which was usually the case, and attempted to go into the house carrying all our "lucks" then Pat would have a fit and chase us for our lives. He would have spent hours getting the house spotless for Ma coming home and if we came in bringing loads of rubbish and dirtying the place then she would say he never cleaned it, so he was very possessive of the house. If he did let us in then he was very strict and would make us sit in the one chair and do nothing more energetic than read.

Most days Harry and I would stand at the close-mouth peering down the street to where the trams passed, and wait expectantly for the familiar figure of Ma, who would usually be carrying a message bag filled with food. The Jewish woman that Ma worked for was aware of our domestic situation and would give her any food that she had left over. Most of it was kosher, but it was all the same to us, and to this day I still have an affection for Jewish food, bagels, egg loafs, pickled herrings and so on. When we saw Ma's figure in the distance we would both run like the clappers towards her, passing the warm, comfortable windows of the three toffy closes. There were nights when it was as cold as ice but we would stand at the close-mouth waiting to see if Ma was coming, or if it was foggy, we would go down to the car stop and stand waiting. Then when she came, we would take the bag from her and carry it, all the time asking what was in it. She would ask us every night why we weren't waiting in the house and we would always put the mix in for Pat saying he wouldn't let us in. The truth was that Pat would, but he had this very effective habit of nipping us if we made one wrong move, so it was better staying out of it. Anyway the streets had a magnetic effect on us. The nightly ritual of getting into the house and around the fire while we unloaded Ma's bag of goodies was great, and while we did this she would make us a meal. Tommy, of course, was very much a street child and he would be out wandering the streets with his pals and doing the things that kids at his age did. Ma would be worn out by the time she got home and, instead of being able to sit down and put her feet up, would have to prepare our meal and then do all the washing up afterwards. We would do small bits here and there but only when told to, because on the whole we were not thinking at that age.

On a Saturday morning Harry and I would get up and go down to the Shan shop at the bottom of our street, and keep a place in the enormous queue, giving Ma time to visit shops to get the things she wanted there. The Shan shop was a Co-op store that sold fresh spoils sent over from the nearby Co-op Bakery and it was very popular as people would come from all over to get the cheap, fresh food. They gave out big bags of broken buns for a penny and we used to get someone at the front of the queue to get us a bag and we would do them all in while waiting our turn.

The local playing park for our part of the Gorbals was the Caledonia Road graveyard and this was the favourite playground on Saturdays when there was no school. It was a disused graveyard, nicknamed "gravey", but next door to it was one that was still being used. During the day and the nights when it was still daylight our parents would send us up to the "gravey" to play out of the road, so there would be lots of the kids from the district up there at any one time, even though one had to climb a wall about eight feet high to get in. We did this by stopping a passer-by and asking him for a lift up, which he usually gave. Once up we would sometimes throw clods of grass at the passers-by. We would play hide-and-seek amongst the gravestones, and there were times when the older kids would try toppling the taller stones over and we would all stand watching. There was this big funny hollow reed which grew up there and looked just like rhubarb: it always grew thickest around the graves and all of us used to eat it. To this day I haven't a clue as to what it was, but it can't have been bad anyway.

I remember we decided to build a Tarzan-type gang hut in one of the gravey trees and we went looking for tools. One of the guys knew where we could get swords and bayonets to help build our hut, so he took us to Commercial Lane behind Lawmoor Street police station. The idea was to get up to the open back window and put our hands in. On top of a locker were lots of weapons, that had been either confiscated or found. One of the kids would clasp his hands making a foothold for another to climb onto. The one on top would then feel about, to get whatever he could. The first trip went very smoothly and we stole two really good bayonets. We made our way back to the gravey to start building our hut all chuffed and excited, certainly not thinking of it as stealing, just good fun.

No one stayed in the gravey when it was dark. The "Fiddler" was the only one who did this. He was rumoured to be an old man who used to go into the graveyard to play his fiddle at his wife's grave each night, so before it got dark everyone would scamper. But first we would hide our bayonets in the next-door gravey amongst the flower pots – nothing was sacred. The Tarzan hut idea didn't last too long as one of the big boys building it fell off the tree and broke his leg. It so happened he was the best dyke jumper in the street. There was a terrific atmosphere in the gravey, it was like a jungle with lots of big weeds and plenty of cover for playing games and it was all free and easy with no adult interference. We could make-believe all we wanted and I had a personal subconscious way of identifying those that belonged there, by whether they had no arse in the seat of their trousers or patches. I don't know why this was but it's a memory that stays with me, just as I remember having a distrust for grown men who wore gloves – even in the middle of winter.

The best nights of the whole week in our district were Fridays and Saturdays at pub-closing time. It was a sort of occasion as all the women would be looking out of their windows for the pubs coming out. This was when all the fights took place and it was great fun watching them, the funny part being that there was hardly ever a policeman in sight at this time. One of the best fighters in our street was a guy called Big Ned and he was always fighting, although he didn't always win. He was always drunk on these nights and after a fight would stumble up the street with all of us kids following him, and when he got to the chip shop he would take us in and buy us bags of chips without paying the man for them, and this really delighted us because mostly when we hung around the chip shop door the same man would kick our arses and tell us to get away from his shop. We used to love it and always looked on it as an honour when Big Ned singled us out. We all idolised him. There would be occasions when Big Ned used to mess his opponents up very badly, and in some cases they were seriously hurt, but the following morning he would walk down the street and people who had seen the fight the previous night would chat away to him as though nothing had happened. In a sense this was socially acceptable and no one ever made a big deal over it.

On Friday nights the men came home from their work and went straight into the pub with their mates, as most of them had just been paid, and those who had no jobs were taken for a drink by their pals. The Gorbals must have had more pubs per head than any other district in Glasgow, as there was one at almost every corner. On Friday kids would be at the pub doors, sent there by their mothers to tell their fathers to come home with the wages before they drank most of them. There were occasions when wives went to the pubs to hunt down their men and rescue the income, but

on the whole this was considered an affront to the husband. Men
filthy from their work would be swilling down beer and spirits
like nobody's business. Large groups of men stood and sat at bars
talking, arguing and singing till nine o'clock when the last call was
made. All of us kids stood outside the pub door listening and looking in, and most of all taking in this man's world. At time up there
would be orders of "carry-outs" (drinks bought to take home) and
the men would stagger outside to the pavement with them, and
congregate there, reluctant to part company and go home.

Just prior to the last call, women in the houses overlooking any
pub would go to their windows to look out, and we kids would run
to the corner of Sandyfaulds Street and Rutherglen Road as that
was the most advantageous point giving us sight of seven pubs.
From there we would usually see where the action was taking place.
Extremities were the norm on such occasions as drunkards would
be on the pavement outside the pub doors, some with their arms
round each others' necks singing songs well out of tune, and alongside them would be two or three others rolling around the ground
in a drunken fight, in some cases with blood all over the place.

On one particular Friday night during the summer months
there were the usual crowds outside the pubs but we sensed trouble in the air. It was still daylight when two of the men, who were
well known in the district, started arguing. The next thing to happen was that one pulled out a revolver and shot the other in the
arm. The injured man ran away through a lane and we followed
him. For us it was a scene straight from a movie, seeing this guy
through drink and gunshot stagger along the road and up to his
house. We then ran back to the pub to find some of the other men
still leaning on each other singing drunken songs as if nothing had
happened. The guy with the gun had disappeared. This particular incident had an unreal quality about it for me. As shootings
weren't an everyday occurrence, I expected it to be a main talking
point, and to cause some local reaction but there was none. I even
began to think I had imagined it until years later, when I asked
the guy who was shot and he confirmed it. The message that came
home to me even at this early age, rightly or wrongly, was that
people talk or gossip about drunken and daft fights throughout

the week, but when two heavies like that fight then people leave it alone and mind their own business.

This was the highlight of our week, going to the pubs at closing time to watch the fights, and there is no doubt that everyone else enjoyed it too. The men, no matter how drunk, would be like homing pigeons and always find their way. Some would stagger up the street with arms outstretched, singing to their hearts' content, and the women hanging out their windows either encouraging them or shaking their heads and rolling their eyes at the drunken character making an ass of himself. From closing time onwards till the early hours of the morning, one would see steady streams of drunks wending their way home, and of course we endeavoured to cash in on this. We would approach them and ask for money, and would either get it or a mouthful of curses, but that was all in the game. There would be the regular characters returning from the boozers full to the gunnels, and one of those who stayed in our street and was looked on with great affection was a guy named Dan Noble. Every time he was drunk he would stagger up the street shouting at the top of his voice "D.N. Dan, my name's Dan, Dan Noble". Sometimes he would throw in that he didn't give a fuck for anybody, and Dan would start this cry from the minute he left the pub till he fell into bed. He would stagger up the middle of the street with the stray dogs following him, barking and adding to the din. Dan would take over the street and any passing cars would have to make way for him while occasionally one of the onlooking women would shout for him to go away to his bed. The best laugh was that when he was sober Dan was a quiet wee man who didn't bother a soul. The way people looked at it was that Dan, who was a widower, worked like hell all week to keep his family and this was his way of letting loose, and as he wasn't bothering anybody then good luck to him.

2

My family situation began to deteriorate and my father's absence began to be felt as Ma was beginning to find things very difficult – this would be in 1951 when I was seven years old. The authorities turned off the electricity as we couldn't pay the bill and things were bad all round as our relatives and neighbours were all feeling the pinch. St Francis Chapel had a poor box and I can remember me and my brother Tommy going to the Franciscan priest there to ask for money to pay for the light. They were usually very good at helping those in need but things were so bad that they had emptied their poor box giving the money to others. Instead they gave us two big candles to use in the house and we took them home. The image of us sitting around in the dark all feeling very sad isn't the impression I want to give here, as the truth was that to us kids living in candlelight was fun a lot of the time as we would use the darkness and shadows to make up games, though it must have been terribly difficult for my ma as she was working like hell and things were getting worse instead of better. One of the few luxuries she had was sending us down for a loose Woodbine. The shopkeeper would open a five-pack of Woodbines as they sold a lot of them in singles to people who couldn't afford to buy more.

When I was about eight I managed to get a job selling coal briquettes from a barrow and got five bob a week for it – including tips. Tommy also managed to get a few bob, selling fish from a barrow. We only worked on a Saturday when there was no school, but these few bob extra helped Ma and were added to the mere pittance that she got from her three part-time jobs. For clothes we would go to the State hand-out people that we called the Parish. I'm pretty vague about its official name but this is as I remember it. It was in the city centre and they used to give out big hairy suits and hairy underwear, but best of all, enormous tackety boots. I was constantly aware of a deep feeling of shame about going to the Parish as it was only the poorest that went there and the people in charge treated us like dirt. I remember that Ma would always get in a state at such times and to add to her embarrassment she knew we hated going because the clothes that one got there were their own stamps of identification as anyone could, at a glance, identify Parish clothes. However, once at the Parish we would play outside with the other kids who were there for the same reasons as us. The Parish was located on, or next to, a very steep hill, and this we loved for when we got our Parish boots on, the big tackety ones, we would go outside and slide down the pavement. One particular guy serving behind the counter was always on the lookout for this, so we would get the kids who had never been there before to go first so that the guy would come rushing out of the door and clip him on the ear then return to shout at our parents about it while we continued to slide. He would tell our parents that if this continued he would stop handing out the clothes and this would result in rare old arguments.

Amongst the kids at the Parish the atmosphere was great as we were all the same and knew it. Then we had to go home and I knew that my brothers felt as I did – inferior. There were lots of families in the district who got free clothing from the state but there was a great deal of teasing and taunting from the other kids about it, and the same went for "free dinners". This was set up for kids whose parents couldn't afford to pay for a meal or were dependent on the State for upkeep. Every Monday morning the teacher would call out the kids who were going to the dinner school for their meal and those who paid for it were called first to pay their moneys and get their tickets and then the teacher would call out the free tickets and the remainder of us would trail out.

In my class at school there was this kid who used to sit next to me and he was well dressed but a friend of mine. The point is we both shared the same desk and there was a strong smell of shit. Naturally all the fingers (those not holding noses) were pointed straight at me and my Parish clobber. There would be days when the smell was so strong that I would suspect the clothes of giving out the sour smell and I would race home, take them off and give the crutch of my pants a thorough sniffing. All kidding aside, I really did have a bad complex about this, until one day in the school playground, with the smell at its height, one beautifully observant kid pointed to the legs of my deskmate and there was the shit running down his wee legs and over the top of his stockings. Honestly I could have kissed him; I felt so happy as the burden of my own complexes vanished completely. When playtime was over the teacher ordered my deskmate to stand where he was and as we left he still stood there almost as though he was stuck to the corner as I bounced all the way to the classroom. I always wondered why the teacher hadn't tracked him down before. After this the poor guy was nicknamed "Smelly" and the name stuck with him for some time.

There was plenty of teacher power in the schools in those days with us not being allowed to speak unless spoken to. My teacher at St Francis was a very frightening female whom I never liked as she would beat the hell out of us at the slightest whim. She was a nice-looking woman too, but that side of it didn't interest us at that age. If you did something that she didn't like then she would get hold of us by the hair or the pullover and swing us about the class like an Irish navvy swinging a pick. There would be the occasional time when someone would threaten to bring up their Ma to her but that was the furthest it went. Although it was a working-class school there were kids in my class that I thought were toffs as they were always nicely dressed, and seemed to be the cleverest. Whenever Teacher asked a question theirs would be the first hands to shoot up and they would answer it immediately. They were a bunch of kids who always played together during the play interval and after school. I personally felt that I was very stupid at school, and mixed this with an overpowering feeling of inferiority due to my circumstances. At one time I wanted to be an altar boy (a child who serves the priest while he is serving the mass) in our chapel but this was at a time when our family circumstances were at their worst, economically and otherwise. Besides my boots, all I had was a big pair of wellies and altar boys needed sandshoes. But apart from this, for some reason or other, these toffy guys seemed to be the ones picked every time.

The reality of the educational side was that never at any time during my primary school attendance did I ever want to do well at my lessons for some very simple reasons. From Primary school there were two schools that the kids in my class could go to after the qualifying exams. One was St Bonaventure's (Bonny's), a junior Secondary, and the other was Holyrood, which we called the toffy school. Now my aim from the minute I went into the primary school was to attend Bonny's, as that was where my older brothers and other kids from my street had gone, so I had already made my mind up that this was where I was going. This meant that there was no incentive for me to go anywhere else and anyway going to Holyrood meant the expense of paying for a uniform so there was no way that this could happen. Therefore it would be Bonny's for me. Expenses aside, the dominating factor that made me always want to go there was that everyone in my street went to Bonny's. Bonny's was for our kind and I knew I'd be happier there. I can still remember the day when they read out the results of the qualification exams, with Smelly and I nearly crapping our breeks (no doubt he did) in case we passed with a high mark and were sent to Holyrood. So, idiots that we were, we rejoiced in failing the exams. If I had been honest then I would have had to admit to a certain feeling deep down of wanting to pass. The strange thing, or should I say obvious thing, was that there were no surprises at exams. Those that wanted to go to Bonny's went, and those that wanted Holyrood went, so on the whole we were superficially satisfied.

There is one thing that perhaps I should make clear here and that is that these kids that I call toffs were not really. It was just a fact that in this vast socially deprived area where poverty was rife, they were fortunate to have had fathers who had good paying jobs that could keep the family clothed reasonably well. The truth of the matter was that they also had next to nothing, but by our standards they seemed to have plenty and the way we judged them was on the way they were clothed, their behaviour and usually the money they had to spend. For instance, we, the scruffs, would take our play-piece into school and just before the bell rang for play-time we would stick the sandwich under our arses and heat it up as well as flattening it to make it look bigger. These other guys didn't do this sort of thing. Even within this class of scruffy kids there was this feeling of inferiority and discrimination that no outside observer would have noticed as there was never any open hostility amongst us; it was just that each kept to his own group as if by some natural instinct.

There was an instance when one of these toffy guys was knocked down by a car and a group of us were sent by the teacher to visit him while he lay in bed at home a few streets from us, in a house which was on a par with the toffy ones in my street. We sat around the bed looking at him like idiots with his father there. I asked for a drink of water and went to get one, but as I stuck my head under the tap and turned it on to drink straight from it, the father let out a loud scream and leapt from his chair as though someone had stuck a pin in his arse. He dragged me away from the tap as though it were about to suck me up and then proceeded to lecture me on the finer points of hygiene and the beasties that wait up taps to jump down the throats of people who drink straight from it. He then made me drink from a nice glass. This is the one thing that I really hated about these people, the way they tended to exaggerate everything to show that they were different. For the rest of the visit he gave us all school lessons, and I couldn't get out quick enough as it was almost as bad as school. The kid in the bed wasn't only suffering from the accident but from his father as well.

After school we would play all the street games of football, headers, kick the can, K.D.R.F. (Kick-door-run-fast). This game involved going to the third flat of a close and kicking every door on the way down with all the people opening the doors after you'd gone to see who was there. But some people were aware of the game so when they saw that it was K.D.R.F. they would run to the window with a pan of water and throw it over us as we came out of the close. We would go to districts away on the other side of Glasgow just walking as far as we could, sometimes getting lost, but always finding our way home. It was all great fun. On a winter's night there would always be some of us grouped round one of the sweet shop windows playing Guesses – this was to choose the name of a sweet and give the others the initial (i.e. C.B.? – Candy Balls) and we would pass hours playing this game. It didn't matter what time of night it was and every mother had the same problem, and that was getting us into the house as we always wanted to stay out, even though it was the early hours of the morning and there would be replies of "Aw Ma, just five minutes."

As bad as my circumstances were, I was always aware of others much worse off than me and I can mind a pal of mine with eleven of a family all staying in the one single room. With all of us we didn't say how crowded it was as we just lived that way, accepting it without question. The resignation to the conditions and the ignorance were probably the biggest sins of all.

The big day came when I was sent to my new school. It was a great feeling to be going to Bonny's as it made me feel all grown up to mix with lots of the tough guys in the district that we looked up to. New kids entering Bonny's were thrown over the walls by the older guys as an initiation ceremony. There were two walls, each about six feet in height, one of which had a drop of about fifteen feet, and the new kids were lifted up and thrown over them. Some kids would be thrown over the wall with the six-feet drop and others over the fifteen-feet drop, but it all depended on whether the older guys caught you nearer one or the other. Trust me to go over the higher of the two. I didn't hurt myself – the fear hurt more than anything. The older guys used to split us into groups and hold "dummy fights" and all of this was frightening. In a way this was when the age of innocence was lost. There seemed to me to be a more serious side to life now and going to Bonny's brought this out because in the school one was "judged" on one's fighting ability. Watching gang fights and drunks brawl was something that was fun and that we, as kids, played no part in; but now in Bonny's I felt very close to physical violence as there were lots of fights going on. This was far away from the atmosphere of the previous infants schools, where the feeling had been that neither you nor the school mattered as you were too young. Although from this early age I had helped steal bayonets from the police station, some fruit and chocolate from shops, we had not thought it really criminal. Certainly I was aware that it was wrong but there was a feeling that it didn't count then, much in the same category as catching hudgies and playing in the gravey, or raking midgies, most of which were frowned on but tolerated, simply because there was nothing else for us to do. I am certainly not for one moment suggesting that parents in the Gorbals condoned their kids in crime for that wasn't the case, in fact their part in the community probably kept down the number of crimes and accidents in the area. The sub-culture amongst the kids was such that the petty "crimes" mentioned were socially acceptable. Yes, their parents would give them a good thumping if caught, and yes, we would go out and do it again after the beating because not only was it something to do but there was no money.

One feature of the Gorbals sub-culture was that the men in the district who were put on pedestals by us, and in many ways idolised, were the likes of Dan Cronin. Although he was dead by the time I was six years old he remained very much alive locally, being almost a legend in the Gorbals for his fighting abilities. There was Danny O'Neil who ran the local "shebeen" – a place that sold illegal booze after pub hours – and Paddy Slowey who was by now replacing the legendary Dan Cronin as one of the great street fighters. There were times when other guys in the district would steal all sorts of gear and sell it to almost everyone at cheap prices, and these were just things that were a regular part of our lives. It wasn't a case of me thinking these men were bad for I didn't, never at any time, nor was it only the kids who looked up to them but a great many of the adults also. It was a great thing for us to see these men even if they were only standing about the street. We were always aware of their presence and would put on acts for them so that we would be noticed.

There was a guy in our street called Big Jim who was not one of our hero figures but typical of our district nevertheless. He would be fighting most weekends. In every sense his behaviour was a part of our lives and he would fight nine Fridays out of ten and walk away, then get up in the morning and go about his normal business like everyone else. However, one time out of the ten Big Jim would be caught fighting and, when reported in the press, be held up as a monster, when in reality the most that was said in the district about him would be along the lines of: "You would think he would grow up", or "He should meet a nice lassie and settle down". If he was sent to prison then everyone would be asking after him.

As kids we were always looking for adventurous things to do, like putting a rope round the branch of a tree in the gravey and swinging on it, or jumping from dykes that had sharp metal railings beneath us. There was this great thirst for adventure and I know that this was what had me first stealing from shops. I can remember the first time I stole. It was a bar of chocolate and I did it more as a challenge than out of need. There were times when my pals and I would steal soap or something else that was of no use to us, and no sooner had we stolen it than we would throw it away. At the same time each of us was a "good boy" to our parents, as we would run all the messages and try to do things to help the domestic situation, or the neighbours for that matter. We didn't tell our mothers what we did, especially me, as my ma would have kicked up hell, but the point was that none of us saw anything very bad in it.

I do remember the first occasion that we stole money. It was a winter's night and I was with two other pals. Two of us cop-watched while the other stole cash from a van driver's pocket. Once we were safely away, my pal started dividing the money up, but I refused to take any as I was terrified and classed this as real stealing as distinct from what we had been doing in the past. However, I let them pay me into the movies after they had shared the money between them. In all, it amounted to about thirty shillings which was more money than I had ever seen – so I allowed them to buy me sweets and ice cream with it as this was quite acceptable to my conscience. Halfway through the film I started to regret not having taken anything and by time-up I was making noises to the effect that they should give me something. By this time a lot of it had been spent; but I did get half-a-crown, which I was very happy with.

It was never hard after this experience. As for the police, we were always aware of them and basically mistrusted them as one was always being told that they would come to take you away. There were only two cops that were familiar to me by name in those early days. One was a beat cop, who was known to all the kids as Foxy, and the other was a detective called Goodall, who was pretty notorious in our district. Foxy was the one that we watched for as he used to use all sorts of tricks to catch us playing football after school; tricks such as taking his hat off and putting it under his coat then sidling up the street to catch us. He was strongly disliked by us all and counter measures would be taken by posting lookouts who would shout "Foxy" whenever he came in sight. This guy would take playing in the street very personally and he had the same thing about anyone loitering on the street corners. The other cop, the detective Goodall, was a different kettle of fish. Although I was only a youngster, he was very well known to me by name, though I had never even seen him. Goodall was spoken of with fear.

All of the kids from my class in St Francis who had qualified for Bonny's were put into the same class there and we were joined by others from neighbouring schools. I was about twelve at the time. Right from the start I had the feeling that things were for real here. All the ruffians were in the same class in the toughest school in the district. There was another school in the district for the Protestants called Adelphi and this also was a very tough school, but it so happened that Bonny's held most of the guys with the "reputations". However, if you went to either of these schools you had to be able to look after yourself both physically and mentally. There was a thing known as "hard men's walks" of which we were all aware and having just arrived at Bonny's we would all try to adopt a walk that was suitable to us. It must have been funny to see us, still in short trousers, swaggering up to school with these exaggerated walks.

The dominant gang in the district, which mostly originated at Bonny's, was the Cumbie, which took its name from the central street in the area – Cumberland Street. There were two Cumbie gangs: The Big Cumbie and the Wild Young Cumbie. To put the picture straight, the Big Cumbie was made up of silly pricks who were what we called toffy guys and who did nothing to merit their being called a gang. They had a history of some really good fights in other districts like Calton or Bridgeton, but at no time did I ever see them fight and throughout my time they didn't do anything that counted, so they were reckoned to be a pretty impotent bunch. Now the Wild Young Cumbie were a different matter, as they were a force to be reckoned with in the Glasgow world, and they were the ones that most of the kids looked up to in our school.

Things at home had improved by this time as my older brother Pat had a labouring job and Tommy had taken a plumbing apprenticeship in a local shop – a luxury that couldn't be afforded but Ma gave Tommy every encouragement and was proud to have a son serving his time as an apprentice – the university of our world. Ma still worked her three part-time jobs. She seemed to be addicted to them, but the reality was that though two brothers were working, Ma still couldn't afford to give her jobs up.

My oldest brother Pat was exceptionally bright and very talented. He was like me in features, but that's where the resemblance ended as he had a great head on his shoulders and by some means or other found he could play the piano and was really out of this world at it. The music he loved was classical, to play or listen to, and this alone was very unusual. He managed to get an old piano and would sit playing it for hours. There was a part of me that loved this and wanted to take lessons from him, but there was another part that hated it as the music was "toffy" and I would get very embarrassed when any of my pals came up to the door for me to find Pat playing this classical music. He was also a talented sketcher and could draw anything in a very life-like way, as could my brother Tommy. But Pat was different as he was on a very high level, one that was alien to us. Tommy was different again and very much a Gorbals kid doing all the things that most of us did. Because of her jobs Ma had grown terribly old before her time. The household tasks had been passed on to Harry and me, with the eldest two now at work, but there was never much to do as no one was ever in the house and Ma would always clean it when she came in. All that was to be done was to put the fire on for them coming in, and I would get Harry to do this as I was caught up in the street activities and would be fully involved with what I was doing there.

In the class at school some of us knew each other and some didn't, but it was very much a new experience for all of us except the teacher, who gave me the impression that he had had enough of the class of his previous term and was therefore going to be master of this one. I say this because he immediately gave us a lecture on the school "hard men", going on to describe all the moves that we would try, and ended his lecture by saying he was the only hard man here. We would all look knowingly at each other, giving sniggers, while he rambled on, as we had heard similar things from similar people.

I went about with three guys from my previous class. We had never gone about with each other before but now we became friends in and out of school. They were Padge Gallagher, Johnny Boris, and a guy called Tam, all of whom stayed in the district. In the beginning we would go round to play at the Molls Mire, which was a big piece of industrial waste ground behind the school. There were lots of places to explore there, and though there would be times when other classmates would join us, mostly it would be just us four. We would play all the ordinary games and we would make a team for going round the lucky didgies sometimes leaving school to go straight to the toffy district to rake them. Eventually we ended up going into shops and stealing cakes or sweets and although I can't remember how this first started I do know that it wasn't by design. We found it exciting and soon we were deliberately stealing, going into the shops on the way home to take whatever we could. One technique was to go into the shop with a penny, wait in the queue, while the shopkeeper was busy serving others, and lift whatever was near us in the way of "good eats".

At school it became known to the other classmates that we were going "knocking" and some of them would want to come. This is how we became the identifiable toughs of our class. We always made an agreement that whatever we stole we halved, or divided equally amongst ourselves, and in this way we became the guys with plenty of sweeties and things that the other kids didn't have and this was a good feeling. Of course there were the others who would come with us and do no stealing but take some of the stolen goodies, and some started going on their own as the stealing habit was spreading. By this time we were becoming known to the shopkeepers en route to and from the school so we had to move on to greener pastures. We had no wish to give it up for fear of being caught. We had now come to like it and the gains that it brought, and we pursued our new pastime with full energy. There were occasions when we were caught lifting cakes by the shopkeeper and would be chased out but on the whole we were very successful by our standards. We would fill our pockets with biscuits and cakes and walk along the street eating them till we got sick then throw the remainder at each other. It was a natural progression from cakes to more expensive things.

In the classroom our crowd, with me as their leader, became noticeable as the baddies, and the teacher would let us know this in a roundabout way. When one of us got the belt there would be remarks passed by the teacher such as "How hard are you now?" but this was just accepted as a challenge to be met by a determination on our part not to show any weakness or emotion. But there were times when we couldn't help it as they would lay the strap on heavily for us. The teacher would always talk to us in a familiar fashion as though he knew just what we were up to, but we knew that he only talked in this way so that we wouldn't think him an easy mark or take him for a mug. In an odd sort of way we regarded this as a form of condonation of what we were doing. This was something that I always felt very strongly about lots of adults, and even cops that I came in contact with. None of them ever made me feel that they wanted me to be any different to how I was.

At playtime everyone would crowd into the toilets and smoke cigarettes and some of the older boys would even, on occasions, drink wine, but although the toilet was always full of smoke, no one seemed to notice. There would be many fights but we, as the youngest group, would never be involved in these and would only watch on. Most of the talk would be about the Cumbie gangs with everyone pretending that they knew the leaders personally. Some of the kids would say that the leader of the Cumbie was their big cousin so that no one would hit them, and in fact the leaders were held in such high regard that this con trick would always work because no one was ever brave enough to challenge it. On seeing the power it gave him the "pretender" would automatically acquire the reputation of a good fighter, which he would make the most of.

On a Monday, Wednesday and Friday after school there would be a big rush as most kids would head for the lucky didgies, or go round the doors of the houses in the district for empty bottles, all in the hope of getting sixpence each. There was a picture house in Cumberland Street round the corner from where I lived and it had a rule on those three nights that the first sixty kids under fourteen would get in for a tanner, hence the mad rush. This was an unbelievable scene as the kids would get the money, by hook or by crook, and would all be queueing up and it was pandemonium with all sorts of fights to get in amongst the first sixty. The adults round about would stand watching the sight of all these kids trying to get in and really it must have made fantastic entertainment for them. The two doorkeepers were brave guys, especially when their counting got to the fifty mark as that's when the panic really struck the remainder. The picture hall was out of this world because, for starters, no one could hear the movie for us screaming at each other. The seating was of sturdy church-like benches made of wood and, if it was raining, water poured in at certain parts of the hall. There was the occasional rat scampering about the feet of the patrons.

If we happened to miss the first sixty, or if we could only get the price for one of us, then one would go in and when the movie had started he would creep over to the exit door and lift the iron bar and a crowd of us would flood in. There was the odd occasion when we would skip up to the balcony but this was real luxury. One time we pissed over it onto the people below. I remember my ma and Aunt Maggie taking about nine of us kids to the Paragon one night and we were all sitting on our best behaviour watching this movie, with the place so silent that a pin could be heard dropping, when this enormously fat woman in front of us let out a great big fart and we kids broke into laughter, and so did our parents and the people around us. The laughter went on and on until the big fat woman got up and left. We all used to go to the matinee each Saturday afternoon and this was the big treat. Harry and I used to wear our Parish trench coats that were coloured black and buttoned right up to the neck. A woman outside used to sell whelks and make a roaring trade so we would all go in with bags of them. All the kids would eat the whelks by taking the centre out and throwing the shell at those sitting in front. After watching the matinee trailers and cartoons, we would all come out, Harry and I with our coats like capes, buttoned only at the neck, running with hands in the air as though we were flying, very much in the Superman tradition, the other kids being Roy Rogers.

St Francis' school had a boys club two nights a week and kids from the district could go there to take part in sports and games to keep them off the street. I went to it and gave it a try but I really wasn't much of a football man and although I did put some effort into it there was always this feeling of being trapped, though I could never really explain what this meant at the time. In many ways it was very like school, which I detested, and there was always the feeling that I was being talked "down" to by the guys who ran it, who for some reason or other would take every high-spirited action as a direct challenge to them. There was one guy who had been a boxer in his army days and lived on this reputation. He constantly reminded us of this in a very subtle, intimidating sort of way. I had always possessed a great deal of energy and the routine of this club wasn't able to contain it. For instance, the club was pretty small (the games area, that is) and if there were between thirty or forty boys present split into five-a-side football teams this meant that the playing teams would take up all the space while the rest sat on benches or window ledges. During the time that I had to sit on the window ledge while the teams played, I was wrestling about with some others and I smashed two windows while jumping all over the ledge. The guy in charge of us didn't like it and I was barred from going back again.

There was no way that I could explain myself; I didn't know how. How could I explain nervous energy when I hadn't even heard of it before? So what if a few windows are broken? Surely the logical step would have been to leave them broken and to let me experience the consequences of it when the wind blew in on a winter's night. If I, or any of the others, had complained of cold then the practical disadvantages of breaking windows could have been pointed out. Eventually the club lost its true purpose as it barred guys like me from coming in when in fact we should have been the ones to be stopped from leaving at any cost. It then became a meeting place for nice kids who weren't prone to trouble anyway, and it looked as though the guys running it were after a quiet time as they became pretty selective. It wasn't nice to be barred and there were nights when we would go round and stand outside the door and try to get back in. Sometimes we would sneak in and try to hide amongst the other kids but the place was so small that we would soon be seen and thrown out. Eventually being thrown out like this became a prestigious thing for us, though it wasn't at first. Inevitably I got fed up hanging around the club doorway and went back to the streets, where I met some old pals from my school.

During the early months of Bonny's I consolidated my friendship with Padge, Johnny and Tam. We were now going around together all the time and the stealing from shops became a big part of our existence. We extended it to the weekends and would go out to shops in other districts on the Saturday when shopping was a busy time and we could really plunder. By now we were lifting more expensive materials, household goods in particular, all of which would be sold to people in the district. We had no shortage of "fences" for buying the stuff that we stole, usually at around the half-price mark. The streets in the Gorbals were always very dark on winter nights as there were only gas lamps lighting the area, which could have a frightening effect on people not used to them. But to those of us who were accustomed to them the streets held a warmth. At nights groups of us would roam about, moving aimlessly from street to street. There was nothing much to do but someone would usually find something for a laugh or out of devilment.

It was on one such night that one of the guys with me took a run at a shop door and kicked it, a little too hard, for the door flew open and seeing this we all ran away down the dark street in case anyone had seen us. From a safe distance we looked back and could see that no one had heard it or come out, so we debated going back. Some were for it and some were against, but everyone was in a state of scarey excitement and I went back with a few others. On reaching the shop door I looked in at the darkness and very slowly moved in, always expecting someone to come pouncing on top of me. I was followed by a couple of others, who left the last one cop-watching. A constant nervous dialogue took place between me and the cop-watcher, asking him if it was alright. The shop was a babieswear one and sold lots of kids' clothes. I was very scared while in the building but at the same time I had this wonderful feeling of excitement at being in a shop with the goods completely at my disposal. There was this constant duality of feeling with a strong fear on one side and a good feeling of challenge on the other. We were only in the place minutes but in that time had jumped over the counter and taken boxes of goods without looking to see what they were, as there was too much panic and excitement. We took as much as we could carry and then ran to join the others who hadn't come, then on to an old washhouse to see what we had. The kids who stayed outside the shop were now wishing they hadn't for we shared the spoils amongst those of us who had gone in. We had no problem getting the goods sold, as everyone who had a child would have bought them if they had had the chance, so it all went very easy for us this first time and the success of the venture made us feel we were "big time".

Up until this, all we had done was shoplifting and as we had become adept at this and felt on pretty safe ground, with full confidence in our abilities, we then began to turn more to the actual breaking-into shops. While shoplifting we would have competitions to see who had the most "nerve", to see who could steal the best and most valuable article without being seen. There was something adventurous about entering a shop, watching the assistant move, waiting till he was in a certain position then, with as swift a movement as possible, lifting whatever was the target. Now that I was into shopbreaking the feeling was that bit more exciting, and far more rewarding financially, with a whole store full of goods within one's grasp.

Certainly we didn't give up shoplifting altogether, but concentration was more on our night-time activities of breaking and entering. With the money gained from the babieswear shop I bought a hacksaw and set out one night to break into another shop, which meant congregating round the back window and sawing through the metal bars while someone stood outside cop-watching. A basic rule was to always have a cop-watcher while the rest were doing the necessary. Cutting metal bars takes a bit of doing when one is trying to be quiet about it as the rasping of the saw becomes exaggerated in the mind, so sweaty hands and bodies were a part of breaking in. This second shop was a painters' and decorators' and once we had gained entry it was a case of having to crawl along the shop floor, as the front was brightly lit, to get to the till where the money was kept. At this stage we didn't realise that most shop-keepers leave "psychological" cash in the till. This is petty cash for thieves like us to settle for and make off with, rather than ransack the place, and in this case it worked because we took only the cash and a blow-lamp and some paint. The knowledge that we could now break into any shop we wanted was really something. When it got round the class in school that we were "screwing" shops the other kids had me and my pals on pedestals and this boosted our egos. The fact that we'd got practically no financial gain from our second job meant nothing as the important thing was the actual success of getting into the shop. By now I was recognised as leader of the thieving gang and also, for some reason or other, as being the best fighter, even though I hadn't struck a blow at anyone, but this didn't bother me as I loved to accept anything like this.

After school there would be lots of kids wanting to come stealing with me as they thought my pals and I were getting lots of money. Many were stealing in twos or threes, but we were the ones getting most money and the ones with nerve, so all the kids stealing at school wanted to be with us. The competition between me and my pals at stealing was really something and it was this strong competitive spirit that made us the best in the school. But despite it being an added honour to have the best nerve in our clique, there was still the rule of dividing equally all that we stole. Johnny, who was the smallest and the fastest, and on the whole gamer than the rest of us, had the best nerve, but only by a shadow.

As well as our activities becoming known to our fellow pupils they were also well known to the teaching staff and they would let us know this in front of everyone with remarks such as, "Some of the class will end up in the Bar-L prison" (Barlinnie). This, in itself, was a sort of prestigious thing, and seemed to give us a form of identity, because when they made these remarks in a general way we would all give each other knowing looks as though to confirm who they were aiming them at. Although there was a lot of dodging school, we were all regular attenders in the early months. But as time went on various tactics and techniques were used to excuse us from school. The ordinary inconspicuous kid could afford to dodge it without making elaborate excuses but the well-known ones like me had to be doubly wise to get away with it. There was usually some woman about who would write a note for me with an explanation for my absence to take into the teacher as though it had come from my mother. Of course there were times when I was caught, as were my pals.

Whenever we dodged school we would go out stealing from shops and off lorries, knowing full well that the following day when we returned the teacher would give us six of the best, but that didn't matter to us. On such occasions the teacher would give us the belt in front of the girls' class. Of course he only did this with our crowd and it was his way of putting us down so as to show us up in front of the girls, hoping we would cry and at the same time showing the girls how tough he was in his treatment of us. The anomaly of this was that the whole exercise appealed to us as it let us impress the girls and frustrate the teacher, who would be disappointed at getting no satisfaction from our tough façades. We would be determined to take it like men even though it hurt like hell, and save our pain for the minute we got outside the door.

The one comforting factor we could support each other on was that the teachers were all bastards and we hated them. This, of course, was my pupil point of view and there were exceptions to this. There was one particular man who was teaching us technical drawing but who had a predilection for talking at great length about the hard men who had passed through his hands at school. This guy would always digress from the official subject matter to go on about his personal experiences with the hard men of the Gorbals and we would all sit loving it. So with this in mind it was all a matter of individual teachers and how to handle them, for they ranged from those who didn't really care to the complete authoritarian personality. I never got on with any of the teachers at school and most of my pals were in the same boat. There was a void between teacher and pupil and that was it. By the age of twelve and a half there was a feeling that the teachers had given us up for lost.

In contrast to this, three of us, including two other classmates, Padge and Joe Regan, took an early-morning milk delivery job in a toffy district. All the week through we would get up very early, me along with my ma at 5 a.m., and deliver the milk round the door steps and finish at 8.30 a.m. We got 25/- for it and would make an extra few bob in tips. I really enjoyed this very much as there was something nice about the world at that time of the morning. The idea of working and bringing money into the house was very important to me, as it was me paying my way. There was also the fact that Ma was completely worn out and needed all the help she could get. The only way I could help was to work as there was no way that she would take anything from me that was stolen. I usually made school at nine in the nick of time, eating my breakfast on the bus, which was normally a roll and a pint of the firm's milk. Of course no one could be told about the job because at this time there was a scare on about kids working without permits, which was all new to me but it was a fact, so the teachers weren't to know about the work. One day the woman who employed us told me that I couldn't come back as she could get into trouble for giving me work. I think she was using this as an excuse to get rid of me as she had already told me that she wasn't worried about the permit issue. Anyway, from there I got another job delivering messages on a bicycle to big toffy houses in a district where I had previously raked the midgies. It was only a temporary thing but I liked it and was sorry when it ended.

3

In about 1957, when I was thirteen years old, a new machine was put into operation. It was a chewing-gum machine and the distributors put them on shop front doors and walls so that passers-by could purchase gum. There must have been a big sales drive, for they were put on lots of shops throughout the district. It was a penny for a packet and, for every fourth one, a free pack was given. These machines made a fortune as everyone was using them, but their accessibility was very tempting to us who roamed the streets. We decided to break into them and wrenched one off the wall, taking it into one of the backs to force it open, but opening it under these circumstances was too much work as there was no means of leverage. However, from this primitive method of wrenching the whole machine off the wall, we developed a technique that was very simple and effective and that was to put a metal spike up the spout where the gum came out and to force the front off, open the money part and take the cash along with the remaining gum. All the kids in the school would get free gum from us but the worst of it was that the method, once it became known, was too easy, and lots of kids were doing them. If someone in the school had a pocketful of pennies then he was sure to have done a machine the previous night. With this competition we would go out at night and sometimes break into four or five machines, one after the other, till the time came when the company refused to repair them as they must have been losing too much cash, so it was a case of hunting at nights for a surviving machine. The pennies that I got from them would be put into an old nylon stocking and stashed up the room chimney. There was never a fire there, so there was no reason for anyone to go near it.

One night we were out screwing machines and it was one of those dark winter evenings. Just as we were taking the cash from the machine two uniformed cops came upon us and we scattered, the six of us, all from the school. As we belted along Cumberland Street with cops well behind with no chance of catching us, a kid who knew us was coming in the opposite direction and not seeing the cops behind us shouted, asking where we were going. On seeing the cops he shut his mouth and started walking as he had before. But it was too late, the cops had seen him attempting to speak to us and as there was no chance of them catching us, they stopped and caught hold of the kid and questioned him. Meanwhile, we split the cash and went home and I was all washed, had my pennies up the chimney and was in bed with my brothers when the cops came in the early hours of the morning; they were detectives.

My ma let them in and woke me up and the butterflies started going in my stomach when I saw who they were. They told me that they had three of my pals in the squad car downstairs and named them, saying that they had admitted doing the machines. With this I gave them the pennies I had up the lum and my ma just couldn't believe it. The look on her face was that of astonishment, but I was absolutely petrified at the sight of the cops. They told me to get dressed as they were taking me away. My ma, who had done her best for me, was saying things like, "Oh no", and asking the cops not to take me. What would happen to me, she asked, and they said that I would be taken to a Home tonight, and all the things about the cops taking me away to a Home were the threats that had been said over and over again by most adults and here it was coming true. I left the house crying and on reaching the squad car was met with wails from Padge, Johnny and Tam, who were howling the car down, and from my close they drove us to the Police Headquarters with us repeatedly asking them to let us go and we would never do it again. We were charged in the police office and locked in a room till a van was ready to take us to the Remand Home. While in this room we were so terrified that we didn't dare even speak to each other and when questioned by the cops we admitted to every machine we had done, giving them the details of each. There was no tough façade on my face now, or the rest, as we were only four wee boys who were terrified at the thought of being put away.

A police van drove us to Larchgrove. The squad car and the police van had the same very distinctive scent. There was this smell of fear in them that I have always connected with police uniforms and vehicles, this sense that is more of a feeling than a smell, but it's there. It was in the early hours of the morning when we drove up to the front door of Larchgrove, which is in Glasgow, and the thing that hit me, even then, was the newness of the place. We cowered in the doorway waiting for it to open and when it did we found the entrance to be gleaming, absolutely spotless, with brass or chrome doorplates gleaming and a strong smell of disinfectant. These places have a smell of their own. The screw that took charge of us on entry didn't really see us. We didn't exist. His way of communicating was to point in the direction, without looking at us, and shout in a crisp, clear voice what we were to do, and we did it. Being in such a state of fear and confusion we stumbled, faltered and fell in the rush to do as he said. He was a giant of a man who neither smiled nor allowed any other expression to enter his face, which I could tell from the glances I stole at him whenever a movement forced me to look his way.

We were made to strip off all our clothes and we were then taken to a big square that seemed to be the centre spot of the place. The man lifted a big bucket that stood in the square and taking a stick from it he slapped this thick white gooey stuff on the end of the stick onto our hair and ordered us to rub it in, which we did with great enthusiasm in the hope of pleasing him. Each of us was given a shower and a locker to put the home clothes in. He led us to the dormitories where the beds were and the sound of crying children permeated the place, silenced only by the shout of "Shut up" from the screw, but on hearing the crying we four broke into loud sobbing that couldn't be subdued because we were terrified out of our wits and I kept asking for my ma, over and over again. I was put into a dormitory with three other strangers all my own age. I lay saying to myself as I cried that I would never do it again and how sorry I was for doing it. I'll never forget that first night nor the boy in the next bed, who seemed to be crying in his sleep or was too afraid to open his eyes, but my own personal pain was tremendous as this was the first time I had been away from the house. The whole thing was terrifying for me, I was physically shaking with fear and didn't dare sleep in case something happened. I honestly couldn't believe what was happening to me. I wanted my ma.

At six in the morning a man came walking along the corridor ringing a big bell and shouting for everyone to get out of bed and make them up. This I did along the with others, following their every move, as I hadn't a clue what was to be done, and everyone made their way to the toilets and spray room or the big room where the lockers stood. Everyone had to get ready as the screws stood about, shouting at anyone who seemed to be slow in doing so. I was amazed at the ease with which some of the kids were taking it, almost in a confident manner as though they knew what they were doing and had been there for some time, yet it was incomprehensible to me that anyone could have been there in that place for any length of time. I was too terrified to speak to anyone, as were many of the others, but there were some kids who even laughed as they were dressing. When we were dressed, everyone was hurried along to the big square we had been in before. There must have been about sixty kids in all and everyone was dressed in khaki short trousers, a shirt and a pair of sandshoes. The screws were all dressed in civilian clothing and made us all stand to attention in complete silence until it was time to march to breakfast. If, on the way, someone made the slightest noise we were about-turned and taken back to the square to wait till we were ready to go in silence and this determined whether breakfast would be hot or cold.

That first morning we were turned around twice and although I heard no one making a noise, I was still incredulous at the thought of someone having the nerve to do so and angry that they should, as I felt this might make things worse for me. After breakfast those of us who were to make court appearances were taken away to be put into our own clothing and made ready for the police van which was coming for us. The screw told us to leave the Home clothes in a neat bundle as we might be coming back. The thought of this almost knocked me over. We all looked at each other with trembling lips. Of course I knew that my ma would take me home once I had seen her; I prayed to God that she would.

Once back in the Police Headquarters where the court was to be held, the detectives came and took the four of us out of the cell and started joking about how busy we had been keeping them with all the work that went into investigating the break-ins. Of course we had told them everything and had cleared their books for them. From here we were taken to a makeshift cell that was used as the fingerprint department and these very tall men in brown coats took our fingerprints, and from there to another makeshift cell that was converted into a photography room to take mug shots of us, and in this way I went officially into the police files. These two things were mind-blowing experiences and added to the seriousness for me. The people doing this were taking it all for granted and herding us about like sheep as though they had been doing it all their lives; whereas I was in a stupefied state, doing things I was told in a very nervous fashion, always afraid that I would bring the wrath of the cops down on me. When I went into the courtroom, which was filled with people, I saw my ma and felt that little bit better as I knew that she would help me. The parents of the four of us were allowed to come across and stand immediately behind us while the hearing proceeded. It was very short and sweet, with the four of us being remanded for four days in Larchgrove, and we were escorted by the police out of the room. It all happened so quickly that we were in the cell again before we realised what was happening. The thought of returning to the Remand Home was worrying me very much as the few hours I'd spent there had been enough and I only wanted to go home and never get in trouble again. But taken back we were.

Larchgrove Remand Home is on the east end of Glasgow and sits in a large estate that has a wall around it. Kids who get into trouble go there up to the age of sixteen and from that age onwards they go to Barlinnie Prison. Kids can lie on remand for nearly four months awaiting trial. When found guilty, they can be sent back to Larchgrove to serve sentences, the maximum being 28 days, so as well as a Remand Home it is also a Detention Centre where kids are sent for punishment. For misbehaving in the place the punishments range from extra scrubbing of floors to being locked in solitary, or to corporal punishment which takes the form of a thick leather strap over the buttocks. Discipline reigned supreme in Larchgrove and each person in there had to maintain a high standard. I felt very much at the mercy of the screws, as I'm sure everyone else did. Everything they said went, and was law. After breakfast in the morning the kids were split up into groups, with one screw taking charge of so many, and each of us was given a bucket and scrubber and cloth. The whole morning was spent scrubbing the floors and the scrubbing had to be very thorough because if it wasn't everyone in that group had to go back to the beginning and start over again. I was in such a daze with the whole experience, I just scrubbed till I was told to move on as I was scared to do anything without being told. In the afternoon, after lunch, we were put into a small yard for exercise, and from there back to scrubbing the walls and cleaning the brasses. It was no wonder the place was absolutely gleaming, and had this continually new look about it: the screws wanted to see their faces in everything, and see them they did. Nothing was left untouched or uncleaned.

At four o'clock we were made ready in the big square for the evening meal and put through the marching procedure. The dining hall was upstairs and I'll never forget this meal as I was seated next to a window from which I could see buses travelling along the Edinburgh Road. At five o'clock lots of men and women came out of the Olivetti typewriter factory across the road. It was a winter's night with lights on and I felt as though someone had torn the heart from me, as here were all these people going home to sit at the table near a fire and eat. To go home! The sight of this hurt me very much. I thought of how, later that night, Ma would come home and make a meal for my brothers. It was terrible to see all these people walking about free, and so I always tried to avoid sitting near a window in Larchgrove. After the meal we were taken to the dormitories and made to sit there while some of the screws went for their meals. At seven o'clock that night my ma came up, as that was visiting time. It was great to see her and I sat so close to her, almost on her knee and kept asking her what would happen to me and could she get me home? She kept asking me if I was all right and I just implored her to get me home and I would never get into trouble again. Lots of kids had visits and most of them looked very much as I did. When they called "time-up" I wanted very badly to crawl back up Ma's womb and stay there.

After the visit we were lined up in the Big Square and had the white ointment slapped onto our hair. We were then given a shower and put to bed. This was the daily routine, except visits were only allowed every second night. There was no acting in a tough manner now. I was what I was, just a little boy.

After four days of this we were taken to court and given two years' probation each. It was pure bliss to walk out of the court with my ma, with all of us kids repeating again the words that we had been saying those past four days, that we would never get into trouble again and this we promised while our parents assumed that we had learned our lesson. My ma told me to keep away from the others or I'd just get into trouble and the other parents told their kids the same. I was told that I was to come straight home after school and stay in, as I was on probation now and had to take great care or I'd be taken away again, so I said I'd adhere to this and anything else as long as I never had to go back to that place. She had to go straight off to work, but was obviously delighted to have me back in the house. Everyone else was out at work or in school and I was so glad to be back in the house; it seemed like years since I had been there as so much had gone on during the last four days.

The following morning it was back to school and on the way there I met some of my classmates, who questioned me about the experience of Larchgrove. By the time I had reached the school the fear of it was fading and I was responding to their questions boastfully, so that before very long I was giving a completely fictitious account of my experience and how I had handled it in a manly way. There was no talk of tears and heartbreak or the pain I had felt. In many ways I was believing what I was saying about how confident and unafraid I had been. When I told them this I was thinking of the few kids who were very confident about the Remand Home, those who had been in many times before and were used to it. All four of us were in the same class and our experience was the talk of the class, and school. Our reintroduction to the class was made by the teacher remarking that four of our friends were with us again and that he hoped they had learned a lesson. Just the previous day the four of us had been terrified out of our wits, but here we were, one day later, putting up fronts and acting the toughies. Even to each other there was this denial that we had been scared and we began to make-believe about things that we knew just weren't true.

However, for a week or so after school time I would return to the house and stay in till Ma came home at nine o'clock, and I would have the fire on and the house tidied as best I could. My pals had parents who were home so they were kept in the house after school, but mine was purely a self-discipline thing as Ma was out at work. There didn't seem much use in sitting in the house alone, so, with this in mind, it was back to the streets, though I made sure I was home for Ma coming in. Harry was old enough to get about himself with his own pals now, so there was no need for me to look after him.

The reality of me keeping away from my pals was nonsensical because we met each other all the time through school and doing messages or playing in the street, so we still went about with each other but made sure our parents didn't see us. Although each of our parents maintained that their son was good and that the others had got him into trouble, this just wasn't true. There was no individual to blame for leading us.

Being on probation meant that I would be under supervision for two years, with a man, the probation officer, paying periodical visits to the house to speak to me and find out how I was getting on. He was a large man with an intimidating sort of way about him and it was very odd having him in the house as it made everyone feel they were under supervision, and I felt very guilty as it had been my behaviour that had brought this man into our lives. Whenever he came we felt that he was observing everyone and looking the house over and the atmosphere of the house would seem to change when this "intruder" entered. While he was in everyone would put on a front and Ma would run around getting him tea and trying to be nice to him. His visits were only once a month but even then it was too much. There were quite a lot of people, adults too, on probation in our district, so he would have lots of clients, but as everyone was keen to avoid him, an early-warning system would go round when he was in the district. This used to happen as well when the GPO were around with their vans for licences or when the debt man was looking for his cash. So whenever he came into the area word went round and people refused to answer the door. After some time he would get fly to this and come through the backs, or when it became very bad he sent letters demanding our presence at his office, but this was better as it kept him out of the house.

One of the kids in our district got a television and though he was the sort of toffy kind of kid his telly endeared him to us and he found himself with more friends than he had ever had in his life. It was the first telly in the street and everyone would try to get him to take them up to his house to watch a programme. We would all be on the lookout for him and really he wallowed in this new-found popularity. I often wondered how he coped with the situation when tellies became more common. One day he took a crowd of us up to his very nice house when his mother and father were out working. He had this grandfather, a grumpy old man who used to moan continuously, but this time he slept on a chair while we all sat in front of him watching *Bill and Ben the Flower Pot Men*. It was fantastic, except that the old guy woke up and started shouting and hitting those nearest to him with his stick. We just moved out of reach and continued watching while this old guy continued to shout; but we were glued to the telly and wouldn't budge.

Another guy in our class at school who was a bit of a nonentity also became everyone's friend because of a domestic phenomenon – a bath. He had moved to a new house and it had a bath in it. The house was in a fringe district of the Gorbals called Oatlands which was quite toffy – very middle class, we thought. They were houses that had good lucky didgies, which we didn't hesitate to rake. Word soon got round about the bath and one day after school we persuaded him to take us along to see it. He had a lovely house with venetian blinds on the windows. It was very impressive, as were the other houses around it. He showed us the

bathroom and we all wanted a bath but his mother came in, which
put an end to that. However, we did get one another day. I thought
how great it must have been to live in a house that one could bathe
and shit in.

Things in school were returning to normal as our parents had
got over the shock of our being inside, so we were now officially
going around together again. At night we would concentrate on
raising money to go to the pictures and one of the ways we did
this was to go round the fruit shops collecting the empty wooden
boxes, breaking them up into bunches and selling them round the
doors for firewood. We sold them cheaper and bigger than the
shops, so the sales were good. At night we would sit in the old
washhouse in the back for hours, using it as a gang hut. We used
candles to light it up and those of us who were Catholics would
get a Protestant pal of ours, who stayed downstairs from me, to go
into the chapel and steal candles for the gang hut as they were too
scared to do it.

The chapel had a hold over us, in a curious way, and it was
the same going to Confession. No matter what sins had been
committed, after telling the priest there was this extraordinary
feeling of being pure. Religion played a dominant part in the life
of our district: the Catholics and the Proddies, Celtic and Rangers
football teams. I was never very strong on this, maybe due to not
having any great love for football, where all the discrimination
seemed to stem from. Also, some of my best pals were Protestants.
There was the annual thing of going on St Patrick's Day from
our school down to the local Proddy school, grabbing anyone we
could and asking, "Are you a Billy, a Dan or an old tin can?" If he
was a "Billy" he was tossed in the air because that meant he was
a Protestant, if he was a "Dan" he was okay as that was Catholic,
and though the "old tin can" meant neither, since everyone
seemed to mention the latter anyway, they got thrown up too.
Though this was more a carry-on than a religious thing with me,
for others it was the real thing as Billys were bluenose bastards.
The Proddies would do the same and so it was a case of give a
little, take a little. In general the real religious bigots were amongst
the grown-ups.

About this time I decided to go into business along with my pals, Johnny, Padge and Tam. We were to use a barrow as transport to sell coal briquettes around the neighbouring districts. We would have to do this on Saturdays, when we had a break from school. There was a family in the Gorbals who hired out barrows to anyone wanting to go out with rags or coal. We went to Coal Hill, a yard in the Gorbals where trains bring in coal for the merchants to load up. We were naive enough to think that the merchants would give us briquettes without payment and let us pay up after we'd sold them, but on seeing us, they chased us away. Obviously they looked on us as daft wee boys, but we didn't see ourselves as such. Eventually we gave up trying to get the coal legitimately and decided to steal it. There was a guy with a big store a couple of streets from me and he sold firewood and coal briquettes and the place was loaded with them. We decided it would be a very simple matter to break into it. We broke the padlock on the store door and took boxes of briquettes, making trip after trip to get them, and so it was back to thieving only months after being released from Larchgrove. When Saturday came we were all up early and out on the streets with the barrow and coal shouting "Coal briqueeeettt-teess", and we would tramp round the streets shouting our lungs out, selling them at 2/6d. a dozen. We sold them all and it was good fun but we had no money at the end of it as we spent it all as we earned it on hot pies and peas, having about four lunchtimes in all. At the end of the day we gave the barrow away to the kids in the street to keep instead of taking it back – we had given a phoney name anyway.

One day we decided to run away and make our fortunes, so the four of us jumped a train and ended up in Edinburgh with a few bob in our pockets. We wandered round the city looking it over and went into a railway yard late at night and climbed into an open wagon that was covered with a tarpaulin. We got underneath and had all started singing and carrying on when a torch shone in – it was a cop. He took us out and we ended up in the police station, where they took our names and put us in a cell for the night. The cell had a big fire with a guard over it, far different from the Glasgow ones and much cosier. In the morning they gave us a stick of Edinburgh rock for our breakfast and that's the truth. The cops told us our parents had been notified and they put us on the Glasgow train, where they asked a man to see that we were okay on the journey. Fool that he was he took the responsibility. By the time we got to Glasgow the man was a nervous wreck as we were running all over the place. It was Sunday morning and as soon as our parents met us on the station we were slapped for running away, but they then took us into the station cafe and bought us breakfast, so it was okay. As usual we were told that we had to stay in at nights but as always we knew that they would have to let us out sometime.

The fear that Larchgrove held for us had completely vanished and I was now out stealing much worse than I had ever done. Now that I was experienced in the game the emphasis was on stealing goods that could be sold for money, only taking stuff to eat when I was hungry. Things like electric shavers and transistor radios which had just hit the commercial market were a good steal as people would buy them, also clothes for kids and adults. Whatever was the fashion, we would get it. Our own fences were plentiful. At New Year we would concentrate on booze, whisky in particular, as it would go as fast as it was stolen. The best targets were lorries delivering to the local pubs. We watched till the guy went into the shop with his load, then we would walk over, lift a case and walk off in full view of everyone around. It would be done so casually that most people would think nothing of it and those who did would just give a wry smile. I was only thirteen and all sorts of adults would be looking for me to remind me that they would buy any cheap Scotch that I got, as people got frantic for it at that time of year. On one particular occasion I had just lifted a case of Scotch from a lorry, having taken my jacket off to look like a delivery boy, walked away with it through the backs and was just crossing the next street, when this guy with a horse and cart selling coal (in the middle of the street) saw me and asked if I was selling it and when I told him I was, he took six bottles from me then and there. I had known him just to see before but obviously he had heard of me, so this was typical of the way things went.

Women who wanted nylons or men's shirts for their husbands or boyfriends would ask me if I had any. Our "fence" wasn't some mastermind Fagin who sent us out to steal or exploited us by buying the stolen articles. It was just ordinary people who took the stuff from us as they probably couldn't afford to pay the full price. If it wasn't me that was selling stolen gear then it would be any number of others, as there was this sort of unofficial "underground" market for stuff and usually anything could be bought at half price or well below that. There was a great deal of excitement about it and I had this pal who had fantastic patter and he would chat up shop owners to buy the gear from us. He was really good and got the best of prices for me. Stealing and selling the gear was good as it gave me a sort of identity; people knew that if they wanted things they could come to our crowd and we would usually find a way.

4

I became very interested in pigeons, not the racing kind, but show pigeons and there seemed to be a fever gripping a few of us over them. We would buy what birds we could from the money we made from stealing, but that wasn't enough, so we started stealing them and to do this we would break into pigeon huts all over Glasgow and bring them home. I got quite a notorious name amongst pigeon flyers in the district for having lots of stolen birds. I used to keep them in the loft above the house and they would make a terrible noise, but the neighbours would say nothing about that as they were only too glad to see me keeping out of trouble; little did they know. Eventually I had to give it up because, whenever birds were stolen, men from all over Glasgow would come to my door knocking, asking for their birds, even when I hadn't got them. One of my pals was still keen on the bird flying and knew an easy pigeon hut to screw in the Oatlands, so one night three of us went up to it and broke in. The hut was empty but while we were there the cops came and chased us, catching all of us.

We were charged and taken through the whole admittance procedure, finding ourselves back in Larchgrove the following day. The hatred of the place returned the minute the police caught us and I was sick at the thought of going back there and very frightened. After being fingerprinted and photographed we were taken to court and sentenced to fourteen days' Detention for breaking into an empty hut. The routine was the same, as were my feelings about the place: the scrubbing, the discipline, the occasional thumping from the screws. My ma was shattered when she came up to see me and I told her the same as I did the last time I was in, that I wouldn't get into trouble again and really all she could do was believe me.

Near the end of this period of detention the screws selected me to go with four older guys of about sixteen to a farm to get manure for the Larchgrove garden. Some of the farm workers offered me cigarettes; I didn't smoke so I took them for the others. It was a great trip as we went by lorry along the Edinburgh Road and getting the cigarettes was a small victory, as the big guys were chuffed with them, saying I was a great wee guy. At night everyone would lie in bed and listen for the loud steps of the Headmaster of the place as he walked from his office to the big square. He had metal tips on his shoes and the sound of him walking on the stone floor could be heard all through the Home. Corporal punishment was always given out at night, after everyone had been put to bed, and no one ever knew who was to get it, so we would lie there listening for the name to be shouted. The place was in silence, with no one daring to even whisper. On this particular night my name was called out. It was a bolt out of the blue and I stiffened with fear, unable to budge. My name was called again, "Boyle". I slid out of bed, the fear inside me reflected on the faces of the others, all of them feeling the pain with me, wondering if they would be next.

On reaching the Big Square the screws all stood in silence as I came along in my pyjamas. The Head accused me of bringing cigarettes into the Home when I had known they weren't allowed. I made a feeble attempt to deny it, but was so surprised at him knowing that I then admitted it. He had this big leather belt in his hands and it was so stiff that it stood out straight. He told me to bend over but I was too terrified to move. He repeated the order but I honestly couldn't move so he put his hand in his pocket, pulled out a sweet (obviously he had experienced this sort of thing before) and threw it on the floor, telling me to pick it up. As I bent down to do so he hit me full force across the arse and I yelled and the tears flowed down my cheeks. I stood with my arse against the wall refusing to turn round and crying louder, hoping he would give up but he shouted for me to turn round and bend over. All the while the others were lying in bed listening to this. Finally he told the screws to hold me and with me screaming all the while, he proceeded to belt me. For refusing to obey him by not turning round, he put me in the strong cell for the night. The following morning I was let out to join the others and they told me that two of the older guys had been caught smoking and had given my name. My arse was sore for days.

I truly suffered with other kids who got the belt in the nights to come as each stroke could be heard throughout the place. The anomalous situation was that those of us who received the belt were looked up to by the other kids in the place even though they had heard each of us crying our eyes out at the time. I had cried loudly and unashamedly when getting the belt because it really was sore, just as it was to every kid who received it. One could hear stories of kids afterwards boasting how they had never cried and I also took part in this boasting, yet we had all heard each other.

Thankfully the day of release came and it was a Saturday at 6 p.m. Our parents were there to meet us at the door. I was glad to see my ma and she gave me the usual lecture. In our world there wasn't much cuddling or embracing of parents, as that was too sissy, so when we first saw our parents it was just a big hello and then the lectures came. I was overjoyed to be out and sincerely meant it when I told my ma that I would never get into trouble ever again. I told her this again and again, and with my whole heart and soul this was what I meant. Why, when feeling like this did I return time and time again? I never wanted to get into trouble and there were times when this feeling was passionately strong, not only in me but in all of us, though we would only admit this to each other when caught, because when we were out in the streets what we were doing seemed so natural. I always felt very inarticulate when I was a kid and could never talk to people like teachers or those who were part of the authorities. My probation officer used to have to drag every word out of me even though it was very meaningless stuff. It was different with my own people in the district as I would talk away naturally with them. Certainly there were lots of kids in the Gorbals who had never been in trouble and lots of them had gone about with me at one time or another. The difference was that although they had taken part in the mischief, unlike us, none of them had been caught.

When we got out of Larchgrove we left the thieving again and after school resumed the practice of going over the Mollsy to play at various games, wrestling and dummy fighting. It was at this time that we decided to become a gang and set about thinking up a name for it. We came up with the "Skull Gang", so we all got white skulls painted on the back of our leather jerkins, which caught on so that lots of kids wanted to join us. It wasn't really a fighting gang but just a group of us who were going around together playing at various games. It all started innocently enough. As the leather or imitation leather jackets were the rage, with backs painted, everyone was all for it. One kid came up to us and asked me if he could join our gang and I told him he would have to go through an initiation ceremony, after school. He agreed to do this. At first I meant it as a joke but during the class period some of us were whispering about what to do. After school hours we all went up the Mollsy with the kid who wanted to join us. Each of us was trying to outdo the other with outrageous suggestions for initiation tests. Finally, as we were walking over the railway bridge, a spot where lots of trains slow down to come in or leave the nearby depot, I told him to drop off the bridge onto a moving train and everyone backed me up on this. So the guy waited with us until a train came along at a reasonable speed then he climbed over the parapet and dropped the fifteen feet or so into the open wagon of the train, which by then gathered speed and went in the opposite direction from the depot. We ran to the other side of the bridge and there was his little head over the rim of the truck shouting that he couldn't get off, and we were in stitches laughing and shouting for him to send us a postcard. I think he ended up in Motherwell or some place like that but it certainly gave us laughs for some time to come.

At nights it was a case of back to playing in the streets at various games, and by this time some girls were going around with us and we would feel them up. It was about this time when I had my first girl and it was a glorious knee-trembler in the back, with cats and rats running about. After it I can remember going home and wondering if my ma would be able to tell from my face that I had had it. The first thing I did when I walked into the house was to look in the mirror but I looked just the same. For some reason or other I thought I'd look different. Sometimes when I went home Ma would be in the house and she would be worrying because my brothers hadn't come home. I would tell her that they were out playing and she used to say that she didn't worry too much about me as she knew I could look after myself.

There wasn't much money about but the shops in the area used to cater to the people in the district. For instance, one of the chip shops, "Greasy Peters", would sell a penny's worth of scrapings – that was the fine bits of batter and potato from the chips and fish. Lots of us would go in and get these and buy a burnt hot roll from the bakers and put the scrapings onto the roll. One shopkeeper used to sell penny packets of currants with candy balls and she made a fortune from this so that when she died the cops found a large sum of money in her shop. Another shop sold penny Vantas, which was a small bottle of coloured water that was meant to be ginger. There was "Dirty Maggies", where the kids could go and swap comics. Her shop would be piled high with them but always well away from reach, as experience had taught her that we would rather swipe them than buy or swap. Most of the shops in the district gave "tick" and this was worked out by people going down to the shop during the week and getting food on tick and paying it back on the Friday or Saturday when the wages came into the house. However, the old favourite was "John the Pawns" – the pawnshop – and the Monday would see queues of great length outside the place. People would have big brown paper-wrapped parcels under their arms to put the man's suit into Uncle John's and the same people could be seen in the same queue on the Friday waiting to lift the stuff that had been pawned on the Monday, and this would go on week after week. Most of these shops were small and very dirty with little lighting in them, but everyone would know where to go. A stranger in the district would find it difficult to believe that the shops were open as they seemed very dark and ill used. One could go into the fruit shops and buy chipped fruit. The fruiterer would cut the bad part off and sell the remainder to us so that nothing was wasted. The same could be done in the bakers for broken biscuits or the day-before's leftovers as these were sold at a cheaper price. There was Paddy's Market in the Bridgegate, which would always be full of people in to buy cheap clothes. My Aunt Peggy had a stall selling old clothes that they had been out hawking for. She would always give us clothes out of the "bag" so if I needed trousers my ma would ask Peggy if there was anything decent in the "bag". The bag was the name for the bundle she carried when out hawking.

There were lots of gangs in Glasgow and this seems to have been the case since I can remember. In the Gorbals alone there were the two "Cumbie" gangs, "The Beehive", "The Hammer", "The Dixy", "The Valley", "The Clatty Dozen", "The Skull", "The Stud", "The Kay", also one or two others that I can't recall. But gangs were very much a part of the place and it was the done thing to join one. Up to this point I had avoided gang fights and preferred watching the many that took place. "The Skull", the gang that I led, were basically a stealing gang and a group that went around together. However, one night as we were hanging around the street corner in a group in Lawmoor Street, a gang of guys from down the street approached us and asked us to help them out against a mob from another district who were coming over to fight them that night. This mob from down the street didn't have a gang name but they were pretty wild and their leader was Mad Owny, who was feared amongst us, so although we wanted to keep our distance, at the same time it was very difficult to turn them down because they may have taken offence. But they had made us feel good by asking us to fight with them. They were slightly older than us and more experienced and we all went to their washhouse ganghut and they gave us lots of weapons, and I was given a metal knuckleduster that was very heavy and could do plenty of damage. There were butterflies in my stomach while waiting on the gang coming to fight but inside myself I was saying that I would just act the part and not hit anyone, though my biggest thought was the fear that I might be injured, so I was both frightened and excited.

Owny's gang had plenty of girls going around with them and there was a lot of showing off in front of them about how we would use the knife or the knuckleduster. As the night wore on, and there was no sight of the opposition, Owny's pals started getting a bit restless and messing us around to show off to the girls, so by this time we were wondering what we had let ourselves in for. Eventually it was decided that this other mob weren't going to show up so one of Owny's boys decided that we should have a "dummy fight", with their gang against ours; having been on the brunt of it all night, I didn't like the smell of it. This "dummy fight" was to take place where we stood, about a hundred yards from Lawmoor Street police station, in the middle of the street, but as the streets were so dark the cops could have been a hundred miles away for all the difference it made. The "dummy fight" started with Owny coming for me with his heavily metal-studded leather belt and fear more than gameness made me strike at him with the knuckleduster, and very hard at that, so almost immediately the "dummy fight" was for real. I burst Owny's head and he started shouting that the fight was only for fun – he was taking fright at the ferocity of my blows. Within this very short period of time I was able to see Owny wasn't so tough after all and when the others also saw this they stepped back a bit and my pals became the confident ones, though a shaky confidence it was. It was amazing the transformation that took place. Owny could beat all of his pals physically and because I had just beaten Owny they thought that I could beat them. The relief of not getting beaten up myself and the total surprise that it was turning into a victory was enough to fill me with an enthusiasm that was circulating the group. Owny was even saying that I was "crazy" and the rest were reiterating what he was saying; so although it was only minutes after the "dummy fight", we were talking about having a fighting gang with me as the leader. We were all for it and I was very excited and chuffed at the idea of being classed as a good fighter, and loved it when they said I was crazy as this was meant as a compliment within our culture. All this adulation was going to my head, with all the birds hanging around, and I was loving it. The ironic thing is that before I hit Owny, I'd been very scared and when I actually struck him it was only through fear, that and nothing else. But just like the Larchgrove experience when I was very afraid, the adulation and kudos that came my way were easy to succumb to after the event. That night I went home feeling great and could hardly sleep for thinking of this new victory. Next morning it was all over the school; everyone there seemed to be talking about it.

From then on we would all meet at night and run around the streets shouting gang slogans and playing around. We would go around the gravey a lot, but about this time there was a big scare going about that a madman was terrorising kids in there. It was said that a man with a cape and big iron teeth was roaming about. After school time there would be literally hundreds of kids from all over the district going to the gravey wall and climbing up. Some of us would take a few steps inside the gravey and shout that we had seen the madman and everyone would scatter and run. This went on for over a week and very soon got out of hand as kids were terrified. The press came on the scene and it so happened that across the street was a small shop that sold fruit, vegetables and comics and some of the comics were horror ones. The press immediately jumped on this as being the cause and before anyone knew what was happening there was a loud cry for the banning of comics. There was also a decision to put an iron railing on top of the wall round the gravey to keep kids out and this was done, so although the bigger kids could still climb it, the gravey as a playground went out of action.

Owny's gang had plenty of experience of breaking into places and thieving, having been at it longer than us. One of these methods was known as "grafting", which was finding a shop with an empty house next to it or above it and making a hole in the roof or through the wall and going in that way. There was plenty of scope for this as the Gorbals was part of a redevelopment scheme. Lots of kids at our school were being rehoused in housing schemes in Castlemilk, Garthamlock and Drumchapel. Some of our neighbours were also being moved. Many people resisted this strongly and my ma was one of them. However, some of my class-mates and pals who had been moved were still attending school and travelling to and fro to play with their old pals. No one seemed to like the new housing schemes.

But to get back to the shopbreaking, all this movement meant that there would often be empty houses next to shops full of goods. When we went out to break into them we would carry a Brace and Bit, a chisel and a hammer, as these tools would take us through bricks and wooden floorboards. Another thing was the using of a stout plank of wood between the bars on the windows of a back shop to force the metal bars apart. At first we couldn't believe it would work, but when we saw that it did we would go round bending bars for the fun of it. The graft was the safest and best as we could cut the floorboards of a house and, using a rope, drop to the floor of the shop below. At least two of us would go down the rope, clean out the goods that we knew we could get "fenced" and pass them up to those above. This meant that a cop passing on his rounds could be checking the doors and see nothing amiss. Our cop-watcher would have warned us of his movements and we would sit in the shop very quietly listening to him pulling the locks and checking the back door, if there was one, and passing on. Once he was well away we would continue our work. There was real excitement about this sort of thing and I really loved it. Of course there was an element of fear, the fear of getting caught, which was always present.

By the time I was fourteen I had been doing lots of breaking into shops and warehouses and fighting with other gangs but I was finally caught for screwing shops and given twenty-eight days detention in Larchgrove. Padge and Johnny were with me again but this time I found it different. I wasn't afraid of it as I had been before. I knew the system and how to work it and although I disliked it every bit as much, it held no fear for me now. I was going in amongst people that I knew, for instance the screw knew my name and asked what I was in for, and at the same time I knew them and how each one liked me to behave and I would handle it that way. The screws knew that we three had been there before and would give us jobs that were cushy but that needed kids who didn't have to be watched all the time. I was put in the kitchen and would sneak into the food store and steal large bars of cooking chocolate for my pals and myself and they would get the perks from their jobs, so we had a better time. Although we were still very much into the disciplinary scene, by this time we could do our scrubbing and make our beds square without any bother. The screw that would give you a cuff on the lug was avoided so that it was usually the new kids that got it. The difference was that I was now one of the confident ones and every morning when new kids would come in looking as frightened as I had once been, it made me think how it was good knowing the ropes. My ma would come up to see me and I would tell her that I was never coming in again and I really believed this, and so did Ma. I caught on to the fact that if I wore a mechanical smile and was subservient to the screws then I would skate through the twenty-eight days and this is what happened. No doubt I hated doing this but it was how one got out and I was cute enough to see that this was what they wanted. On Sundays they would take us to chapel at St John's Approved School, which lay in the same grounds, and during mass I was able to see some of my pals who had been going around with me there and other friends I had made in the Remand Home. The place was full of old faces I had known.

After discharge from Larchgrove I was back at school the next day and each time I came home from the place I was put on a higher pedestal in the class and school by all the other kids and most of the teachers left me alone as I was looked on as a real troublemaker. I was left with a year to do in school but there was nothing to justify my being there as lessons were secondary to everything else that went on. The funny thing was that until about this period I had been a pretty mild pupil, and though I had a bit of a carry on I was always manageable and afraid of the teachers. At this time I was still wearing a leather jacket and an army belt with metal studs hammered into it and the trend was to see who could undo their belt the quickest to use in a fight, and most of the kids were pretty quick at this and would pass the time practising.

We had this big teacher who talked just like a man in the street, a very rough one, in comparison to teachers as we knew them.

One day in class he lifted his foot, put it on the desk of a pal of mine and leant on his knee as he continued to speak to us and the next thing he knew, we were all in stitches laughing at him as the sock he had on was full of holes. We thought this hilarious as it was one thing for us to have holes in our clothes but not the teacher! Anyway this big teacher took offence at our laughter and pulled out one of the boys and was about to strap him. The boy was Johnny, and I told him to leave him alone and swore at him. By this time he was really angry and he left Johnny and came for me. I stood there like Billy the Kid, and tried to loosen my belt to get it off and hit him but, unlike the other times, it wouldn't come so I ran away, with this big teacher chasing me around the class, and just at this time the bell rang and everyone scampered out, leaving me getting chased around the class with him calling me all the little bastards of the day and me trying like fuck to get the belt loosened, but it wouldn't come. When he did get me, he pounded the shit out of me and at that moment the cleaner came in to clean the classroom and the teacher turned to tell her to get the Headmaster, but she took one look at me and said she was calling the police as my face was in a bit of a state. I managed to get away from him but by that time my lip and nose were burst and a black eye was on the way. All the kids were looking in the classroom window and when I got out they cheered me. There was no way I could lose. Due to the state of my face I had to tell my ma, so the next morning she took me to see the Headmaster and after a long discussion it was all forgotten and I was allowed a few days off.

By this time we were drinking wine in the toilets and smoking. Another gang had sprouted up in the school and we would fight with each other and one time I sat in class with a bayonet down the side of my trouser leg as a fight was looming with the other gang. I ended up fighting with the leader of the gang and he pulled a flick knife on me during the fight – which was supposed to be a fair one. A "Square-Go" is one where the fists, head and feet are used, but no weapons. When this guy pulled out the flick knife it was one of my pals who saw it and shouted to me and I got it off him and kicked it to my pal but the Headmaster came in and caught us, taking both of us to stand outside the door of his room. While there, we never spoke but the other guy's face was in a mess and mine was okay. All the girls had to walk past the Headmaster's room to get to their classes and it was good to watch them seeing his face and asking if I had done it, with their teachers shouting at them for speaking to us. The other guy was looked on as the best fighter in the school so this was a big victory for me and I loved it. We stood there for some time until the police came, which surprised me as it had been a fair fight. They let the other guy go and the two uniformed cops took me between them and walked me all the way to Lawmoor Street police station. I walked past neighbours who asked me what was wrong and I shouted that it was okay and that nothing was wrong. The cops said I was to be sent away and they left me in a small room for a couple of hours but then they let me go and nothing further happened.

By this time Johnny Boris was sentenced to an Approved School, and a new kid, Johnnie Crosby, who had just come out of one, joined our class. Johnnie's uncle had been sentenced to death and reprieved so this was a big talking point for us and he joined our gang. There was a lot of coming and going in the school at this time due to the new housing development. Some of my pals who used to come down to our district at nights after moving house started making new pals up there and from this there grew more gangs, some of which became rivals of ours.

Meanwhile, my reputation was expanding amongst the kids of my age, and with the police, who were keeping a close eye on me. Our group took up street fighting more seriously though we still did the odd bit of stealing. This meant that we would meet and go to other parts of the district and fight rival gangs. At nights we would all be standing around the corner when someone would say that members of a rival gang were nearby and we would go for them, just like that and they did the same with us. There would be frequent meets to have a full gang fight but these took place very seldom as by the time we had made arrangements the cops would usually be on the spot though there were times when we would be fully into it before they arrived. All sorts of weapons were used: knives, hatchets, bayonets and swords, but they were for show rather than for use. The main rival gang to us in the Gorbals was "The Stud" and we fought continually and went for each other individually when we met on the street. Eventually there was an arrangement made for me and the leader of the "Stud" to fight each other on a one-to-one basis. The fight was to be on the "Stud" territory, in a place called "The Raw", a piece of waste ground that had once held houses which had since been knocked down. It was a "Square Go" and by the time we had got there the place was filled with people from all over the district. The area was in complete darkness, with everyone squeezing around us to see what was going on, so there was little space left to fight. Anyway we went ahead and flew at each other but the minute both of us rolled on the ground everyone started booting the two of us. The boots were from each of our supporters trying to help us, but thank Christ someone called that the cops were coming and this scattered everybody and we made off. If they hadn't called out, the chances are that the two of us would have been kicked to death. I spent days looking for guys who had kicked me but it was hard trying to find out as they had all been at it.

Not long after this the "Stud" began to fall away and we went looking for greener pastures. By now it was all a case of getting a reputation and this was only gained through fighting other gangs. We started fighting the gangs in Castlemilk, some of whom had been our pals and part of our old gang, but they became as much against us as we them. We beat them without any bother. All during these fights no one was badly hurt as they were only boys' fights, till one hot summer's night in a desolate part of the district we had a fight with a gang in Govanhill, which is a fringe district of the Gorbals. Most of the guys in the gang there came from the Gorbals and we all knew each other pretty well. All of us were armed to the teeth and I had a butcher's knife, the others had their own weapons. As the two gangs came into sight of each other they broke into a run, throwing bottles as they came. This usually broke the groups up and we met and fought the individual who was nearest. I was fighting this guy who had a hammer that kept bouncing off my head and during the struggle we ended up in the close-mouth with me on top of him. I hacked the butcher's knife into his face and slashed him, the skin parted and the blood started pouring over both of us. Between the blood coming from him and from my head, we were covered in it. On seeing us most of the others took fright and bolted but we were each helped by our pals.

This was the first time I had slashed anyone and really I didn't feel any remorse or pity for the guy as my head was sore and cut and I was cursing that I didn't give him worse, with my pals telling me not to worry as we would get him again. Certainly I had hit Owny with the knuckleduster but that was different as this time I had gone out to fight with a weapon intending to use it. The reason that I didn't feel any sorrow was that all the other fights had prepared me for this and I was actually looking forward to using the weapon, as were the others. In the other fights I hadn't slashed or hurt anyone seriously although we boasted amongst ourselves as though we had. So when it did happen it wasn't just an idle boast and in fact it lent credibility to the earlier boasts and fantasy tales that we had been spreading. Another aspect that, for me, made slashing all the more a proper action was the injuries I'd suffered myself, a couple of gashes and bumps on the head from the hammer blows. They were a great prize in a strange sort of way because they let the others see that the victory was all the more deserved. It didn't take that incident long to circulate the district and other gangs outside. Within days I was a force to be reckoned with and some kids were saying that I was as "mad as a brush". There was a sort of hero worship about all of this and I was placed on a higher pedestal by all my own gang, but like reputations in other fields, you've got to deliver the goods otherwise you're in trouble.

By this time I was becoming pretty well known in the Gorbals as a thief and a fighter and the older guys in the district would use us to carry out what we thought were important tasks. For instance there was the shebeen runner who put us to good use. His shebeen was run from an ordinary house in Lawmoor Street and each weekend he would stack it full of cheap wine and other booze. It would open after the pubs closed during the week, but the bulk of the business was at the weekend when all the parties would be taking place. He would get the booze at wholesale prices then sell it for more than the retail prices, therefore making a good profit. The rumours would fly about frequently that he was paying the cops off, and locally this was felt to be true as his shebeen was only 100 yards from the cop station. We would make some cash for standing about and telling strangers looking for the shebeen how to find it. Taxidrivers would bring clients, and prostitutes would bring American sailors and ordinary "johns" to it for booze. If they didn't know where his shebeen was we would refuse to direct them till we got more cash out of them and this would always work. Some of them were only too glad to give it to us as they were usually in need of a drink.

It was great watching the shebeen owner move about, as if he was a mini Al Capone, with a big black car and the usual henchmen. They would get all their booze from the pub at the corner and we were fascinated watching them load up. They had cases and cases of booze and it was incredible to see all this being done with no one saying a word. It was as though they were a law unto themselves. Occasionally there would be a fight in the shebeen but never as many as one would expect in such a place. There was lots of singing and Yanks screwing the brass nails (prostitutes) in the closes nearby, which we used to watch. Lots of local people used the shebeen and they could get tick but only if their names were good. The local men also used to play Pitch and Toss at the street corners, which was tossing pennies in the air and betting whether they landed heads or tails. There was a banker who would hold the cash and do the betting and the local men would play this through the week. We would be told to cop-watch for this and it was always good for a few bob bung from the men. We would approach the winner afterwards and tell him we had been cop-watching and a good bung would be handed out. Sometimes we would shout that the cops were coming when they weren't, and they would scatter, taking all the heavy cash with them, leaving the small change lying on the ground, and we would jump over and pick it up, but we could only do this occasionally. However, on the Saturday and Sunday there was a big Pitch and Toss held in the Moll's Mire, run by the shebeen owner. This was the big daddy as there would be lots of money changing hands; most of the men from the district went there, in fact men came from all over Glasgow. There was no way we could get to cop-watch this, the adults did it, but it was rumoured that the cops were paid not to come near though on occasions they made a token gesture.

Some of the local safe-blowers blew a safe in a Post Office and took lots of postal orders and the stamp to ramp them with. In order to get rid of them they got some of us together and asked us to go into the local shops to change them, giving us so much from each one. This meant a lot of money for us by any standards. Each night after we had been out cashing them we would go into the local pub and pay them the cash. They would buy us a pint and this was fantastic, sitting there in the pub at fourteen, drinking. The publican would say nothing as they were all pals, which was good for us as we could now go into the pub. It was great for us to walk home from school at lunchtime and go straight into the pub with other kids from the school looking on. All week we would go out stealing, save up for the weekend and sit in the pub, buying the older people drink and putting it back ourselves, although a few pints would have us full to the gunnels. Before we were allowed into the pubs we would buy cheap wine and go into the backs and sit round a fire drinking it or in someone's house if none of the adults were in. We would hold parties with girls and have fun getting drunk out of our minds.

Boozing became a big thing for us and when we got drunk we would do crazy things like smashing shop windows and fighting. I would waken in the morning wondering what I had done the night before and go round to my pals and find that they were in the same state. From there we would walk along the street and see windows smashed in the shops and would then recall that we had done it. Sometimes it was so bad that I wouldn't even remember. Now any booze that we stole we kept for our own parties unless it was an excessive amount. Our stealing was now for booze money and there would be times when we would be going into school with a hangover and bleary eyes. Kids at fifteen would try to bluff their way into the pubs and be turned back and we would be sitting there a year younger, getting away with it. These were the things that I and my pals valued most. The things that I would do in drink were unbelievable. I went round to the Big Cumbie and challenged them to fight and had the shit kicked out of me by one of them for being a cheeky wee bastard. The situation got so bad that all of us were going around becoming near-alchoholics at the age of fourteen. The pitiful side of it all is that never at any time did I get the least pleasure from drinking. I really didn't like the stuff, but drinking was the done thing so I did it. All my life the men of the district had hung around the local pubs. The pub was where it all happened, and this was the good thing about being in with the right people as you could always get that bit more. At the night's end we would fall out of the pub with the drunken men and women.

The worst thing about breaking into shops at night and stealing goods was having to sell them as it meant taking another risk selling the stuff, so it was much better to get the cash whenever possible. About this time I hit on another seam and that was breaking into the shops during their lunchtime closing hour. The owners would lock the front door putting a token lock on, as they would only be gone for an hour or so and who would break into the shop in broad daylight? We would and we did. This was really good as we would spend our school lunchtime walking around looking at the shops, usually knowing which ones would be going for their lunch. We would watch till they had gone and wait till the street was vacant for a good stretch. It didn't matter if people were a good distance up the street for all they would see was a kid running and kicking the wall, or what looked like the wall from their vantage point and how many times have we seen this happening? I would go in and clear the till and search around as some shopkeepers usually kept cash hidden in biscuit tins or other hidey holes. The tills were usually packed with money and I would load it into my pockets and fill a bag with cigarettes or any other easy-selling articles and walk out. The money to be made at this was really tremendous when comparing our other hauls. Usually we would go back to school with about ten pounds each in our pockets, a great feeling as this was a lot of money for us.

I remember the first time I scored during a dinner-hour break-in, we got over ten pounds. It was a rainy day, the sole of my shoe had a big hole in it and my sock was soaking wet. All afternoon I thought about getting another pair of shoes but how could I wear them into the house as Ma would see them and kick up hell if she thought I had been out stealing. At four o'clock I took this guy in my class with me to the cobbler shop in Rutherglen Road. He always had shoes for sale that had been in for repair but hadn't been picked up by the owners who couldn't afford to pay. I made a deal with this pal in my class that I would buy him a pair of these, as he too had holes in his, if he would come home with me so I could use him as my alibi. He agreed so I told my ma that this guy's mother had given me the shoes and he confirmed this. Ma gave the shoes a thorough going over and when she saw that they weren't new, she accepted it. I had to go to such lengths with schemes such as this to fool Ma, otherwise she just wouldn't have it. So there was I with plenty of money and a good pair of shoes asking myself, "What more did anyone want?" Apart from booze, we spent the money on paying everyone into the movies and smoking the cigarettes that we stole and though I didn't smoke I would puff twice from a cigarette and throw away the remainder. We really felt prosperous at such times but no sooner was it there than it was gone. Easy come, easy go. One time after a few rapid lunchtime raids the cops came up to the school with a witness as we were lining up to go into the classes. The cops took the witness round everyone in the school to see if she could identify the raiders and passed me by with a lot of the money in my pockets. After this scare we cooled it for a while.

It was about this time that I got really desperate and with a few pals wearing balaclavas went into some of the local shops and held them up. In one shop the woman told us she had no money; we opened her purse and a holy medal was in it so we all ran out, not bothering to take the cash from the register. We got nothing from the four shops that we tried to hold up as it was real desperado stuff and with the masks off all the shopkeepers knew us. However, all of us were arrested by the detective Goodall and put on an identification parade. When the witnesses came in to pick out the raiders we called them by their names and they us, asking what we were doing there. This was a close call so we decided to put an end to that one.

Just before leaving school I could see that no one was interested whether I stayed or left so I took the latter course and went looking for a job. I went to a lemonade factory and they employed me. When they asked for my insurance cards I said I would get them soon. Of course I knew that when starting a job one gets about three weeks' grace before the cards are demanded. I went round the shops with a lorry, taking the crates in behind the counter and while doing so, I would take what I could and smother it in the crates of empty bottles that I was taking out. My favourite "steal" was small packets that held 10 in silver and I would always be on the lookout for these and get a couple as well as other goods. The driver was a suspicious bastard, but he was also a lazy one and his downfall was caused by sitting in the back shop eating or drinking tea. I had this job five days and looted almost every shop I went into. On the Friday the driver went into a cafe for his tea and left me out in the van; I was standing on the back of it. I knew where the driver kept all his smash collected from the lemonade sales, so when some guys came along that I knew I told them to steal it. When he noticed it missing later he questioned me but I denied it, so he went to Lawmoor Street Police office to report it while I sat outside. That night I lifted my wages, getting about two pounds odd, but I was laughing as I had been scoring all week. If they came near me then I would say I was too young to work. On my way back to school one morning I saw the same driver delivering lemonade to a shop and he stared at me, but he had another van boy.

At fifteen I left school and in every way it was like leaving prison. I had no regrets. I felt a real sense of freedom. There was a dance held for those leaving but it was made plain that we weren't welcome. That was okay by us as none of us wanted to go anyway. It was great to be finished with the dump. For the last few months I had been going around with this girl, who would cop-watch for us at night while we screwed and fought. She was sixteen, and after school she would come up and wait at the gate for me. There would be no more of that now as I was no longer a child.

The school didn't have a very good success story, as I continued to meet guys from my class in prison.

My Class

Johnny – Approved School, Borstal, Prison and now serving
   Life Imprisonment.
Andy – Borstal, Prison and Life Imprisonment.
Johnnie C. – Various institutions, Prison and Life Imprisonment.
Padge – Various institutions and a long-term prison sentence.

There are at least four other kids from classes younger than me serving life sentences. All of these listed were for separate charges of murder in different parts of the country. There are lots serving sentences of varying lengths. But there is always that bond of having been Bonny's boys and we look back on our times there as fun. My vision of a future when I was leaving didn't stretch very far as my only ambition was to get a job so that I could buy a new suit. All I could think of was a labouring job, as a trade was a luxury and the money was too small. I had done nothing at school and found it hard to be articulate. It was easier to stand and nod or shrug my shoulders than to talk.

All of this led to me taking a job with the *Evening Times*, a Glasgow newspaper. The job was about all I could get and about all I wanted as it meant delivering the newspapers as van boy. The good point for me was that in between rounds I would go to the shops not far away, as it was in the city centre, and steal. By this time I had a good seam worked out. I would go to the shop, usually a large one, with an old classmate, and give him my jacket and I would roll up my sleeves. I had stolen a key to the display windows which fitted lots of them as they seemed to be standard. I would pick an appropriate moment and enter as though I worked in the shop and was doing my work. The space outside the window would be filled with customers looking at some of the goods that I was in fact stealing, but they would never guess. I would take what I wanted and leave, locking the window behind me. I would go back to work and complete my round then sell whatever I had stolen that particular day. The job was easy and so was the stealing, so I was quite happy with my lot. Now in the paper jobs it's all slack till printing time when the papers are parcelled and ready for delivery and then the rush is on. This particular day, I was at the railway station and missed the run and this upset the guy who was my immediate boss and we had a clash. He wasn't a bad guy but I didn't fancy him much and I became a bit awkward. Then he had a go at me one day and that was it. I was unemployed.

I went back to gang fighting and full-time stealing. Most of us from the school still went around together and by this time I was well established as a good fighter amongst my own group. Whenever any of us got caught out stealing the golden rule was to say nothing and plead not guilty and the rest of us would get bail money. A few of our pals got caught and the rest of us went out stealing to raise the bail money. We stole lots of gear and sold it and I went round the guys' parents giving them the dough to help with the bail, or to get them some food while they were in. I went to one of their houses and the mother took me in, but not long after the step-father came in and he didn't know me. During the conversation we had, he started talking about Boyle who had led their son astray. His mother, standing there with a fistful of readies, was holding her face at her man's bloomer. I just got up and walked away and laughed like hell when I got outside the door. If it had been me I could imagine my ma saying the same thing. There was always a great deal of loyalty amongst us in that respect.

It was around this time, while breaking into shops, that I stole my first safe. We had taken the complete set of bars from the back shop window and decided to lift the small but very heavy safe out. When moving it from under the counter and turning it over, the cash inside the safe rattled and this gave us great delight. Though we hadn't a clue how to open it we decided to take it as the sound of the cash was just too much to resist. After getting it out of the shop window we put it onto an old pram and wheeled it to a back-court in Lawmoor Street, where we tried to open it with hammers and chisels. While struggling with it to get it into better positions the money rattled and this in turn brought the householders to their windows. We pulled iron railings out of the fence nearby and attacked the metal box with these, the noise bringing more spectators to their windows. One man threw us a heavy hammer to try to open it with but it was all in vain. As the night passed into morning we decided to call a halt, putting it in the nearby midgie and covering it with ashes then going home to bed.

I felt very tired but it was a rich sort of tiredness with the money in the safe, feeling as though it were in my pocket. We didn't touch it during the daytime but spent the time speculating on the contents and what we would do with it. The more we speculated the higher the sum got as we all forgot that it had come from a wee store; but we lived on these daydreams and they were good while they lasted. It's very difficult to try keeping anything a secret in our district, so by afternoon it seemed as though everyone knew about it and other kids were asking us for a look. Some mothers, on hearing it, didn't let their sons out that night; but it was in vain, as a night's sweat was all we got and each of us were thoroughly frustrated with it. Spectators threw suggestions thick and fast but to no avail. We even carried the safe up three flights of stairs and dropped it over onto the back but the ground was all mud and it sank a good deal into the ground, leaving the safe unmarked. The rattle of cash was enough to keep us at it, but we had to return it to another midgie for the night and no sooner had I got to sleep when I was awakened by one of my pals as the men were emptying the midgies. So we went round and started throwing stones at them and they ran away to get the cops as we were stopping them from doing their job. While they were doing this we had the safe in the pram and wheeled it to a safe midgie. On one occasion we wheeled it past the Police Office, on the other side of the street.

The next day I went to this guy who was a safe-blower and asked him to open it and he gave me instructions to take it to the "Raw" and he would get it. That night we made the meet and he came in a big car, took me away with it and into a house. He had hardly got it into the house when within a few minutes he had the back of the safe torn off and was extracting the contents. I watched, fascinated at how easy he had made it. There was £90 odd and we split it up, giving him a good whack for opening it. By the time I had divided it between the rest of us there wasn't much. Had we worked like we did for Wimpeys they would probably have given us more. However, to look on the bright side I now had the know-how to open a safe and had made another good contact. Most of these guys like to know kids who can shut their mouths and the experience was good. The safe incident was looked on as quite an event and everyone thought we were loaded: they of course were working on the same assumption as I had been, that nobody puts a little drop of cash in a safe, that's where all the big cash is kept.

Two days later I was picked up by the cops – detectives – and as I walked into the squad room one of them told me to take a good look – he was referring to a safe with the back torn open but I played dumb and gave him a quizzical look. The two detectives in charge of the case had been onto me since I was a kid so we knew each other. They had this crazy act where one would be the baddy and the other the goodie with the big melting warm heart. It was very difficult not to laugh at them as they went through this routine. The baddy would always go through this taking-off-the-jacket-meaning-business routine while his partner would restrain him and offer me a cigarette. This would go on and on, with them throwing in that they had my fingerprints on the safe, but I said nothing, till they eventually put me out. I used to wonder why they went through this routine over and over again till it struck me that it may have been worked with others, but even so, why continue it with me when they had tried it so often and it had failed? By now I was smart for all the games the cops played and followed the golden rule of saying nothing till I had seen my lawyer. I didn't really hate the cops at that time, although I was certainly very wary and in some cases frightened of them. They were by now the recognised enemy and the less one had to do with them the better.

Although only fifteen I was drinking quite openly in the pubs and mixing with older criminals, listening to them talk of their exploits and in some cases their dealings with the police, how the police planted evidence on them and told lies when giving evidence in court against them. All of this I would listen to and nod as though believing it but there was this innocence that made me not believe it deep down. I had the odd thump from cops, but I also had the odd thump from teachers and a gaffer, amongst many others. Any dealings I had with the police were of a superficial nature, whereas these guys were on a more intense level. So the innocence was still there in me and I wasn't aware of the politics of crime – the real politics. These older guys had been where I was yet to go and had the experience that I was yet to gain.

So apart from my own petty clashes with the cops, I was also gaining through the experiences of others. I can remember the case of a drunk guy being lifted on Hogmanay by two beat police. There was a crowd round them trying to persuade the cops to let the man go, saying some of them would take him home. There was obviously a lot of feeling from the people as New Year is an emotional period when everyone likes to be in their own home. However, the cops weren't going to let the man go so a struggle started between the crowd and the cops, with one of the police going for assistance and leaving the other to watch the drunk. The remaining cop said that we were to wait till his mate had gone out of sight and then he would let him go. There was no doubt that he was frightened. It was on such occasions that I began to get to know the cops. I looked at them the way most people do, with a basic mistrust, but then I had had that bit more personal experience than most.

Around this time the "Wild Young Cumbie" were very active, getting involved in lots of heavy fighting scenes and getting the name of being the best fighting gang ever to come out of the Gorbals, both collectively and as individuals. Some of them were involved in a big fight that was reminiscent of a Wild West saloon brawl in the Gorbals and there was a big court trial afterwards where John McCue, Artie Austin and three others were involved and all given sentences. John – four years – and Artie – eighteen months. The press made a big deal of it and labelled John as the leader. The fact was that another guy was the leader. This was all part of the image-building process of the press. All of us younger kids would pore over these newspapers, and the press coverage only confirmed the years of adulation that we had given them. Being in the papers was a great thing to us. All of the kids that went about with me idolised these guys so when they were jailed and put out of the way we saw fit to change the name of our gang from the "Skull" to the "Cumbie". Our activities on the gang scene became more intense. I was intent on making a name for myself, and the only way this could be achieved was by violence. There seemed to be plenty of rewards for the gamest guy, and I was intending to be him. Certainly the punishments were pretty severe, but when living this existence it is difficult to think about getting caught so this didn't really enter into it.

Violence now entered our thieving and when we broke into a place it would be done quite openly by walking up to the premises, smashing the window, jumping through and loading up with what we wanted to take. If any good citizen tried to stop us we would face up to him, but almost every time we did it unheeded. The dialogue and rumour that went on about the gangs was what gave us, as individuals, a boost; so the more daring or cheeky the event, the bigger the impact. The same thing went for gang fights as the one giving out the most stitches got the reputation. It also made others think twice before coming near you. When anyone did come for you, it was usually the real thing with no messing about, so there was a dangerous side to it, but I must have accepted the risks because that's the path I trod. This sort of attitude was held in almost every gang. There were times when we would talk about losing our "nerve" or "bottle" and this was a great fear amongst us.

Some kids that had gone about with us had fallen away to get a job or go with a girlfriend. This to us was "chickening out", which was something we didn't want to do and which we were afraid of. I would frequently "test" my nerve, setting myself tasks which would usually take the form of stealing. My ma used this old pram for taking her house washing to the "steamy" (washhouse). One night I borrowed it and went to a small pub, jemmied the front door, went in and took lots of booze, loaded it onto the pram and got away. We used to hang around this old guy's house with girls and so I took the load of booze up there where all my pals were and surprised them with the drink and we all had a party. This was looked on as being really game, but most importantly, these were things that I used to do to prove to myself that I hadn't lost my "nerve". The old guy whose house we used would get very drunk and we would be lying on the floor with the girls and he would shout to me (he was an old sailor) to clear the deck and we just laughed. We found that lots of older guys would hang around us as they were sure to get booze; but usually they were the weaker ones. They were district characters with fantastic lines in patter and they would tell us stories of how they did lots of depredation ('dep' as we called it). The important thing for us was that these guys were putting our names about to the older guys in the district, making us known to them, so it was all part of climbing the ladder into the real criminal world.

5

My lone journeys of testing myself came to an abrupt end when I stole a cash box of money from the Carnival during the Glasgow Fair Holiday, and on the way out a squad car with detectives who knew me pulled up and spoke to me on a routine questioning thing, searched me and found the cash box. So once again I was inside. I went through all the old familiar procedures and ended up in Larchgrove. Then there was a court appearance where I was put on remand for Approved School Reports. The reports proved positive as I was assessed as eligible for Approved School and sentenced for an indefinite period, which meant up to three years. This shocked me even though I had expected it, but the reality was far worse than I had ever imagined. I felt as I did the very first time I had ever been arrested. My ma was in court crying, and so was I at the thought of going away for three years.

I was taken by car to St John's Approved School, barely fifty yards from Larchgrove. I was left standing by the front door for some time until a man came along, took my name and one or two other particulars, then left me. Much later, as though by accident, a guy who I knew came along and to his surprise found me standing there, so he took me to change my clothing. The place seemed empty as these were the only two people that I had seen in the two hours I had been there. As I walked along the corridor quizzing him I looked over the surroundings in trepidation. Coming in the opposite direction was an old guy in robes and as we drew near him, he reached forward and pulled me to him and struck me full on the head with something hard, watching as I fell back. Not one word was uttered between us. This was my introduction to St John's. I was then told that the old man was one of the staff and that he had hit me with a billiard ball.

I was given the school uniform to wear, a green shirt and a pair of trousers, by an old tailor who had bomb shells and hand grenades all over his desk, which he apparently collected. Such was my introduction to the place. This approved school was run by a team of religious Brothers who wore black cassocks. The place was not only for kids like me who got into trouble, but also for other kids who didn't get into trouble but were in the place for "care and protection". Most of these boys had been in orphanages all their lives but when they became too old and foster parents couldn't be found for them they were put into St John's. There were some kids who had done the full three-year period but these were exceptional cases. The common period of stay was fourteen months, though a great percentage went straight to Borstal from there. My first few days there were hellish as I hated the place and wanted to get out of it very quickly. The fact that I met plenty of old friends meant nothing. I was intent on running away at the first possible chance and kept telling them this but they just said that everyone feels the same when they first come in but I would get used to it. The action of the old guy hitting me meant nothing to them as this sort of thing happened all the time and obviously they were used to it. They were right and within a few days I had settled down somewhat.

In the morning we would get up, make our beds, then go downstairs to the toilets, where everyone would wash. There were about a hundred and fifty boys in the place and we would all wash at the sinks then line up and be marched to the chapel, where mass would be said, with everyone closing their eyes for sleep more than for prayer. After mass everyone was marched downstairs for breakfast and prayers, which were said before and after the meal. We would then be lined up in the big yard and taken to our particular workshop. I was put in the joiners as a few of my pals were there and they said I was to come with them. At lunchtime it was back to the dining hall and while we were saying prayers the meal would be put on the table. I'll never forget my first meal. The time between meals was pretty lengthy and there was always talk about being hungry, so that while the prayers were being said two kids seated on the opposite side of my table leant forward, one of them spitting in his own dinner and the other extracting his false teeth from his mouth and placing them on top of his meal. I watched, puzzled, and laughed at it, thinking it was a joke, but later on I found out that they were recognised as being the weak ones and therefore more likely to have their meals eaten by the others. This prevented that from happening. It was just a survival tactic.

After lunch it would be back out to the yard for football then back to work. Work ended at 4.30 p.m., at which time we were all lined up for a shower. There was a big communal shower section where about twelve boys could shower at a time and one of the Brothers would stand looking in, ordering us to wash our necks or something else. From there it was to the dining hall for the evening meal, after which the rest of the evening was our own. The school had a swimming pool in it, which was the favourite attraction for everyone.

Kids came to the school from all over Scotland. It was a senior approved school, which meant it took boys in from the age of fifteen upwards. There were a number of civilian staff but they were usually the workshop instructors, though some would come in at nights to supervise. There were a number of Irish matrons who did the cooking and the laundry and they stayed in the buildings as did the Brothers. There was one night watchman; he too was a civilian. The system was such that kids who were in for a certain length of time would be allowed to visit their homes on Saturdays and Sundays. When kids didn't return it was often said that it was because of mass rather than anything else, as the prayers that were said in that place were unbelievable and really put me off the Catholic religion, which was already coming out of my ears. The only kids that went home at the weekends were those who were within travelling distance; anyone who lived beyond Edinburgh had to stay in. The ones in for care and protection had no homes to go to, but those of us with homes would be able to take one of these kids home for the day so that he could have a day out at a friend's house and get a good meal. So for this reason the kids from Glasgow and Edinburgh had the advantage and those from far away would try to keep in the good books.

The kids from the smaller towns and villages in the outlying districts would look up to the city kids, as did those from the orphanages. Most of the talk during the working hours and the recreation periods was centred around crime, as we from the cities would be impressing those from the small towns. When one of these kids went out with a city boy to his home for a meal it was often the first time he had ever been in the city so he would be easily impressed. The Gorbals had a bad reputation, so they would be afraid but also fascinated by going there. The approved school must have been like a university of crime for these kids, as they learned more and newer techniques from it than anything else. But this went for the city boys too as we were making new contacts in other districts, so it was exciting all round. The orphanage kids, who had no previous criminal inclinations, were soon up to their necks in stealing, some of them getting put in Borstal from St John's for committing crimes while there. Stealing was new and exciting to them and they would go out on Saturdays and Sundays to enjoy the adventure of it all. It gave them a sense of independence as they didn't need to ask others for handouts all the time. The approved school gave us 2/6 a week, which was for the work we did. They used to march us all down to the State picture house on the Saturday afternoon for the matinee and our seats would be segregated from the kids that stayed in the Shettleston area. There always sure to be kids running away under the darkness of the film.

After the initial shock of entry I soon hardened and became very much a part of it, trying to gain a position in the only way I knew possible, by violence. Certainly I polished the floors along with everyone else and did my bit as all new boys do, but eventually I asserted myself and sat back while the weak put their shoulders to the wheel. Bullying was commonplace and was very much a part of what the approved school was all about and the same could be said of homosexuality. These two activities were rife within the place and it was through them that one asserted one's position. It was either that or be on the receiving end. It was a very tough place and every kid had to be tough to survive it from the official and the un-official stand-point. For sleeping arrangements the boys were split into dormitories, there being four dorms in all, each holding from twenty to forty beds. One nightshift man, who was on constantly, moved between the dorms and his own office, which meant that we hardly saw him. This would allow us to sit up talking all night or having pillow fights and at times drinking booze which we had smuggled in. There was very seldom any homosexuality at these times as it was too open and this was usually reserved for stolen moments in dark corners. One of the worst insults to another boy in this place was to call him a poof, because if the name was given often enough it would stick and guys would be up trying to prove it. There were the few kids who were that way but on the whole most of them were forced into it.

The ordinary staff in the school were very much like those that I had met in schools outside and there was always this feeling of distance between us. During my whole period in St John's I never got close to any of them, even to talk to on a superficial basis, as all of us kept our distance. There were barriers there and the only one ever to penetrate these barriers was the head man, Brother Paul. He was an admirable person, one who was interested and who cared. He was the one man who made any impression on me, who wasn't afraid to get to know the kids or to give a part of himself to us. He did strange things to all of us with the relationships he tried to build with everyone. He made us all feel very guilty about doing things that were wrong. It's not that he had the chance to get to know any of us really well as he seemed always to be swamped in administrative duties, but when he was about and when he spoke, his actions made every one of us pay attention. He cut through all the phoneyness and we were able to see that he was the genuine article. His presence was a luxury, but the unfortunate thing was that he was the only one with this attitude and sensing this he would take progressive steps to include us by discussing things, such as the money that was allocated to him each year. He would inform us as to how it would be spent and ask for opinions. The fact that he brought us into it even though we didn't always under-stand gave us some sense of responsibility, so that if we ran out of table tennis balls, for instance, at least we knew what it meant so we tried to ensure that they lasted. Apart from the Brothers who would be prone to using violence there was one other who had a predilection for pornography, and kids would make themselves a good day with him by getting porny photos.

The staff in the school would always use Borstal as the big threat, so in many ways it was a challenge and it seemed that I would go there automatically. The Approved School surely played a vital part in my criminal development. It gave me connections that I was to find useful in my adult days. It gave me an introduction to guys from towns and cities throughout Scotland and from many areas in Glasgow, many of whom grew up to be the top thieves or fighters in their areas. There is no doubt at all that most of them gained, in a criminal sense, from their approved school experience. Two names worth mentioning in this context are Ben Conroy and Larry Winters, but there were very many more who were to be quite close to me in my adult years. The fact that we had the same experience by being in the same place was a binding factor and put us on a par with the old-boy network that is so effective in other circles. The work within the school was non-existent and I would spend my day in the joiners' shop with some pals, sitting at a stove-type fire, getting warm and skipping out the door to try to steal potatoes from the kitchen so that we could stick them in the fire and cook them. Things were usually monotonous, though there was plenty of football but, as I said, I wasn't a keen footballer.

A few months later I was given leave to go home. It was great to be with my pals again having parties and drinking so when the time came to return to the Approved School I decided that I wasn't going. I had been looking over a new shop that had just been opened in the district which was loaded with electric sewing machines. These were in great demand, with lots of women wanting them, so I went with some pals early one morning to break into it. With the shop just opened it was still not fitted with an alarm system so it was lying there very vulnerable. We hit it when the beat cops were changing shifts at 6 a.m. or so. We made off with a load of them and got away successfully. The demand for these machines was something, so we had no trouble selling them. We had been talking about the idea of going to London for some time now and I and this other guy finally decided to go on the day that I was due back at the school. The guy with me played the guitar and was really good with it so the idea was that he would get work with a band and I would be his manager – that's how crazy it all was. I had all the cash, so off we went.

I can remember the feeling of going there and how everyone at home had said that the streets of London were paved with gold. Somehow I had taken this literally because I was surprised when I was actually in London to see ordinary streets and buildings. Both of us had some clothes in a soldier's kit bag and we took turns carrying it, although it pretty soon ended up back in the left luggage at the station. From there we wandered all over the place, finally getting to the West End, and hunted out the "Two Eyes Cafe" where Tommy Steele and other singers were "discovered". But it was empty so we wandered around buying junk from stalls and shops. We slept the first night in a "Model" that was full of old men and passed ourselves off as being of age. We had heard that everyone robs everyone else in these pitches, so we sat and looked at some of them as they stripped, putting their shoes under the bed legs and sitting the bed on top of the shoes so that no one stole them during the night. They put the rest of their clothing into the pillowcases so we followed suit.

Within a few days our money was all spent so we wandered around trying to get dish-washing jobs. We were hungry and had nowhere to sleep until we found a back close, where we huddled together with our jackets over our heads. During the day we went to the train station and slept on the benches. If we had tried to sleep there at night, the cops would have picked us up and discovered that I had blown from the Approved School. One night we were wandering about when the cops came and arrested us and took us into the police station. They questioned us but we already had stories and false names prearranged so, when they separated us and found our stories corresponding, they let us go. A few nights later when we were very hungry we heard two guys speaking with Scottish accents so we asked them for some cash. They had just come back from a night at the dog racing and had done very well so they took us for a big meal and gave us a couple of pounds. This really made our day. It is a great feeling to find people like that when you have nothing.

A few nights later, in a state of hunger, we were walking along this road looking for a place to sleep when lo and behold there in front of us was a shop window lying broken and inside were transistor radios. We looked about and the place was very dark and quiet so I reached in and grabbed a transistor and as we turned to go the lights and engine of a car across the street came to life and made for us and we were pounced upon. It was the cops. Apparently this was an old trick. If a window was smashed and the stuff stolen before the cops arrived, then they would lie in wait for the first unsuspecting victim. In many ways it was the most unexpected thing that could have happened to us. Even though the musician's job was becoming a dream in the distance, then the dishwashing, the last thing we expected was to be arrested, because we had been keeping out of bother. But something had to give, as we couldn't carry on in this way with no real sleep or meals. After a brief court appearance we were taken to Shepherd's Bush Remand Home, which we found to be much easier than Larchgrove. On the way there, we were being driven in a police van along a busy street when, by sheer coincidence, I saw my brother Tommy, who was in London, working. I shouted out of the window to him and he came along to the Remand Home to visit me. My pal and I were always hungry and we were a joke in the place for when they shouted that extra food was available, no matter what it was, we would make a mad rush for it. After another court appearance, I was ordered back to the Approved School under the supervision of one of the Brothers, who had been sent down for me. My pal was remanded for probation reports.

On the train journey, the Brother brought two packed lunches and I consumed mine immediately while he fussed and pecked over his, much to my annoyance. Eventually he fell asleep, leaving a sandwich and an apple on the table in front of him, with me sitting there looking at it. So while he slept I ate his apple, saying to myself that I could tell him that it rolled off the table while he slept, but as he didn't waken for some time I ate his sandwich too.

I knew he had to wake up and I knew he would be raging at me, so I started thinking up elaborate excuses about where the food had gone to. Instead, when he woke up, I closed my eyes, pretending to sleep and I could hear him searching about for his food. I kept my eyes closed for a long time and when I did open them he sat reading a book, looking bloody furious. When the trolley came round for coffee he bought only one for himself and said nothing to me.

As a punishment for running away I was to be kept in and not allowed home for a long time. I also had to wear short khaki trousers for a period. The standard punishment for kids running away from the Approved School was the "pants" (a leather belt battered over the bare arse) but for me this was the easiest part. I had a great deal of respect for Brother Paul so that being brought back and having to face him was the hardest part of it all as I felt that I had let him down, and in many ways I had.

When I returned from absconding to London, I painted a lovely picture and exaggerated it saying that the streets really were paved with gold. Within a few days, lots of kids were absconding and heading for London, some being caught on the Edinburgh Road, trying to hitch a lift. Now some of them had run away before and knew full well they would go to Borstal if they did so again. But it made no difference. There was this glamour part to it all that as kids we could never see past. Around this time there was an outbreak of gang fighting in Barlinnie Prison when the "Scurvy" gang were making headlines and lots of stabbings were taking place. We in St John's loved this and would all talk about it, saying that we would prefer to be doing our time in Barlinnie rather than here, as that was where the real tough guys were.

Brother Paul had a scheme going by which kids in the latter part of their sentence could get an outside job in preparation for going out. I was given a chance on this and it meant going out in the morning to a job and returning afterwards to the school each night. At the end of the week we would hand in our wages and get ten shillings spending money. I got a job in the Gorbals Sawmills that was known locally as a "slave camp". The hard labour of it didn't really matter to me because it allowed me to go home for lunch. I lost the job but didn't tell the Brothers this as it would have been a set-back in terms of my being released for good. At the same time I had to make up the wages so I went out stealing and would go in on the Friday to the room where the Brother took the wages of the workers and marked them in a big book and when asked for my wage slip pretend I'd lost it. It was a struggle for me getting the wages each week, but this carried on for about three weeks. One Saturday night I arrived back in the Approved School after my day out and quite by chance bumped into Brother Paul in the main entrance and spontaneously asked him when I could be liberated. He simply turned round and told me to go home. I too turned round and ran into the night where it was dark and the rain was cascading down beautifully. I jumped on the first bus, afraid that he would come after me saying it was all a joke. I sat on the top floor next to the window watching the rain cleanse the city streets and in a strange way wash away with it the strain that I had been under. My entry to St John's had been very strange but then so had my exit.

In a way I left it a much harder person as it tore me from my family for a period, giving me confidence amongst kids my own age who were unknown to me, letting me see that I could more than hold my own.

On leaving the Approved School I was able to get a job with my brother Tommy, who by this time was working in the shipyards in Govan, but I only stayed there for a short period. Although free from the school, I was still on Licence for a year, which meant a form of probation under the condition that I could be recalled at any time. The person doing the supervising was the school Welfare Officer and I didn't see much of him though he was quite a nice, helpful guy.

I left the job in the shipyards to return to London. Once there, I got a flat in Elephant and Castle. One night I wandered over to King's Cross, where most Scottish guys hang around and there I met plenty from the Gorbals and in particular, Frank Wilson and Artie Austin. I was very glad to see them and they me. These were the guys that I used to idolise, as did all the kids in the district, so I had a feeling of awe being with them. Frank was small with fairish hair and broad shoulders. He had a strong good-looking face with white, even teeth. His eyes were blue and penetrating and seemed to mirror his mind, which was quick and very smart in a business-like fashion. His fighting abilities were something to be admired as he was very tough and had a reputation for being able to knock out men taller than himself with one punch. When he was a kid he was keen on amateur boxing and dabbled in it for a spell, but he was more interested in street fighting and became entangled in the "Cumbie" gang. He was the leader and was well respected and feared in the gang circles. Frank stayed in a room and kitchen in the Gorbals with his mother, brother and sisters. He was always a serious sort of guy who gave the picture of being straight out of Chicago in the twenties. He could name all the gangsters from that era and go into detail on the set-up of organised crime in the States. To date he had been in Remand Homes, Approved School and had served one or two small petty prison sentences. From an early age Frank had also been running around the streets and learning all the tricks of the trade which one could pick up.

Artie Austin was over six feet tall, with broad shoulders and going prematurely bald. He had a fantastic personality, good looks and was full of life and would start singing at the first sight of a stage or a party. I started going around with them and we kept very much to ourselves, though through stealing we had to mix occasionally with London guys to fence our goods. But we kept away from the known thieves. If I had plenty of nerve before, I had double the amount now as I was intent on impressing Frank and Artie, though I would never admit this to them. London was a dream as it was so big that one could hit different parts of it each day and so remain anonymous. I stole anything, specialising in nothing. I would take things from lorries, shops and anywhere else that was vulnerable. Life was a merry-go-round of wastage with me stealing to socialise. I would take pills (purple hearts) and wander around the West End in a daze. These pills as well as keeping one awake gave one a strong urge to talk, and I would look for an empty ear and bore it to tears. I would go into a shop to buy something as simple as a newspaper with the eyes popping out of my head and fall into a long drawn-out discussion with the shop assistant almost striking him catatonic with boredom. In the local pubs there were lots of prostitutes and I would hang around with them. They were trouble as they would start fights knowing someone was there to do their fighting, but they were good-hearted. It was fun for me and one of them from the Glasgow area, Irene, used to take me to this club where marijuana was sold and we would get stoned. It was great listening to all the kinky stories that they told, and being with them broadened my sexual experience.

Sometimes we would get fed up with London and return to Glasgow for a spell and this was when I would bask in the glory as Frank and Artie were looked up to by the local kids of my age and those older than me. I was climbing the local social ladder and quite frankly it was going to my head. But mixing and going around with these older guys I felt that I had to continually prove myself. Neither Frank nor Artie put this pressure on me but it was just something that was happening, the pressures of my situation. I still got on with the guys of my own age and drank with them and there was no need for me to boast as it was the talk of the district anyway. I would do crazy things very much to test myself and although they were crazy, they seemed sane enough under the cloud of booze and pills, and I thought nothing of them.

On leaving a party one night, in a house full of my pals, I went round to a rival gang corner where the "Bee Hive" loiter and started shouting "Cumbie" slogans and attacking the leader of their gang with a brick. No sooner had I done this when they pounced on me, throwing my face down in the street and pinning me there while someone smashed beer bottles over my head (screw tops) and started cutting my on the back of the neck and head with the jagged glass top. The group made off. I got to my feet feeling the liquid running down my neck and back, thinking I was badly cut and that it was blood, but I continued to shout the slogans. I was still standing there, soaking wet, full of pills and booze, shouting "Cumbie", when the Black Maria arrived and I was thrown into the back of it. In the van I started to argue with the cops and they didn't take too kindly to that. Arriving at the cop shop, even more bloodied, I was charged at the police bar and spat a mouthful of blood on the desk sergeant.

This infuriated them which they made plain to me physically. I woke the following morning in a white tiled cell with a sore face and head, my clothes sticking to me with blood. I was charged with breach of the peace and making a nuisance of myself. When asked what had happened to my face I told the magistrate that I had fallen, so was given a fine and let loose.

There is no doubt that when I was sober, alone and faced with reality I hated myself, almost as though I was aware of the self-destructive course I was on but unable to do anything about it. I was lost. The only way out was to get involved in more devilment and booze. It wasn't as though I was getting into all of this and had no feeling about it, for I did, but there was just this completely lost feeling, as I felt myself getting deeper and deeper into it. Yet on the other side, when I was with my pals, there was the feeling that it was okay and that having attacked a gang single-handed the previous night, I had in some way proved myself and gained enough confidence to fight alongside them. I had this hunger to be recognised, to establish a reputation for myself and it acted as an incentive being with the top guys in the district at sixteen. There was this inner compulsion for me to win recognition amongst them. There were times when I could see that the others were feeling the same but none of us would put it to each other in words.

Things in my home were going smoothly enough and though I was getting into a lot of trouble, my ma hadn't a clue about it. Other wives and mothers in the district would hear of it but wouldn't tell my ma, as there would be this protective thing going on. This wasn't for my ma only; it was a common thing and basically due to the fact that neighbours didn't want to give the mother any more worries than she already had. There was also the fact that people minded their own business. Occasionally I would return to Ma's and stay for a bit as in many ways it was like re-entering the womb, where I could recuperate from the pressures and tensions of the wild side of life. I'm sure Ma heard the occasional rumour; I can't believe they escaped her completely. If she did she seldom said and maybe she thought that I was as much a man as I'd ever be and, with not staying in the house, was leading my own life. This is not to say that she was objective about it. There is no doubt that anything she did hear would have torn a piece from her heart as she loved me and all of us very much. If Ma did mention anything then I would deny it, even though it was probably true, as I could never have admitted my way of life to her.

My two older brothers were working and Harry was still at school. I was the occasional lodger. All of us got on fantastically well together and there was this very strong family feeling amongst us which extended to my aunts and uncles. We were very close and loyal to each other. Ma still held her three part-time jobs and seemed to think that she couldn't do without them. I was stealing materials that would have made her household work easier but there was no way that I could even attempt to bring this up as I knew she wouldn't have any of it. I had one aunt that I could talk to about this and I asked her to persuade Ma to take some of the goods but she wouldn't try either. I thought this was crazy as some of my pals would give their parents stolen goods and I would have liked to have done the same. There would be times when I entered the house after being absent for weeks and I would be accepted as though I had never been away. Of course there were times when I would tell Ma that I was working in London, but this wasn't a lie for lying's sake but because I knew it would ease her mind. I'm not sure that she believed me at these times but I felt it would give her an alternative version to the other rumours she might hear. I guess I worked on the principle that most mothers listen only to the good about their own brood.

Artie Austin and I started working as a team while Frank and the others went their way to do their own thing for a spell. We worked out of Glasgow, taking a plane to Birmingham, Manchester or London and stealing whatever came our way. Artie was a guy for the good times and we swept along together on this. Sometimes we would go to these places and not touch a drink while we were working but, returning home, life would be a haze created by booze which cleared long enough for us to take another trip to make more cash to spend on more booze. In many ways it was great as Artie could sing very well and we would always be at parties having a good time. He was Americanised and wore clothes from the States and had a Yankee way about him. With his balding hair and me looking like a kid, we were an odd-looking couple of pals. One day he disappeared to the States and the next I heard he was in New York.

PART TWO

PART TWO

6

Meanwhile I was busy thieving and fighting, still trying to gain a position for myself, which I already had but couldn't recognise. Even if I had, I doubt if I'd have stopped. The law of averages meant that I had to "fall" again as I was exposing myself to the law too much, and before very long it came. I was arrested for shopbreaking, only this time I was taken to Barlinnie Prison.

Although quite new to me, going to Barlinnie didn't hold the same fear as the Remand Home had. There was apprehension and excitement on facing the unknown but there was also this feeling of having "arrived". I was just coming on for seventeen when I went to Barlinnie. I was taken in the prison van with lots of others, mostly old men who had been there many times before. Each of us was taken into the reception area and locked into very small boxes, two to a box. There was a piece of wood nailed to the wall meant for us to sit on but there was only room enough for one. The box was about three feet by three feet in size and about eight feet in height. These are what are known as the "dog boxes" as that's just what they're like. The old guy locked in with me tried to kid me that this was where we slept but I was familiar with the prison routine as I had heard others describe it time after time. There was barely room to stand in it never mind eat together, but they gave us lunch in a small bowl with a spoon so that we had to stand and eat out of the bowl and rest the cup of soup on the small wooden strip that was meant to be the chair. A bolt on the outside locked us in and the doors would be opened by "trusty" prisoners who had cushy reception jobs. Usually these were posts filled by the white-collar criminal.

I was called out and taken in front of a desk where a screw told me to undress in front of all these other screws and "trusties". I did so while he marked all my personal belongings and property onto a card. I was then asked a series of questions: Have you ever been in a mental institution? Ever had venereal disease? Any insanity in your family? A long list of questions while I stood there with a towel wrapped around my middle. I was then given a bath – we were only allowed three inches of water, which a "trusty" measured out with a key that he had for the taps. After a couple of minutes a screw came along, telling everyone to soap off. At first I thought he was joking – I hadn't had any time to put soap on. From there, the group of prisoners were taken to the prison hospital and made to drop our trousers while a screw came along to inspect us for crabs. Anyone who had them was whisked away, shaved and put in isolation. The rest of us were taken to the untried hall. It was a massive place and the sound of men's voices, feet on metal stairways, keys jangling, and the loud bang of slamming cell doors was what hit me at first. Those prisoners out doing working tasks would all look over the galleries to see who was amongst the newcomers. The head screw at the desk gave each of us a cell to go to. I was on the third flat, but on going upstairs I was shouted at by a number of familiar faces, coming from either the district or the Remand Home or the Approved School. It was a comforting feeling to see so many people I knew and I felt better now that I had met them. On reaching the third flat I was put into a cell with two other guys, who had been there for some time.

When the door was closed there was the expected questioning about what I was in for and where I came from and vice versa. There was one single bed which was a board nailed to the floor, and a bunk which swayed at the slightest movement and I got the bottom bed there. The blankets were filthy, with lots of burn holes from guys smoking. The cell was filthy and there was an overwhelming stench of urine that came from the three stained chamber pots in the far corner. There was no escaping from this stench. There was a table that we were to use for eating on but it was covered with dog ends. There were three old mugs and these were for our water to last us through the night and for our tea when it came round. Men in the untried hall could stay there for nigh on four months waiting on trial and this could be extended by the court. The prisoners were locked up twenty-three hours a day and allowed out for half an hour in the morning and afternoon to walk around the prison yard. There were fifty cells on each flat and four flats. Sometimes there were over one hundred men in the fifty cells. The stench in the halls was appalling as there were only two toilets for each flat and men would have to "slop out" their chamber pots in these toilets. Each man wore a suit of prison clothes, ill-fitting, with either or both of the sleeves or trouser bottoms rolled up.

This was where I was, locked in a cell with two strangers and determined that I wasn't going to use the chamber pot, come what may. I would lie there bursting for the toilet and refuse to do it, hoping the door would open soon so I could go to the one outside. The other two guys in the cell were used to it all and used it without any hang-ups and when they did, I would turn to the wall as I felt very embarrassed sitting there watching them sitting on the chamber pot. The meals were piled onto a small wheelbarrow and pushed round the gallery. A screw would come in advance and open the cell door as the barrow reached it. "Trusties" would give us the food in a metal bowl and a screw would be behind the barrow to close the door. All this took a long time, which meant that the food was always cold. A hot meal was never to be seen. The screws opened and shut doors and ordered us about but nothing more than that. They never seemed to ask for anything in a normal voice, everything was said in very loud shouts and this struck me forcibly when coming into prison for the first time.

The daily routine was for the doors to open at 6 a.m. and all the prisoners would rush out and form long lines to empty their chamber pots and get water for shaving and washing. Then it was lock-up and breakfast was brought round the doors after which we would sit about the cell either lying with our eyes closed or speaking to each other; but there were often long periods of silence. At mid-morning we would be opened up for half an hour's exercise and if it was raining then we would be marched round the gallery on the second flat, which meant a crowd of men would be crammed in together walking round in circles.

Exercise gave me a chance to see all the guys that I knew and there were plenty of familiar faces. All the guys from the district greeted me warmly and we talked about things, getting the latest news from the guy last in. We would talk about what each of us was in for and what our chances were. Some would be in for serious offences, and others would be in for minor ones. I was tipped for a Borstal Report and Borstal. The guys from my district in the prison were well connected and saw that I got books, papers and other small extras. All these things were the wee perks that made it seem better. After the morning exercise, it was lock-up for a period, then lunch would come round, then we'd be locked up again till mid-afternoon when the second half-hour exercise period would be allowed. After that we would be locked up till after the evening meal then a few minutes to slop out and then that was it till the following morning.

I didn't smoke and I would watch the guys in my cell roll up their dog ends into cigarettes then roll up the dog ends from that. It was horrible watching this, as being a non-smoker, I hated touching dog ends let alone finding them floating in a tea cup; but these were things that happened in a cell with two strangers. At night, guys locked in cells would shit on a piece of paper and throw it out of the window rather than have it lying in the cell all night. This was called "bomb throwing" and we would lie in our cells at night hearing the bombs hit the concrete yard outside. The screws would go round with a prisoner in the morning with a barrow and he was nicknamed the "bomb disposal man". It was either an old meths drinker or a first offender who got this job. Sometimes the screws patrolling the yards at night would catch a guy for it and he would be put on a disciplinary charge and be labelled "the mad bomber" and he would keep the name till the next one was caught.

Each of us in the cell would have a small metal basin to wash and brush our teeth in. Frequently guys would crack up and everyone would lie very quiet while someone smashed up his cell by breaking the small windows and the table and anything else that he could. If there were two others in the cell they would stand by and let him go ahead knowing that the guy would have to get it out. Afterwards he would be taken to the punishment cell on the bottom flat, where at least he had privacy. There were three cells there including a padded one. I had a visit from my ma and she was able to put some sweets in for me as this was a privilege reserved for untried prisoners who had not yet been found guilty. The visit was fifteen minutes and I had to speak through a glass and wire grill. It was difficult to hear each other as it meant bending way over to do so.

I was taken to court and given a Borstal Report by the judge and remanded for twenty-one days in Barlinnie while the report was being compiled. On the last week I was sent for and an Assistant Governor took me into a cell. As he went in the light conked out, so he sent for a bulb and got me to climb up onto the table to fix it in. I spoke to him for a few minutes and he said that by the way I had climbed the chair to put the bulb in I evidently needed more experience in burglary, so he was recommending me to go to Borstal. It was all said in a jocular fashion. When I went back to court I was sentenced to a Borstal Training. During the three weeks of my reports this was the only official I'd seen. It seemed a crazy system, not one to be taken too seriously. There was a great deal of overcrowding in Borstal at that time so the boys had to remain in one of the halls for convicted prisoners for about six or eight weeks till there was a vacancy for them. The system was the same as in the untried hall, apart from the fact that we were taken to work for a few hours each day, but as there was practically nothing for us to do we would be made to sit around or clean out our cells and polish them. We all had Borstal uniforms and not prison ones. The time went very slowly, though it did give us a chance to get to know the others who would be going to Borstal with us.

The atmosphere was very much like Approved School only this time we were in prison. The majority of us would have preferred to have done our time in Barlinnie rather than go to Borstal, where it was all bull and kids' treatment. We all classed ourselves as men. The talk was all women and crime, but crime was the main topic and we all boasted about what good crooks we were and exaggerated the size of our hauls. I would love it when the guys in my district smuggled over tobacco and sweets to me. This was a good prestige thing as tobacco was the prison currency and I could give it to one of the guys who smoked and he would buy me toothpaste and soap from his wages. Not all of the kids waiting for their place in Borstal had been in Approved School, so it was very much a time to weigh everyone up and make new friends while at the same time trying to establish a position so as to know where we stood in the pecking order. Amongst us were a few kids who had previously done their Borstal training but had fallen into trouble again while out on licence. This licence thing was the same procedure as in Approved School where hardly anyone did the full three years but for the remainder of that time they would be kept under supervision. These guys had been out, fallen into trouble and were now back in, but rather than return them to Borstal they were put into Barlinnie and called "Borstal Recalls". Those of us who hadn't done our Borstal were always quizzing them to find out what it was like but they would only tell of the good laughs they had had and would reminisce in a pleasant nostalgic way. They told us a bit about the strict and petty bullshit that went on but they seemed to gloss over this.

At last my time came to go there and I was taken in a van along with five other kids, one of whom had been in Approved School with me. We said we were sick of being treated like kids. We also felt very apprehensive as we'd heard a lot of bad things about the screws in the Borstal. So in a way we were reluctant participants before we even arrived. We were taken into a reception area and given Borstal suits, which were coloured black and called Battle Dress, and a red striped shirt with heavy black shoes. The first small rebellion from me was with the screw giving out laces for the shoes and demanding a "Thank you, sir" from each of us. When he came to me I refused to answer him. It was very interesting as he had been full of confidence up till that moment and he now became unsure of himself as I was an unknown quantity. He glossed over the affair and put it down as nothing, but to me it was a moral victory.

Borstal was made up of what they termed Houses, and newcomers, or "Rookies" as we were called, went into Douglas House for the initial two months of bullshit, and from there we would be put through to either Bruce, Rothesay or Wallace Houses. Wallace House was reserved for the baddies as they had cells for the occupants, whereas the other Houses had dormitories. Douglas House, where I was as a rookie, had single cells the same as Wallace House and each cell had a bed, a small table, and a rough wardrobe for hanging up the battle dress suit. Everything was made of wood except for the bed and every one of these had to be scrubbed, thoroughly scrubbed, each and every day.

The daily routine was that a pail of water had to be taken into each cell the previous night (a bucket, cloth and scrubber were in every cell) so that immediately on rising everyone would box their bedding in military fashion and then proceed to scrub every wooden article in the cell while a screw came round inspecting to see that we were doing it properly. If he had cause to enter the cell he would shout for the borstal boy to stand to attention while he went round looking in corners for dirt and even if none was found we could be told to do it again. Hundreds of kids must have scrubbed the cell I was in before I came, for it was spotless and I reasoned that it couldn't get any cleaner than it was so I would never put too much effort into scrubbing except when I heard the approaching screw. I could never make a bed military style and this was my weak spot as it would be torn apart by the inspecting screw every other day. I really hated this. Everything in the place had to be done "on the double", so that after scrubbing the cell we had to dress immaculately with shining shoes and best dress and stand to attention, just like all the other places I had been in, and then march single file for breakfast. This was in the main area on the bottom floor of Douglas House. After breakfast we were lined up and stood to attention then split into groups, some of whom would go to a classroom for school lessons while the others would scrub the hall area and other parts of the Borstal.

My rebellious actions took the form of never standing to attention and I would do this when the screws shouted during the line-ups, so that they could never see me. In many ways it was me retaining a part of myself. The minute the screw's back was turned, I would do nothing, so if we were scrubbing and the screw went to look at someone else or do something else then I would wipe the floor with a wet cloth to give it a wet look or I would just rest my knees, which would be sore from kneeling down. I was caught at this once by two screws and they came across very heavy, shouting at me, but I told them I had been doing it properly. They kept shouting, as they stood over me, telling me to scrub but I got up and threw the bucket of water over the floor and was locked up for it. This was being "put on report" and an offence against good discipline. The following morning I was taken in front of the Headmaster, who was called the Housemaster, and he punished me by giving me a fine. The group who scrubbed in the morning went to school in the afternoon and vice versa. We were given physical training every day and taken into a gym for this. There were rumours that the gym teacher was a black belt at karate, although it was just as likely to be judo. I'm sure these gymnasium teachers used to spread these rumours themselves as almost every institution that I had been in had one. The P.T. class was very hard going and we would be pushed to the limits.

It was amazing the number of kids that I knew in the Borstal from elsewhere. Due to be liberated was Ben Conroy, and coming in just behind me was Larry Winters. Many guys from my district were in other Houses and sending me over toothpaste, soap and tobacco. The wages for Rookies were very small, so receiving these extras from my friends was very helpful. It meant that I didn't have to rely on the wages made from scrubbing, as the favourite punishment was to take money off someone's wages for the slightest thing. There was a great deal of discontent amongst the kids in the Rookies and with this there was always talk of rioting, which would raise itself to a very intense level. I would like to have led one but it was all talk and never seemed to come off.

One night, while lying in my cell, I was particularly dreading the thought of getting up in the morning and going through all the scrubbing. I had had enough of it and wanted to get away from it all, so I put all the furniture from my cell in front of the door, barricading myself in. I lay there and listened to the nightshift patrol making his way along the gallery, looking through judas holes on the way. When he came to mine he shouted for me to clear the judas hole and I told him to take a fuck at himself and just lay there. He went away and I listened to every noise. It was great to lie there feeling that for the first time in months, I was able to decide something for myself. I heard reinforcements coming and they tried to put the door in but I had it well and truly barricaded. Eventually the Governor was called in and they tried to talk me out. It was a big thing for the Governor to be called in at night. It was near morning when I came out but while I was locked in I felt really good and very much my own man with these people speaking to me as a human being for the first time, even if it was only to get something out of me. It didn't really matter what happened from there as I felt I had nothing more to gain by staying in. When I came out one of the people responsible for running the place was there, along with the patrol screws and I was taken to the punishment cells, known as the "Digger". We went through a series of corridors to parts of the Borstal that I had never been to before. All the time that I walked I was expecting to be attacked by the screws as I heard there were lots of beatings going on in the place. However, no one touched me, and I was taken into this hall area that was full of cells. At the end of the hall a section of the bottom flat was partitioned off and I was taken through a door there and downstairs to a sort of dungeon place and this was my introduction to the "Digger".

I was put into one of the cells and fell asleep, but was soon wakened by a loud bell ringing which meant that I had to get up and box my bedding. My door opened, I was told to put my bed outside the door, then it was closed again. I was given a pail and scrubber to do the floor and there was no dodging it as someone stood over me all the time. I was given breakfast and then taken out for P.T. into a small yard. Halfway through the morning I was dressed up and taken to the Governor's office. I was marched in and told to give my name and number, which I did, and was given seven days in the punishment cells. There were only a couple of kids in the Digger with me and three times a day we were taken to the P.T. class and put through a very gruelling circuit. Between trips to the gym we were taken to a small yard and made to scrape rusty beds with wire brushes and at any moment while cleaning them we would be ordered to stop and start running round the small yard in circles with our big heavy boots on. The whole day was made up of going from one of these tasks to another so that within a short period there was that super-fit feeling, but no healthy mind with it as I hated the bastards. I was always aware of the helpless position I was in down in the Digger so I didn't provoke anyone.

Being under the ground and well out of the way, there was this constant feeling of isolation. They got at me twice while I was in there. The first time a screw came in and shouted at me to stand to attention which I did, but apparently I had clenched fists and that's not the proper way, but a boxer's way, so he asked if I could fight and I said yes, so he slapped me on the face while I just stood there, not daring to hit him back. The other time was when I was caught dodging the scrubbing. The screw came in with another, punching me on the back of the head and kicking me on the side as I pretended to be scrubbing my floor. They had crept up to the judas hole and had been looking through for some time, furious at seeing me sitting there resting. On both occasions they left locking the door, leaving me inside with my anger and my impotence. There were times when I could hear other kids getting it but all this harsh treatment was to make sure that we didn't come back again. After my seven days, I was taken up to Douglas House and back into my old cell. Barricading my cell door was considered a game thing by the kids and it had the same effect on them as my Larchgrove experiences had had on the kids in Bonny's. They began to put me on a pedestal and in this way I was asserting my position.

Visits from home would be every three or four weeks and the "Rookies" had their visits from their families together. My ma and auntie would come up with good butter on bread rolls and hot pies from the local bakery and I would gorge myself on these luxuries. Both Ma and Aunt Peggy would cross-examine me as to how I was doing and I would tell them I was doing great. They brought me up to date with all the news of the district, which I was eager to hear. Things went smoothly enough for me because the screws left me alone, not wanting to stir things up too much. I got into a fight with another boy one day and scratched him with a dart. I saw an elderly man dressed in an old coat and hat standing in front of me watching. I thought he was the janitor but in fact he was the Governor, John Oliver. I was to find this out next morning when I went in front of him and was given ten days in the Digger. No doubt they thought I was a nut for going back twice but there I was. The routine was the same but it didn't seem so hard this time as I was familiar with it all.

Eventually I was allocated a place in Wallace House and put in the next cell to a boy from my district in the Gorbals. The routine here was the same as the "Rookies" for a newcomer. There were lots of guys I knew and it was like a meeting of old friends from old places. One hot summer's night the guy next door and I were lying on the floor speaking through the side of the cell wall to each other. This was made possible by way of the heating system which was a metal pipe running from cell to cell. We could hear the night patrol going round as we complained to each other about all the scrubbing. I suggested to him that we should go through the actions of scrubbing the cell as though we were sleep-walking and he agreed. My neighbour set to it but I didn't and I could hear him scrubbing and moving furniture while I lay under the bed covers and laughed like hell. The night patrol man lifted the cover of the judas hole and probably could not believe his eyes. He called the guy's name softly but he continued scrubbing so the night man left to get another screw and they both took turns to look through, till eventually my neighbour returned everything to its rightful place, pulled back the bedcovers and went to bed. When the patrol left we got up to the pipe and laughed together at it. The following morning while scrubbing the floor my neighbour was called down and he vanished for the rest of the day. Late that afternoon he returned and told me he had been taken to the doctor's and given a thorough going over and was taken outside for some tests with wires to his head. We had a right laugh at this and all the more so when he was excused scrubbing for a spell. I met another guy in there from Glasgow, Willie Smith, who came from Govan. Willie had done Borstal Training before and this was his second helping. He had a bad scar on his face from a knife fight. Both of us were to become very close pals.

While in Borstal I was taken to hospital and put through an operation for glandular tuberculosis. This was a shock to me as my health had always been very good. In many ways being in hospital was fun and I enjoyed the good food which the rest of the patients seemed to dislike. An old man in the next bed told me to watch out for the Borstal boy who was up the ward somewhere but when I told him that I was the Borstal boy, we started speaking about it and got on very well. I met a nurse there and fell in love, but it only lasted till my second operation. She was a very nice person although she lived in a different world from me. I was eventually returned to Borstal and given a period in the hospital there, which seldom had a patient in it as it was more a show place than anything else. I was to be given injections every day by the hospital screw. During this period in hospital I should have been given my liberation date having been in for the appropriate time, but with me in the hospital, the Board, who decide such things, seemed to forget all about me. So when the screw came in to give me my injection I told him to stick it up his own arse and I refused treatment till my case was reconsidered. So they gave me my liberation date, which was two months away. I was given light tasks till that day came.

During this time there was a tremendous rebellion by a lot of the kids. The Digger, which had once struck fear into the hearts of the majority, lost its reputation, which was upsetting for the screws. There was a crowd lying down there who were refusing to do anything and smashing everything that they could get their hands on. I would constantly be engaged in smuggling them down tobacco and other small luxuries while it lasted. Most of the kids involved in this were boys from St John's or my district, though there were one or two from other approved schools and this breakdown of obedience resulted in the kids being split up and one or two being sent to Barlinnie to complete their terms. By the time I was released I had been in nearly fifteen months and during that time I had made lots of new friends and consolidated many old friendships from earlier places. When the guys and the screws asked what I was going to do when I got out I pretended that everything was all set up for me and that I would go out to plenty of good things. I had nothing, and was going out to nothing, and felt terribly insecure. Although I would never have admitted it, there was a feeling within me that I was being torn away from a lot of good friends and relationships that I had built up. All I had to wear was the Borstal clothes, although they gave each guy a jacket and trousers when being released, but these were such crappy clothes that no one would be seen dead in them and this only added to my insecurity. I was put on the train with the other liberated guys. We were all feeling great and played cards on the journey home with me winning all the money. That eased my feeling somewhat as it gave me a couple of pounds. As loyal as ever, my ma and the other parents met us at the station in Glasgow. The Welfare man was there too to organise our licence arrangements and fix us up with a man to visit every so often to report on how we were doing.

It was great to be back in the Gorbals as fourteen months was a long time to be away, certainly my longest. The streets were the same, with the kids running all over the place, horses and carts carrying coal and all the same guys loitering on the street corners, some drinking out of bottles. Some of them shouted for me to stop and they asked how I was. Neighbours were stopping Ma too, speaking to us and giving me a couple of bob. I loved the place and felt very warm and happy to be back. As I neared my street I could see a few buildings had been knocked down and the contractors were in putting foundations in for skyscrapers. People were being taken out of the houses around us and put into new housing schemes. These skyscrapers were about the first to be built in the Gorbals, but there was Ma saying that she refused to leave as she was happy in her own wee house with neighbours that she had known all her life. She made it plain that if they wanted to get her into a new housing scheme they would have to drag her there bodily. There was a lot of fear about this in the district and there were people staying in buildings that had been vacated, refusing to move till they were rehoused in the Gorbals. There were numerous cases of people being moved to new housing schemes only to come back to houses in their old district.

Ma made a big breakfast for me when we arrived home. It was great to be in the house and see all the small everyday things that I had missed. I remember the surprise when I lifted a cup to drink my tea. In Borstal all cups are pint-sized mugs so the small household cup felt like a feather. I ate all my food then made for the house of a girlfriend. I had been going with this girl off and on as she went about with our gang for a time. She was at home as she had heard I was coming out. It was great having sex again. I screwed this girl silly and it was beautiful.

The Borstal doctor had made arrangements for me to see my own doctor, which I did the next day. He said that I would have to go into hospital for more treatment and made arrangements for the following day. I was sick at this news as I was just out and I wanted time to see everything; but I went anyway. The treatment in the hospital meant daily injections. Everyone in the place had T.B. of varying degrees, but I got on very well with the people there. I was the luckiest guy there as my illness was only minor in comparison to some of them who must have known they wouldn't live very long. What hit me forceably in that hospital was the dedication of the nursing staff and the lengths to which they went to help the patients. Some of us were allowed out into the grounds for a few hours and it was very nice. One day I was lying there in bed when a group of my pals came up. Amongst them was John McCue, who had just been released from his four-year period at Peterhead. I had known of John and had seen him lots of times but I was only a kid then and he wouldn't have remembered me so I was very chuffed when he came up with the others. John was known as a bit of a crazy guy. When fighting he had a fantastic sense of honour about him and there was a lot of respect for him. I had pangs of longing to return to the district and one night while walking the grounds of the hospital a taxi pulled up with two of my pals inside. They had just come into some money and wanted to see me and give me a few pounds. The temptation was too much; I found it just too easy; so I jumped in with them and we headed for the Gorbals.

We went into one of the bars that we used and Frank was sitting there so it was a night for celebration. After closing time, we went to look for a girl that we knew. On reaching the house we went upstairs to fetch her. I lifted a coal hammer from a bunker that was standing on the stairway. I did this because I knew that this girl had brothers who were pretty tough and who didn't like the liaison between their sister and us, and we were expecting them to be there too. We had to enter a very dark lobby to get to the door and sure as hell the brothers came out with a giant of a friend. Words were exchanged and I could feel the trouble about to start. A glass struck my hand so I brought the hammer down on them and that ended the whole matter then and there. We got the hell out of there. I split from the others and went to another girl I knew. The following morning I woke up to find a policeman at the door wanting to see me. I had immediate feelings of dread, but these passed when he explained that the hospital had reported me missing, so I told him I'd be returning. When I got back I was taken in by the nurse and given a bawling out as I had put many of them in trouble. Apparently the other patients, noticing my absence, had pulled back the covers making it look as though I was in the toilet. This worked for some time till a matron doing her rounds during the night suspected. I really felt terrible, especially when they saw my cut hand, which was pretty bad, and the bother they went to to stitch it up and take care of it. I felt the proper heel. Of course while I was lying there, friends of the guys I had hit the previous night were going around searching for me with the intention of doing me serious injury. During the rest of my period in hospital I was a saint, all I wanted was release. When I got out a few weeks later things had settled down somewhat and the trouble had ceased to be prominent.

John, Artie and I were going around together and it was one long party. Most of the time we were hanging around the Gorbals. By this time the gang thing had ceased to exist for us and it was just pals. We would never shout Cumbie or anything like that as we had grown out of it and as a matter of fact all the other gangs that had existed and fought with us had all dispersed too, or had joined with some of their rivals on a friendly basis. For instance, Tam Comerford and Willie McPherson from the "Dixy Gang" were now hanging around with us. But although this had happened we were replaced by younger guys who became the Cumbie and such like, so the gang system was being perpetuated.

We were using two pubs as a base in the Gorbals: The Moy Bar and The Wheatsheaf Bar. The chargehands of these pubs were good to us and gave us more or less what we wanted for the sake of a quiet life. When I say a quiet life I mean just that as it had always been, with fights in their bars, either from the young gangs or others with too much booze in them. If young kids were out trying to make reputations and saw that the barman was a good friend of ours then they would cause no trouble, so it was in his interests to be good to us. There were other bars where we would go at the "demand" for booze and money, but not in these two. About this time the big breweries were taking over lots of the pubs and the guys in charge would be skimming off for themselves so they would end up in debt or with their books in a mess. So they asked us to see that they were robbed and this would be done and the robbery would usually clear their deficiency, and bring their stock situation back to square one.

Guys whom I met in Approved Schools and Borstal and Prison would frequently look me up to sell things for them that they had stolen or ask me to take part in jobs with them. We were all making the best of our institutional experience. We had come through the humiliations and degradations of these places together. We might never see each other from one year to the next, but when we did there was that special bond that may not have had a great deal of strength but was immediately recognisable. If any one of our friends in the prison wanted booze or pills and sent someone over to us for a contribution, then it would be given. This was called "putting a parcel in". So it wasn't a case of the guys on the outside forgetting those on the inside when they left prison. I can say without question that it is ex-prisoners who do more for ex-prisoners than any official organisation such as the After Care. It's just the done thing and something that the guy outside takes for granted and the guy inside really appreciates. Of course there is the odd guy who will leave one of these places and pull some stroke that is against the "code", but this doesn't happen often as he usually has to return to prison at some stage and that's when he will pay the penalty.

The "criminal code" isn't a thing that has been written up by top gangsters. It is an unwritten code of ethics. There are done things and things that are not done. It isn't the done thing to "grass" or inform on anyone. It isn't the done thing to "bump" or cheat someone from a robbery that you have all taken part in. There are lots of these unwritten rules that could fill another book but these are just two examples that exist between guys in crime and on the whole they abide by them.

In Glasgow three guys were causing quite a stir in the criminal world around this time and were becoming pretty big. They were Willie Smith and Malky and Willie Bennett, all from the Govan area. Willie Smith and I were firm friends and we would go down to Govan to see them all the while building a stronger friendship. All of us were young and not really established yet.

Meanwhile back in the Gorbals, Artie and I were moving around and picking up money here and there. We were in The Wheatsheaf Bar one night when two brothers, part of a large family of brothers who were very much a mob on their own, came in and tried to hassle the chargehand for booze or cash, so he called to us. We spoke to the brothers in a nice way because we didn't really want trouble with them. We walked outside the pub and along Rutherglen Road. I had a knife in my coat pocket, the brothers had bottles of beer and one had a tumbler. But while we walked the atmosphere began to get very hot and it ended up in a fight with the older brother jumping on my back. I pulled the knife and stuck it into his face while Artie grappled with the other then they ran off. We knew they were going for the rest of the family so we made for a street corner in Cumberland Street where we got together a group of friends and we all went looking for them, but they were not to be seen. However, on the way back we came across another group that we had had trouble with, and a running fight took place in Crown Street. There was quite a bit of stabbing and cutting going on and with the pubs just coming out the streets were crowded. To make matters worse there was a large crowd round a car accident blocking a part of Crown Street, so there was panic when the fighting took place amongst them. When the police finally came the whole thing broke up but as a result lots of innocent people were injured.

I found Artie in a close covered in blood. He had a slash wound running the length of his face but when the blood was wiped off it was only a superficial cut and though it would leave a fine mark it wouldn't leave a bad scar. We were walking along Cumberland Street and I threw away my knife as police cars were all over the place. When they saw us they grabbed us, threw us in the squad car and took us to the police station. By now the political criminal code was very much ingrained in me and I said nothing to them. Any questions they had to put were met by a wall of silence. We were charged with seven serious assaults and locked up. Other guys had been injured in the fight but they wouldn't dare come forward for fear of being charged. Later we were taken to the Police Headquarters, charged again then locked up in the cells. While we were lying there the brothers we fought with had been to Artie's house, kicked the door off its hinges and raided the place, hoping to get him as he lay in bed. But only his old mother was there.

While lying in the cells awaiting these charges, I wasn't too upset as there had been a good fight and I wasn't thinking of it in terms of society but simply from the gang-fight point of view. At no time did I express concern for any of the people who were injured or give them any thought at all. The only feeling of any kind was my own misfortune at being caught. All through the night, a long line of detectives from the junior ranks to the most senior came in to see us, looking through the square judas hole and shouting names to me as they did to most prisoners. It didn't really affect us and I would laugh at them when they said it in the hope of showing them that it didn't matter what they said as they were the enemy and all bastards anyway. Both of us were given a series of Identification parades the following day, which was a Sunday, and we were allowed to see our lawyers. On the Monday morning we were taken for fingerprinting and photographing, but by now I was familiar with the whole procedure. There was no more fear of the unknown.

Both of us were remanded to Barlinnie Prison and taken there. By this time all the guys in the place had heard we were coming and had the usual odds and ends like toothpaste, soap or sweets and reading material ready for us. There had been a lot of publicity about the assaults, describing innocent people being injured, and though the press made a big thing out of it, the guys in the prison saw it in another way and they were immediately sympathetic to our getting caught. They asked what our chances were of getting off and how the I.D. parades went, and there they were assessing and judging the whole thing, as we did with each other's cases.

From any point of view the situation was bad but there was this unfeeling thing about it. Both of us were held till after the Christmas and New Year periods and I was given bail in January 1963. As I walked out of the prison gate I was met by Frank and we went home. We went back up to visit Artie and took him the things that he was allowed while waiting trial and we brought him up to date with the news.

About this time the gang of brothers were looking out for me and rumour had it that they were intent on crippling me. I was walking the streets with a revolver and a knife, ready for anything. Not long after being released on bail, I was buying the morning papers which come out the night before and I had a knife wrapped up in the newspaper, folding it very neatly and in my waistband was a Walther automatic pistol. I was approached by two beat cops who asked what I was doing out, and I told them that I was on bail awaiting trial. They followed me part way along the road little knowing what I was carrying. I had decided to leave for London as that was where Frank had been for a good few months and I felt I would be better off down there for the moment. But needing some cash, I managed to do a job stealing a load of whisky and was in a pub one night waiting to see a guy about selling it. The pub was near the Clyde waterfront and there were two exits, one into the main road and the other into a dark side street, and I chose the latter. It was extremely dark and the snow was lying pretty thick on the ground when I walked out. Without any warning I was hit on the side of the head, a mighty blow, and my immediate reflex was to go for the weapon I had on me, but I was hit from the other side and dragged towards a small van. I began to struggle as the blows were systematically landed on my head and spreadeagled body. There was quite a group around hitting me with hammers and hatchets on the head, but paying particular attention to my kneecaps and my hands. I lay there feeling every blow land but shock seemed to wash away pain and all I could think of was would I live and all the while sickening blows were landing all over my body for what seemed an eternity. I was left lying unconscious in the snow in the middle of the street.

When I came to I saw people passing by in the main street and cars and buses flashing past. It all seemed very normal and I crawled over to a nearby dark close that had a faint gas light glowing and lay there trying to feel the extent of my damage. I knew that I was pretty bad and the pain was crippling whenever I moved. When I finally managed to get onto my feet I saw that gut was hanging out of my trouser bottom, and the blood was running down my face from head wounds. Every move was an effort as I crawled to get a taxi but I found it hard as they took me for a drunk man. I finally managed to get home to my ma's and it was just like a "B" movie as I crawled into the house in a terrible state seeing the horror reflected on her face at my condition. I lost consciousness as I sat into the chair. Ma had two aunts in the house and they all came to the decision to call an ambulance, which was a mistake because calling an ambulance meant the police would automatically arrive. I kept coming and going and remember the cops trying to get out of me what had happened and me saying that I had fallen.

I woke up in hospital. While the doctors were patching me up they told me that I would be in for some time, but I had other ideas. My problem was being unable to move, but this was resolved by the presence of Frank, who had heard that I was in hospital and had come up. I signed myself out and he got transport and we left. No sooner had we arrived in my ma's house when the cops were at the door – detectives. They were told that I was still in hospital but they went downstairs and waited in the car probably thinking that I hadn't arrived home yet. I was helped down to a neighbour's house to stay the night, every movement an agony. My legs at the knees had stiffened up and my back was a mass of bruises from the hammer blows. A large, deep wound was below my left knee-cap and my head was cut in several places, all of which had stitches in them. What was worrying me was that the cops, knowing what was happening, were intent on arresting me on a holding charge as they anticipated all sorts of gang wars breaking out. Sleep was slow in coming that night as the pain was excruciating but I had time to think over the night's events. There was no fear now, unlike before when I had been grabbed by the mob; that was real fear. All my thoughts were on means of revenge, as a "come back" was important. This was a sign of strength in any group, as it would make others think twice about coming after me, if they knew I would come back for revenge. The following morning I was taken to a safe house to lie and rest.

The brothers who had done the damage were dropping it around the district that I was lying in the hospital crippled and that anyone else looking for trouble would know to expect the same. Within a few hours the rumour was going round that I was in a bad way and would never walk again. I discussed this with two friends and we decided that there was no way for an immediate retaliation but that we should blow these myths going round. I was half carried to a car and driven to a pub in the Gorbals. All my injuries were hidden by my hair and clothes, only the hand ones showed. The point was to blow the cripple thing and just to be there would discredit the rumours and the other mob. We managed to get some of the big mouths into the pub and when they saw me they immediately started talking about the rumour going round. We had a good laugh at them, though it was hurting me, but it was important for us to show a good front. We knew that when this reached the other mob they would be puzzled as they knew only too well that they had given me a thorough going over. The fact that I was sitting in a pub was the last thing they would be expecting. It was a small consolation but it was all worth it.

7

By this time the cops were getting really hot in their search for me and putting the pressure on, so I left for London. When I got there I started moneylending with another pal, using a pub that we frequented as a base. Moneylending at this time was a flourishing business in Glasgow and though illegal was very much an acceptable thing in the districts. It worked by us lending money to people in the area, or who we knew were regulars in the pub. For every £1 that was loaned out, the borrower paid 20p interest (4 shillings in the £). If the borrower didn't pay or missed a week then he payed a further 20p and it went up 20p each week till he paid. We had to do something with the money we had otherwise it would be squandered, so we decided to make it earn more for us. The guys who were borrowing it were usually thieves and crooks of various sorts. They would ask for what they needed and it was given. It also meant that we didn't have to expose ourselves to taking risks daily as that was something I couldn't afford with this forthcoming trial. So while in London we kept mainly to ourselves apart from the guys we met in the moneylending. There was the usual existence of girls and clubs. Life was easy and things were very good for the short period I was there, but it came to an abrupt end.

One night in the West End I was stopped by an ordinary beat cop. He was being very nosey and persistent, wanting to know things and I could see that he was set on taking me along with him, so I punched him and put him on the ground. We ran with him in pursuit, so we stopped and beat him up and tried to put him out, as my injuries meant that I couldn't get off on a good run. Finally we got him down, but while we were running police cars came and they caught me. I was taken to a cop station and put into a cell. In the cell I could hear a lot of cops outside and knew that they were coming in to have a go at me because no one has a go at the cops without getting their just beating. True to form, they all came in, kicking and punching me to the floor, and left me lying there. To be honest it wasn't very bad, my head had some bumps and my nose and mouth were cut, but on the whole it was next to nothing as they seemed to get in each other's way more than anything else.

Their pound of flesh taken, they took me and charged me with police assault and the following morning I appeared in front of the Magistrates' Court, where I pleaded not guilty, thinking I would get bail but they remanded me till the afternoon for trial and I thought I'd defend myself. The trial lasted only half an hour or so and the Magistrate found me guilty. After a short talk with the Prosecutor, who told him that I was awaiting seven charges of serious assault, he gave me six weeks imprisonment in Wormwood Scrubs. I was taken to the prison where I did my time then was allowed to go free but as I walked out of the prison gate, two detectives were waiting for me to take me back to Scotland for trial the next week.

The trial was at the High Court Buildings in Glasgow, but it was a sheriff and jury trial. This meant that the maximum sentence the sheriff could impose was two years but if he felt that a higher sentence was appropriate then he could remit us to the High Court for sentence and they could give us whatever they wanted. The trial lasted two days and we were both found guilty of two charges and, as expected, remitted to the High Court in Edinburgh for sentence. The following week both Artie and I faced a High Court Judge and were sentenced, Artie to three years and me to two years imprisonment. We were taken to Edinburgh prison. The press made a big deal of the reporting of the case and, true to form, Artie was described as the leader of the Cumbie and I as his second-in-command. Edinburgh prison was usually reserved for first offenders so Artie and I were taken back to Glasgow and

Barlinnie as soon as possible, but that was fine with us as we preferred Barlinnie.

This was my first time in Barlinnie as a tried prisoner and with the publicity from the trial I was immediately assured of having an "identity". I was only eighteen years old so was split from Artie and put into a hall with the under-twenty-ones. I was beside lots of kids that had been in other places with me, amongst them was Ben Conroy. We went around together along with a lot of Gorbals guys, but Ben went out quite soon after that. In this hall there were young men doing sentences from ten days to four years. The bulk of these were the very short sentences, most of them petty offences committed through drink. The prison garb was brown moleskin suits and they were usually ill-fitting so most of us would get our trousers taken in as was the style in those days. Prisoners doing a relatively long period would split into cliques and I mean cliques as distinct from gangs. These were formed out of companionship as guys would share their tobacco and exchange reading material and any other odds and ends that came their way. Although the under-twenty-ones were separated in the hall they were celled in, the working arrangements were such that we joined up with the rest of the prisoners.

I was taken the following morning and put into the mailbag party beside Artie and there I was introduced to lots of guys that Artie knew, most of whom were from Peterhead but down in Barlinnie for local visits. These were all guys who had big reputations in Glasgow, so in many ways there was lots of excitement in this for me. All of us would sit on the long hard wooden bench with mailbags over our knees to keep us warm and a needle and thread in our hands as though we were working. The truth is that there was no need to work if one was sitting in such company. These were the real fighters and the screws would try to keep well out of their way. Due to his age and sentence, Artie was to be sent to Peterhead, which is the long-term prison in Scotland. The bus transferred prisoners there every month. All prisoners serving six months and over were allowed nine hours of visits per year and these were spread out to allow three twenty-minute visits every two months with a bonus for the long termers in that they get three thirty-minute visits after the first ten months. The visits take place in very small cubicles and the prisoner is put into it with the visitor on the other side of the glass and wire partition with no privacy to speak to his family. Kids of the prisoner would come in and try to get to their father, but the glass and wire would prevent them. Screws would walk up and down each side of the partition listening to what was being said.

I was in a single cell which had a chamber pot, table, chair and bed. There was a heavy steel frame with glass panes in it at the window and a set of thick steel bars. The routine in prisons is very rigidly structured and almost the same in every prison in Scotland. In the morning there is slop-out and wash-up then breakfast, either in the cell or in a dining hall. Work at 8 a.m. then lunch at noon; after lunch there is an hour's exercise either in the prison yards or round the gallery of the halls if it is raining. Back to work till 4.30 p.m. then evening meal. Lock-up at 5 p.m. till the screws go for their tea then slop out at about 6.30 p.m. Those prisoners eligible for recreation are allowed out to the dining halls which act as the recreation halls for an hour or so, then it is lock-up and the screws go away at 9 p.m. The only variation is on Saturdays and Sundays when the screws go away at 5 p.m. till the following morning, and on both these days it is lock-up most of the time.

The sentence that I was doing was quite big for a guy of my age with no prison sentence before but I wasn't really horrified at it. There was a sort of pride in it as I felt really good to be in beside lots of hard men as I was on the way to being one myself. When we were in our cliques it would be all "façades" and tough talk, but that wasn't what prison was to me. To me at that time prison was just a hazard of the life I was leading. It was all part of the sub-culture for everyone to go about trying to impress everyone else.

The fact is that prison eats your insides out, and ties your stomach in knots, leaving your heart very heavy. All of this takes place when you are alone, but it wouldn't be the done thing to let this be seen by other people. At nights I would get up to my window and look out from the top flat and could see the cars and buses and people walking in the streets and, though this hurt me, I never said that I wouldn't be back because by this time I was fully involved in being a criminal, and I only knew that I wanted to be out and be big in crime. I felt all the feelings but could never get it all together to see what I was doing to myself. Instead I took these feelings as signs of personal weakness and would never dare let anyone see them. What the fuck is it all about? What kind of thing made me pretend that prison had no effect on me? All the frustrations that I had in Approved School and Borstal about being treated like a child, all the bullshit that I always imagined would be resolved when I got to prison didn't turn out that way because they were here but in a different form.

I was allowed to write one letter a week to my family and all in-going and out-going mail was censored. The screws were very petty and would concentrate on small things just like the prisoners. They would come in and search your cell and person. You could be put on report for hanging pin-ups on the walls. Some of us serving lengthy sentences would bribe one of the painters (prisoners working in the painters) to steal some paint for us and we would paint our cells as they were only painted every seven years by the prison and they were filthy. For this the prisoner would lose remission. I lost remission for very petty offences. One day I was walking along in single file with over a hundred others when this screw started shouting at me like I was dirt. Maybe I was, but as far as I was concerned so was he; so I thumped him on the jaw and was dragged off him by some other screws and taken to the bottom flat of the hall and thrown in the punishment cell, after having my clothes and shoes taken from me. While sitting there in this totally defenceless position a group of screws came in and attacked me. I knew that if I did anything back there would be more charges so I more or less took what they gave giving token resistance and they left. Much later I was taken to the hospital in the prison and gave the reason for my injuries as having fallen. The following morning I was taken in front of the Governor and the screw described what had happened and I agreed with it and was sentenced to fourteen days. The fact that I had heavy bruising on one side of my face didn't raise the Governor's curiosity.

I returned to the punishment cell and decided that I hated all bastard screws. What I couldn't accept was their rendering me absolutely helpless before coming in and attacking me. I spent all the fourteen days trying to get my anger out on them, but I never could. The solitary period was spent lying on the floor of the dark and very cold cell and this was interrupted for my one hour's exercise each day. There were days when I didn't take this as I couldn't stand the company of the screws who would walk along with me. I recognised the importance of this sentence as it was establishing a reputation, and what better place to do this than a prison that held a conglomeration of criminals from all over Scotland? This was the place to make important contacts and signs of weakness would do nothing to strengthen these, so all emotions had to lie underneath. When I was allowed out after my fourteen days punishment in solitary the guys in the hall greeted me well and gave me one or two luxuries that I hadn't been able to get – a Mars bar and a girlie magazine. I continued to get into trouble and the days were spent with me looking for the screws to slip up and vice versa. They had all the advantages as there is a rule forbidding almost everything in prison, even those allowed in the rule book, as it's all a matter of interpretation.

One day I was pulled out of line for having tight trousers and locked up in the punishment cell. They took the trousers off me to act as evidence, giving me an ill-fitting pair to take their place but I refused to wear them. When the time came for me to go in front of the Governor for a breach of discipline I went in my shirt tail, refusing to dress. He sent me to solitary for seven days but I still refused to wear them. While in solitary confinement I was opened up three times each day to slop out my chamber pot and I would walk to the toilet naked. After doing this for some time the door opened and my old trousers were thrown in. When my punishment was completed I was taken in front of the Governor and told that I was being put on Rule 36, for subversive activities. I was informed that Rule 36 is not a punishment but that I was just being segregated from the other prisoners as I was a bad influence on them. I was taken to a cell at the far end of the hall above which was the Hanging Cell, and outside the window were the unmarked graves where the condemned men were buried.

Rule 36 meant that my routine was exactly that of punishment only they put it under another title and told me that it wasn't punishment. During the day they would give me a load of mail bags to sew and at the same time take out my bedding so I couldn't lie in bed. But I would spread out the mail bags and make a bed out of them, not doing any work as there was nothing they could do to me. I had reached rock bottom and they were playing on my being too bored to sit doing nothing, but even if I had been, there was no way I would do their fucking bags. The days were spent lying thinking and there would be times when I would walk up and down on exercise beside the unmarked graves and think of those lying there. I knew the brother of one and the relative of another. There were stories of them that went round the prison. One of them had attacked the screw before being hung and had broken another one's nose. Screws would tell prisoners the tales of their time on the Deathwatch and how the guys always thanked them for being decent. It was all so eerie sleeping there between executioner and graves. I remember seeing letters that someone had stolen from the files of condemned men and these were crank letters that struck real terror into my heart.

After two months of this solitary I was told that I was being allowed to circulate with the other prisoners but that special arrangements had been made and I was being transferred to the adult hall where all the older prisoners were as that would keep me in line. So without much ado I was transferred to "A" Hall. I found the atmosphere there totally different with prisoners roaming the place loose and free within the hall area. I was only eighteen and the age for this hall was twenty-one and over. I was met with a barrage of greetings as most of the Gorbals guys were there and others that I had met from other districts and they were running the place. So I was given lots of freedom and lots of luxuries as they had fingers in different pies and this was beautiful. There was no bullshit or regimentation here, it was all wild and woolly. Most of the guys that I knew were the tobacco barons and were getting parcels in and there would be the occasional smuggled booze and small parties.

Stabbings amongst prisoners were common occurrences and there was never any great hassle or upheaval over them; the prisoners took them for granted. Prison stabbings are usually well set-up events and those carrying them out would take pride in doing a neat job. I did one of these and it was against a guy from my district who had been causing some trouble amongst our group. In things like this the done thing is to make a hit and make it quick because everyone weighs these things up and if they see people getting off with things then they think you're soft. So I set this deal up while walking through the corridor, the main "hit" place, as the prisoners walk single file through dark corridors. It usually takes about four to do it, with the guy who is making the hit carrying the knife, with two in front of the victim and two behind. The guy walks up, makes the hit, then passes the knife to the guy in front of the victim, and this was what I did. Before the screw can notice that someone has been hit the guy is well away, and only the victim is left, the weapon concealed by this time in a pre-arranged place. When getting to work there is a discussion as to whether it was a good hit or not. In this context, you have the art of violence in which the manner of its execution is very much appreciated just as works of art are appreciated in another culture. People in the art world understand what art is all about whereas in my world we think it's a load of balls, a big con; just as people in most sections of society view our cutting and maiming each other as hideous. The fact is that this is how we lived and if someone were to cut my face I wouldn't like it but I would accept it knowing that it was a hazard of the life I was leading. I would be intent on getting back at whoever had done it, but on the whole slashing, stabbing, shooting and death are to be expected amongst those of us who live like this.

So, ten days after being transferred to the men's hall to be "kept in place", I was being interviewed by the cops for a stabbing. The cops had been through this so many times that they knew it was a waste of time as no one ever talked. The victim would usually say he fell. The following morning I was taken in front of the Governor with three others and we were all placed on Rule 36. I was put in a cell on the bottom flat of the hall. One can only be put on Rule 36 for a month at a time and each month it usually gets reviewed by the Governor, who can extend it. It was the same routine as last time and I lay on the mail bags like most of the others.

Around this time there were a lot of "brew ups" taking place in the prison: this means guys making their own alcohol from stills set up in the workshops or anywhere else. It was a paint extract that they were using and lots of them were being treated for burnt stomachs. Meanwhile those of us on solitary had received a "parcel" of drugs and were lying stoned out of our minds. The parcel consisted of purple hearts and sleepers and during the day the purple hearts would pep me up so that I would be lying in my cell singing, as they had the effect of making me want to talk to someone. When night approached I would take sleepers to get me to sleep. It was during this period, as I lay in this drugged state, that news came over the radio that President Kennedy had been assassinated. This was shouted out of a cell door by a long-term prisoner who was allowed a personal radio, but through the haze of the drugs I thought it was some unreal dream that could never be true. Later, when the drugs had worn off, it hit me and I was strangely sad.

Each month I was taken in front of the Governor and told that I was being kept in solitary confinement. As the months went on I hardened myself to expect this, but deep within I thought I might be allowed off as the rule is that if a prisoner behaves, then he is supposed to be let back into circulation. The wording of the rules are different by far from the humanitarian interpretation that is given when the authorities are questioned about them. As far as I was concerned I was putting all my concentration into showing no emotion at all and to appear as though it didn't bother me. For six months, one after the other, I was taken up and told that I was being kept on solitary, but I always knew that they could not keep me forever. It was a case of giving nothing and getting nothing, the result being that pure hatred was allowed to grow.

The incident with the brothers that I had had was still continuing on the outside with lots of skirmishes and one particularly big battle in which several of my friends ended up in hospital, and one or two of the other side in later clashes. In fights like this guys who get cut quite badly don't always go to doctors; they prefer to see to the injuries themselves rather than have it made official. There were a number of shootings in which charges were made, but when this happened all efforts were made to keep the matter out of the hands of the police. There were also other fights taking place in other areas of the Gorbals and in these some of my pals were badly cut and scarred. If you give it out then you must be prepared to take it and that was the dominant attitude amongst us. There was one guy who was shot in his home and he "grassed" on his attackers. They had certainly taken a liberty in going into this man's home with his wife and family there, but it was still seen as no excuse for his grassing on them. In such cases as this the guy will usually blame it on his wife for putting the guys in jail. Fortunately all was seen to and the guys charged were let off. I was lying in prison during all of this and was very frustrated as I felt that I could solve it all by plunging straight in and defeating the enemy but these were only fantasies brought about by the frustrations of incarceration. My life was crime and all I wanted to do was make a reputation for myself and get money. I was lying in solitary confinement and when my thoughts were not on the events taking place on the outside then it was projecting all my hatred onto the screws who continued to make my life in there a misery with their petty rules and regulations. I would dream of being at the gate when they all came off duty and shooting them all, but I soon found that this was almost every prisoner's fantasy.

Eventually I was let out of solitary after six months. This was the longest time in my life that I had been locked up alone like that and I felt very strange. I felt the tension of living under solitary conditions; my head felt funny and it was very strange being with other prisoners. I couldn't speak for very long as my vocal chords would hurt and the back of my throat would dry up. I always needed a glass of water nearby till I got used to it. The others on it with me were the same. The Authorities gave me a nice cushy job for the remaining few months of my sentence, which was now not far away.

8

I was let out one September morning and met at the prison gate by Willie Smith and John McCue and we went straight home to my ma's house. By now she was staying in the Oatlands as our old house in Sandyfaulds Street had been demolished. My ma and other neighbours were retreating into the other tenements in the district rather than leave the Gorbals. The Oatlands had once been a sort of toffy district but now we were in it, and it had changed since those days. When the Sandyfaulds Street house was being demolished my ma and some of the neighbours wept as they all went to see it go. It sounds all sentimental and guffy but they had lived in these old houses all their lives and hated to see this happening. Instead of driving home I would have preferred to have walked, in order to see the ordinary things that prison deprives one of. It's not the expensive or luxurious things that one misses but the basic everyday things everyone takes for granted – people walking in a street, sitting on a bus, buying something in a shop; the sound of children and of feminine conversation, away from the coarse male environment that one is subjected to day in, day out.

It was nice to see my ma and all the family and as it was 7 a.m. they were all in. We had very hearty greetings but, for some strange reason or other, actual physical contact in families that I knew was very limited. I would never think of coming into the house after this long absence and cuddling my ma or giving her a kiss or for that matter shaking my brothers by the hand or embracing them; these things just weren't done. That was all sissy stuff, therefore not for us. After a drink and a good breakfast, Ma and I went into the room – the new house was the same as the old one – a room and kitchen. Ma pleaded with me to keep out of trouble. She was very old then and very worried and I loved her, but though I was well aware that I could be in trouble the minute I left her house I gave her the answer she wanted to hear. She knew I didn't mean it and I'm sure she knew that I was not wanting to hurt her, but what could she do?

From here, Willie, John and I went to other districts in Glasgow to see old friends and, as is customary, have a drink. At the same time money is given to the guy just out, which is usually the done thing. From there all three of us went to the city centre to get some girls. We went with them to a pub party and a house party afterwards. Life was so good at these times. Without delay I was bedded with a girl and giving her all the hatred stored up over the last eighteen months. I stayed there till I was satiated and that took most of the day, after which it was in another celebration period, making a glut of myself and making up for time lost.

By this time we were looked upon as the top mob in the city and our strength lay in the fact that we were a conglomeration of fighters from surrounding areas. People looked upon us as a group of young guys with plenty of "bottle" who were best avoided. There were other individual guys who were in very strong positions within their own district but all of us were on friendly terms and these guys were very shrewd cookies who had things pretty well sewn up, whereas we hadn't established that kind of stability yet. Because we were a force to be reckoned with this didn't mean that we could rule as a group without opposition, let's say the opposition was limited. Glasgow is a pretty violent jungle and one is never without opposition there, no matter how strong one may be.

At this period I was living between the districts of Govan, the city centre and the Gorbals. Govan was where the moneylending and shebeen rackets were, and I along with some others were pretty loosely involved there by keeping an eye on things in the capacity of "heavies". At nights we would go up to the city centre and collect girls who were prostitutes, take them to the Gorbals for a booze up and back to the Govan area for a party and bed. Govan was an ideal district for rackets as it took in all the shift workers coming in for booze to the shebeen. We used a two-apartment house run by a friend. One room would be filled with crates of booze, and some women would sit in there throughout the night and sell it while we lay in the other with birds. One room filled with booze and the other with mattresses. This way we were always handy for any trouble that arose, but this was very seldom as it was a well-known fact that we were associated with it, so the trouble was kept to a minimum. Both of these rackets were borderline "illegals" and not recognised as potentially dangerous by the cops. People who were short of money would come to the illegal moneylenders as they knew cash would be given then and there without having to put up a guarantor or household goods. They did not have to sign official documents or wait any length of time for the cash.

The shebeening was a different matter as all sorts of strokes would be pulled by strangers in the night gasping for a drink, willing to resort to anything for a taste of the stuff. There always seemed to be more desperation for the booze than for money. Therefore stricter rules had to be laid down regarding it and the principal one was that no credit would be given to strangers or doubtful characters.

After prison I was feeling sexually deprived so I would buy enough provisions for three days and head for a house with a girl, locking myself in. I concentrated on foods that were rec-ommended energy restorers; steak, cheese and fruit. These were beautiful times. There was the time when Willie, John and I were in the city centre and we picked up two girls with the intention of taking them back to Govan. We were walking along Sauchiehall Street looking for a taxi, when we saw, parked by the kerb, a white Jaguar with the driver trying to start the engine. We gave him a push to get it started and he gave us a lift to Govan, dropping John off at the Gorbals.

In Glasgow at this time hardly any of the guys in the criminal scene took money from the Labour Exchange but in court this was used against them when the Jury were told that they had no visible means of support, especially when they were seen to be spending a lot of money. So for the first time everyone started taking their dole money. The morning after the lift in the white Jaguar I went to the Labour Exchange in a taxi. As I went in confronting the man behind the desk, I sensed something was wrong as he was acting very strange. It all fell into place when cops came jumping out from the doors round about, pounced on me and whisked me away in a car. I was taken to the local police station, where I was stripped naked by the cops and had my clothing searched piece by piece. The only thing that worried me was that I had a dose of the clap and the card for the clinic was in my pocket, so when I heard them sniggering behind me I knew what it was. I could see from the glass reflection in front of me that they were passing it around. The arrest was to do with a four-figure robbery that had been committed in the city a few days earlier and our crowd were the chief suspects. I told them I was just out of prison recently and had done nothing but they knew all of that and referred to the expensive clothes I was wearing. They then went on to relate how we had been seen driving in a white Jaguar the night before with classy birds in it. It got a bit ludicrous when they suggested that I was the brains behind it, Willie the heavy and John the driver. I was kept there for hours then released and told to attend an identification parade at a later date.

When I returned to Govan to tell the others how the cops had reconstructed the crime, with us being the arch-villains, we had a good laugh, but this didn't last long as they raided our families' and relatives' homes, searching and tearing them apart. It was as if a campaign against us was on as the cops were on our tails every move we made. There was nothing we could do as all of us had records, so they could pull us up and search us whenever it pleased them. There was no danger of us making any official complaint about it. Life got so bad that we had to make rules to combat it. I was getting my experience first hand and I was now saying the things that I had heard the older guys say years before. If the cops approached us in the street to search us then we made a rule that on seeing them coming we would immediately stop the first passer-by and ask him to search us first in case the cops planted anything on us. The funny thing was that this was a quiet period for us and we weren't really causing any trouble. Although we were hanging around the moneylenders ready to deal with any trouble that might arise, up till this time all had been quiet. Life now became very serious and we began to live cautiously.

I took up going with this girl, Margaret, but the scene was really crazy and should never have been. I don't think I was ready for any involvement. Like the others, it should have been a one-night affair, but for some reason it didn't happen like that, even though I knew deep down that it was all wrong. Even at our closest there was always a distance between us. I was weakened by the fact that I allowed it to go on when it would have been better for every-one concerned to bring it to an end. But then how many people say the same thing in retrospect? The point is that I knew within myself that I wasn't ready for a binding or steady relationship and my behaviour went a long way to substantiate that. Never at any time could I imagine myself getting married or settling down. This made me different from other people of my own age who would be wanting to get married soon after leaving school. But I allowed the relationship with Margaret to continue, knowing that it was on a course for disaster, very much like my own life.

It was around this time in December, 1964, when the cops burst into my house in the early hours of the morning as I lay in bed with Margaret. They told us to get up. There were about eight of them, all detectives. The atmosphere was really tense, and it was obvious they were going to give the house and me a thorough search. I was very angry and was asking what they were wanting and what this was all about. No one answered but I could feel the hostility very strongly. Margaret was allowed to dress and I was given a blanket to throw over myself. All the time I was watching their every move, so between waking up and trying to find out what was going on and watching them I was finding it difficult to think clearly. I stood in the centre of the floor with the gold-coloured blanket draped over me and watched as they tore open furniture in their search.

I couldn't, for the life of me, think what it was all about as I had been doing nothing actively criminal lately. Certainly the cops had been having a go at us by using harassing tactics but this wasn't the usual thing; the atmosphere was especially tense and serious. They piled up lots of household objects that they were intending to take away and most of my clothing. One or two of them made snide remarks at me but this was just part of the usual behaviour and it didn't really bother me as I knew they wouldn't dare make them when they were alone with me. Initially I thought they were just "noising me up" and I could see that they were intent on frightening me, but just as I was thinking this they told me that I was being charged with murder. This word and all that it means is very frightening, even in the criminal world, and the impact of it on me was tremendous. I really felt weak at the knees and a terrifying chill ran through my body. Their attitudes and actions now fell into perspective, but within me there was this inner defence mechanism telling me that the cops were at it and that their tactics were always to make things worse than they really were in order to frighten the person into giving information or getting him to admit to a lesser charge. I was caught between the seriousness of their behaviour and my past knowledge of how they work and it was this basic uncertainty that prevented me from at once facing up to the reality of a murder charge.

Wearing the blanket and a pair of shoes I was taken off to the Central Police Headquarters and it was then that the reality hit me. Standing behind the bar of the station was a line of top cops, the head of whom was Goodall, who stood there, pipe in mouth, staring at me. All the cash taken from me and from Margaret's purse was placed on the bar top in front of me and Goodall remarked that I knew what the charge would be. The uniformed Inspector with them then began to read out the name of the dead man and the charge being Capital Murder, which I could be hanged for. I was asked if I would like to say anything about the charges against me and I told them I had nothing to say. I was now functioning in the way that I would with any other charge, and the old rule of "saying nothing till I saw my lawyer" prevailed, even though I was wanting to burst out screaming my innocence at them and telling them that they had made a terrible mistake. But I couldn't and wouldn't. The cops all stared at me and I at them, none of us saying anything, but the enmity between us was very obvious.

I was taken in front of a Doctor Imrie, a pathologist, and gave him permission to examine me for injuries to my body and allowed him to take material from underneath my fingernails. I was then taken upstairs to a cell with a cage front door on it that was specifically built for observation. Many times when I was a kid along with others I had found myself in this cell while waiting to go to the Remand Home, but now the significance of it hit me. I was given some blankets and sat on the floor with them around me. A uniformed cop was sitting on the other side of the cage door watching me. My mind was in a turmoil. I was charged with murdering and stealing money from a man called Lynch, whom I had neither heard of nor set eyes on. I was also charged with seriously assaulting another man with a knife. I had no knowledge of this man either by sight or name. I was very frightened because although I knew I was innocent, the inescapable fact was that I was lying in this cell charged with murder. By now I was well versed on police tactics of planting evidence and other underhand methods to incriminate known criminals with previous convictions. At this stage, however, I had very little knowledge of what it was all about apart from the charges read out by the cops, so it was difficult for me to try to work out where I was when the damage was done. All I could think of was that I was being framed by the cops. I knew that Margaret had immediately gone for a lawyer but that didn't help me, lying there wondering what was going on.

Meanwhile cops appeared at the cage door looking through at me, calling me all the bastards and other names of the day. Some of them referred to me as a murderer and all of them were infer-ring this by the manner in which they spoke, but rather than blow my cool I sat there pretending that I didn't hear them. I sat there staring straight out at them, putting on a front that belied my true feelings and anxieties. As far as the cops were concerned I had done it, but I didn't expect anything else from them as they very rarely admit to making mistakes, and usually presume that everyone arrested is guilty. I was relieved in the morning when my lawyer came to see me. His first question was to ask if I had done it. I emphatically denied it so he then took down the few details

I could give and he advised me to sit down and think over all my movements of the previous evening.

On the night in question, from approximately 7 p.m. I had been in the Wheatsheaf Pub in the Gorbals with two girls, one of whom was Artie's sister, Bertha. I had sat drinking with them till time up and we'd left the pub together. It was Saturday night and I had walked part of the way up Crown Street with the two girls. The street had been very busy with pubs and cinemas emptying. I'd had a silly argument with a guy as we walked up the street and it had ended up with me chasing him and falling flat on my face in a muddy puddle, which made me very angry. My clothes had been saturated with mud and water and the two girls looking at me had burst out laughing and so had I, as it really was quite funny. I'd left the girls and had asked two kids to call me a taxi. One of the kids had been on the "run" from Borstal and I had offered to let him sleep in my house but he'd declined. When I had got home, Margaret helped me strip off my filthy clothes, then I'd cleaned up and we'd gone to bed.

These had been my movements the previous night but I sat in this cell going over and over them trying to remember who had seen me or who I had spoken to, any little thing that might assist me or my lawyer to clear this whole matter up. I spent the whole of Sunday going over it all and giving it to Bill Dunlop, my lawyer, when he came to see me. He had managed to get some more information to tell me and we compared notes and tried to build a full picture. It was great speaking to him as he had complete faith in my innocence even at that early stage. I needed that sort of reassurance otherwise I'd have cracked up, as the enormity of the charge was tremendously worrying for me. Later that afternoon I was put on an Identification Parade and witnesses were brought in. Amongst them was Artie's sister, Bertha, and she was in tears as she pointed to me saying she was sorry for doing it. All the other witnesses walked past. I was taken in front of a Magistrate the following morning and was remanded in Barlinnie Prison for further inquiry. Once the fingerprinting and photographing procedures were over, I was taken to the prison.

I was put through the usual reception procedure, but after being issued with a prison uniform I was taken to the hospital block and placed on observation in a cell with armoured plate glass on the door and kept there under "strict observation". My day was spent thinking over every little detail concerning my situation and I would jot down on a piece of paper all that I felt was relevant to it and discuss it with my lawyer. After a few days I was allowed into an open ward beside the other untried prisoners. The hospital wing is reserved for psychiatric and murder charge prisoners. There were three of us awaiting trial for murder and the rest of them, ten others, were in for various charges. In the bed next to me was an undertaker in for rape. There was another guy who would lie on the floor and refuse to move except to wrap his body around the legs of the washbasins in the toilet and he would have to be pulled out. There was another who walked about with an imaginary dog, and he would pause to let it do the toilet. All of us slept in the same ward and it was under such circumstances that I had to concentrate on my case.

A couple of days after entering the prison the police were advertising on television for witnesses in connection with the case against me. After discussing this with my lawyer we asked the television company for the same facility to try to contact the taxi driver who had driven me home that night but they denied us this, even though the same people were doing it for the cops and the requests were identical. The kids who had called the taxi for me would be unreliable as witnesses, as they had previous convictions, and the one who had actually called the cab was on the run from Borstal. With the taxi driver no other witnesses would be necessary and it seemed unlikely that the taxi driver could forget picking up a customer in the condition I was in after falling in the puddle. While awaiting trial there were times when I was very hopeful and others when I was thoroughly depressed and thought it all looked hopeless. But overall the fighting spirit was dominant and the support from my family and friends was very strong indeed. I lived with a pen and paper at my side, as my whole life depended on memorising everything that took place that night.

All of my family came up regularly and though worried they were fantastic in the help they offered and the loyalty they showed. Visiting conditions in this sort of situation are ludicrous. Here was I awaiting trial for a charge of which I was completely innocent and the prison regulations stopped me from discussing it with any of my visitors. A screw would sit beside me throughout the visit, and before it began he would warn me not to speak about my charge and that if I did so then the visit would be terminated. How does one sit on a visit with one's mother and not talk about something that has had such an impact on the family? I would have very heated arguments with the screws on this matter but there was no deviating from this rule. There was one occasion when the visit was ending and we rose to walk out and my ma asked me if I had done it. It was a great relief to be able to say that I hadn't as we had never been able to during my spell on remand. For years my ma had been asking me if I'd done things that she had heard about and I had always denied it, even when I had done them. This time it was different as it was very, very serious and there was no room for any games. Both of us knew this.

The person that was able to give me a real boost was my lawyer as he had done a tremendous amount of work on the case and I was always eager to see him. Artie, who had just completed his three-year sentence, came to see me and told me that his sister said she had been threatened by the cops, which is why she had to witness against me in the identity parade. All this sort of thing had been done before to other guys in the criminal element. Similar tactics, similar threats, the same methods employed. In a case such as this it becomes an extreme "Them and Us" situation between the police and the accused. As far as the police were concerned, I was guilty. There was also the fact that they looked on me and my friends as a constant source of trouble.

It was early in 1965 and although the debate on the abolition of capital punishment was on, it was still in force at the time. As my trial date approached they went through the formality of cleaning out the Death Cell because legally I could be sentenced to death. However, days before the trial Abolition became a reality. It was strange this debate going on in Parliament while I was waiting on trial for Capital Murder. This was a warning to me on how easily a mistake could be made.

On the day of the trial I felt edgy but there was a silent confidence within because I felt that I knew I was making this appearance for nothing. I was cleared of the Capital Murder charge and the following day I walked clear out of the court into the street. It was beautiful walking from that dock as the front benches were crammed full of cops, and they were looking very sick indeed. All of my friends cheered and we embraced and this was what it was all about, Us beating Them. The feeling of enmity and hatred flowed between us and the cops. Although I had done nothing to merit being in court, all of us looked on my walking free as being a victory. The pressure was lifted from me completely with the acquittal. Lord Cameron was the presiding judge who told me I could leave the dock. I had had to work like hell during those past three months to get acquitted as had my lawyer and family and friends. The feeling throughout was that the official side couldn't give a damn if I went down for life or not – innocent or guilty.

The press mobbed me on leaving court and to avoid them we jumped into the first car available, which turned out to be the *Daily Express* car. It took us away from the crowds to the house of the reporter in the shadows of Barlinnie Prison, where he set about getting a story and photographs of me and Margaret. There was lots of noise in the reporter's house and this brought his mother into the room to ask us to be quiet as his father was in bed ill and she had had to call in a doctor to attend him. I had heard that reporters would do anything for a story and this sort of thing verified it. I told everyone we should leave, but in the car journey home the reporter was slapped in the face and messed about, and years later this was being exaggerated as it is now said that I put a knife at his throat. The *Express* certainly showed their dislike for me in later years.

It was great to be back in the house again, and to be in the streets of the Gorbals. The celebrations lasted a long time as drink was plentiful and parties were constant. People within the district were telling me to go away to London as the police would wait for their first chance to get me and would make sure the next time.

This was said time and time again, but I didn't pay any attention as I felt that I shouldn't be made to leave my district or leave Glasgow and one thing for sure – I wasn't going to run from cops. But there was this feeling that I would be set up by the cops. I was now number one on the police list and there was an open hatred even amongst cops not involved with the case.

While I had been awaiting trial, John McCue had been arrested for firing a shotgun and was charged with attempted murder and he lay on remand in Barlinnie. This left Willie Smith, another guy, Willie Bennett, and Frank, who had come up from London with a broken leg, although he soon went back down again. I was still celebrating and there is no doubt that the whole thing went to my head. After my release I was the main talking point in the criminal world and lots of guys were looking up to me as it's not everyone who walks out of a murder trial.

There were a number of people in the district who still believed I was guilty and as there was a certain adulation attached to this I didn't go out of my way to deny it. Just like the other times, it enhanced my reputation, which is what I was after. It was just like all the other fears I had experienced while in Larchgrove, that once I was out of it the fear left, and I began to cash in on it. Within myself there was a conflict as I felt a bit of a cheat; I felt I had to prove myself to myself. So ten days after being acquitted, while travelling home from the pub with my younger cousin, both of us the worse for drink, I provoked two guys. I recognised one of them as having been in the old "Bee Hive Gang", and I ended up attacking them, which resulted in a fight with me hitting one of them with a bottle and taking one of his eyes out, and cutting the other on the hand. I felt much better after this as though I had somehow "proved" myself, and in doing so created a more terrifying picture of myself. The following morning the cops were looking for me so this meant that I had to go into hiding, but only as far as the city centre where Margaret and I had a house. I stayed in a lot as the cops were raiding houses looking for me. We would go out occasionally and one of these times, while in a big store buying fruit for the movies, I was grabbed by the arm and told to come to the police station; it was a detective who knew me.

I was surprised and I thought he was with others as the place was crowded; but as we were going outside the store door and I was giving Margaret all the money in my pocket and instructions to contact my lawyer I noticed that he was on his own. At this, I grabbed him and beat him up and made off while Margaret blocked his way. I managed to get over to Govan and was told some hours later that Margaret had been arrested for police assault and obstructing justice. For this she was put into prison, but we were able to get her bail at the soonest possible moment.

Things were hot and I went back into hiding, but it's terribly difficult to lock oneself in a house as it becomes very much a prison. Being on the "run" is a tense situation; one is always on the lookout for cops and every waking minute has to be taken up with watching for them. There is no doubt that this wears one down and becomes very frustrating.

During this spell Tony Smith (no relation to Willie Smith) was released from Peterhead Prison after serving a four-year sentence. Tony, like the rest of us, had a reputation for being a fighter and he came from the Blackhill district. He was met at the train by Willie and some others, and parties were the result. Also at this time Frank came up from London, with his broken leg healed. So there was Willie Smith, Tony Smith, Frank, and Willie Bennett (who came from the Partick district of Glasgow) and myself all hanging around together.

This was quite a bunch by any standards and one particular night we had arranged to meet in Govan. From there we headed for the city centre for further fun and Willie Smith's girlfriend came to meet him as it was her birthday and they were going for a meal. They left us and we went about our own business, drinking. Eventually at pub closing time we made our way to a party that we knew was taking place in the city centre. Going up the dark, winding stairway we could hear music coming from the house where the party was. To get to the house, one had to enter a long and very dark lobby. The place was full of people, some on a bed to our left inside the doorway. Willie Bennett was standing immediately inside the door and on seeing us the party went quiet. I had scarcely entered the house when a voice from inside shouted my name and it turned out to be Irene, the prostitute from London many years ago, so she came out and we went into the dark lobby to renew our acquaintance. We were surprised to see each other, and while we were talking a fight broke out with bottles flying out the doorway and thuds and crashes. I went towards the door but it closed, locking me, Tony and Frank in the lobby with Irene, which meant that Willie Bennett was inside so we began kicking the door down and we finally got in, pulling Willie out. Bottles came flying and fighting took place on the doorstep. Frank was almost scalped by a guy with a big knife, but we got out and made our way downstairs. I grabbed Irene, intending to take her with me, but decided against it. We all made off to a house in Blackhill and saw to Frank's head wound, which was pretty bad. Some home-made butterfly stitches were put on the wound which seemed to stem the blood. The wound was a long thin line along his hairline and his skin could be lifted up. There were other cut faces and bruising, but nothing else serious.

Blackhill is a crazy place. It was now almost three in the morning and we went into the street where some guys were sitting round a bonfire singing Celtic songs and drinking wine almost in the middle of the street. The atmosphere was very similar to that of the old Gorbals that was now being destroyed by demolition squads. We sat around drinking and it was as though it was the middle of the day rather than the middle of the night. Eventually a van came to pick us up. The driver was a big strong guy who was drunk. He ushered us into the van and then took off. Our conversation was trying to find out what bastards were at that party earlier on as they hadn't half given us a beating. We knew that things would be different in the morning when we pursued the matter. Our attention was taken from this by the high speed of the drunken driver as the van travelled towards the city centre. On the way, he told us that the van had no brakes, which had all of us on the verge of shitting ourselves as he pelted on. We were going to my house in the city centre so I had to be up front guiding him. I pointed out the folly of his speeding as the cops were looking for me for assaults. At this he put his hand under the van seat, pulled out a sawn-off shot-gun and reassured me that I'd be okay. All of this was very matter of fact, with us casting glances at the guy as it was apparent to us that we were in the van with a madman. Be that as it may, he did prove to be true to his word in getting us there, but I'll never forget that nightmare journey. He made miraculous swerves to avoid hitting oncoming vehicles and it was with a sigh of relief that he pulled up, though I'm not sure how he stopped the van.

When we arrived at my house, we were informed by Margaret that the cops were looking for all of us for murder, as a young guy had been stabbed to death in that house. Immediately we got onto the phone and found out how true this was as cops were flying round, entering houses in search of us. Within minutes people were visiting the house and one of the first to come was Willie Smith, who had left us to take his girl out, earlier that night. All of us sat very tense, waiting for news to trickle in to bring us up to date. The room went from complete silence to nervous noisiness. Different people reacted in different ways. Willie Bennett was guzzling large amounts of booze in an obvious attempt to knock himself out. Tony was quite calm on the face of it. Frank was pretty shaken but very much in control. I was much the same, the only difference being that I had been on this road before. All of us were finding it very hard to take.

The situation was that now all of us were on the run. I had been on the run for some time with the cops looking for me so in a way I felt disassociated from the murder thing. I was already used to the hunted feeling, but all of us would have to live with it for the moment. There was no way that we would go to the cops, give ourselves up and ask what this was all about. People have to understand the intense feeling of suspicion and distrust that both criminals and cops have for each other and that the best policy for the criminal is to keep out of the way until the heat dies down. With the cops already looking for me I couldn't carry a knife as they could use it as evidence. So I was now unarmed and feeling pretty naked.

News came back to us that two brothers had been stabbed at the party, one of them fatally. The house had been full of people but most of the respectable ones had taken off as they didn't want to be involved, or have their names associated with the house or what was going on that night. There were others very much like ourselves who had left for obvious reasons. This left those who were too drunk or too frightened to get away for the police coming. As soon as our names were mentioned the police went on a raiding spree. What a golden opportunity for them, with all of us involved in the one case. They raided house after house looking for us. Arrangements were made for us to go into hiding, Frank went back to London to carry on his normal life there. Willie Bennett and Tony Smith went to New York and I stayed where I was.

Two days later the cops were still raiding houses. They went into Willie Smith's house in Govan and arrested him for the murder and the serious assault. I went to meet his girlfriend and she told me that she had been to the Procurator Fiscal to explain that Willie and she had left us earlier that night to go for a meal and celebrate her birthday. She gave the time, place and details of their movements. The cops have their grasses and their ears to the ground. All their criminal contacts had informed them that Willie Smith wasn't even near the house that night. So he was now in prison for something he had nothing whatsoever to do with, even in the remotest sense, but they weren't going to do anything about it. He would await trial and no one on the official side would lift a finger to assist him. This is what we in the criminal world call "being slung to the wolves" and this is the very reason why most guys with a criminal record avoid the cops when they are looking for them, not out of a sense of guilt but out of common bloody sense.

A few days later while in my ma's house – I had barely crossed the threshold – there was a knock on the door and I answered it. I was confronted by the cops who were astonished to see me, although they recovered quickly enough to pounce on me. I was hustled down to Police Headquarters and charged by detectives for taking a guy's eye out and cutting another on the hand. From there I was taken to the Northern police station, where I was charged with murder and serious assault. Detectives made the charge and cautioned me, asking if I had anything to say, to which I replied no. I was then taken in front of a uniformed police inspector where I had the charge repeated and I made the same reply. The murder charge worried me a lot as I knew the cops would be very reluctant to let me walk out of this one a free man. Their attitude towards Willie Smith made my speculation even wilder. So it was a total surprise when I was confronted by a cop and told that I could walk free if I gave them a statement. This told me that they were groping in the dark and it made me feel somewhat easier, but not much, as I knew they were going to make a determined effort to put us all in. Anyway, it was nice to be able to tell the cop to stick his offer up his arse.

One of the fears one has when being charged by detectives is that they are prone to writing down what they think you should be saying rather than what you actually are saying. This is called "verballing". When an accused person is charged by the cops he is usually told of the charge and asked if he has anything to say. This is called "cautioning and charging" a prisoner. The accused person is then taken in front of a police inspector at the station bar and here he is formally cautioned and charged. The police inspector isn't present in court, but the detective is, and it is he who is asked whether the accused replied when cautioned and charged. It is here that he reads out what they say the accused said, which is usually not what the accused actually said. This, of course, can seriously damage the defence of the accused. The inspector at the bar hasn't a stake in the case so if comparisons were made in cases where verballing was suspected, then I'm sure there would be a vast difference in what the detective's notebook said to that of the ledger that the inspector puts in his book. Of course this would be explained by saying that the accused said a different thing on each occasion. At the end of the day it's a difficult thing to prove for eventually it boils down to either the jury believing the police or the accused. There is also the point that most lawyers don't like to directly challenge the police by calling them liars, as it will put their clients at a disadvantage. Most juries take the side of the cops and as "verballing" is usually done with accused people who have previous convictions, then it means that by attacking the Crown witness's character, the defence leaves their characters open to attack. As the accused with previous convictions stands to lose, he has to pray that the other evidence will be so weak as to render the "verballing" useless.

Both Willie and I were remanded in custody but kept in separate parts of the prison. He was in the hospital and I was kept under strict supervision on the bottom flat in the untried hall. Now I was awaiting two trials and the charges against me amounted to three serious assaults and murder. This was heavy by any standards. When I was first accused of murder, it was fairly generally accepted that I was innocent, now they were saying otherwise, even though they hadn't heard the full story. They were making flash judgements and condemning us without any qualms. I didn't give two fucks what they said. Screws would make remarks behind my back which would come back to me; they were thinking just like the cops as they all had the same sort of minds.

After I had been in custody for some weeks, I received a letter from the Procurator Fiscal informing me that the charges of murder and serious assault against me had, for the moment, been held in abeyance. Willie was released but I was held in on these other charges and refused bail. The press made a big deal of it. This was the first time such a thing had happened in a murder trial. Meanwhile the cops were continuing the search for Willie Bennett and Tony Smith, who were languishing in New York.

I received an Indictment for the other two serious assaults and was taken to trial in front of a sheriff and jury. My younger cousin had been charged with me although he had played a very minor part and was let out on bail after his arrest. The two guys identified me for attacking them and the jury eventually found me guilty and I was sentenced to two years imprisonment. I started these two years with an advantage in that I was a known personality on my own merits in the criminal sense. So from the start things were pretty cushy and I was given a nice easy job and allowed the usual perks. The prison routine was still the same and old guys told me that it had been pretty much the same since they first came in. Doing time in this prison system does nothing to penetrate or give a person any better understanding of what it's all about. But every time I went into prison I broadened my criminal horizons by making more and more connections in different areas. These were people who knew what the nick was all about, would go into prison, do their time and go out again to take up where they left off.

I met many of the old guys who had been sentenced by Lord Carmont. There was a time when he had made an example of guys charged with serious assaults and had given them sentences that were meant to shock and put an effective end to razor slashings. In practice it was not an effective deterrent, though certain reactionary sections of the Scottish society still shout for more Carmont sentences. They say how well Carmont cleared up the situation but one only had to look at the guys like me who were doing these sentences at that moment.

A few weeks after Willie Smith was released from our murder charge I got news that he was lying in a Glasgow hospital with his throat cut and waiting to be charged with murder. He had been badly wounded in a fight in which the guy he was fighting had died. This was a shattering blow as we were very close, but it also carried other implications. He was now in great danger through these further disastrous circumstances of being recharged with the murder charge that was being held in abeyance. When we first got those letters of abeyance we saw them as the Authorities' clever way of getting out of a situation that could have become embarrassing for them as they had no real evidence to support the charge. However Willie Smith's latest incident changed everything. I was lying in my cell trying to weigh it all up and I became very apprehensive and went to the prison Governor, Duncan MacKenzie. I told him that due to the change of events, I wanted some sort of guarantee from the prison officials that, if the police came up to recharge me for this murder charge that was in abeyance, I could have independent witnesses standing beside me as I was afraid of "verballing". This was agreed to. Willie Smith recovered from the cut throat and was charged with murdering a guy in Govan and was transferred to the prison hospital for treatment while awaiting trial.

Within a short period of time, the other two, Willie Bennett and Tony Smith, returned from New York and were also arrested. That meant that all four of us were in custody, so the preparations went ahead for the trial. Willie Smith was now facing a harrowing situation as he had two murder charges to face and hadn't even been near the first one. By now, the cops in the Glasgow force were all very much aware that Willie had not been with us that night, but that Frank had been. But they weren't interested in Frank as he was in London and no bother to them, whereas Willie was a tremendous source of trouble.

During this period some funny things began happening to the witnesses who were under police supervision. Word was seeping through to us that they were now saying that Willie Smith had committed the murder in the house that night. This was very frightening because if this is what they were saying about Willie, who had not been there, then what the hell were they saying about those of us who had been present? All our lawyers were finding it extremely difficult to get hold of the witnesses for statements. This was all very strange indeed and had our minds working overtime. At the pleading diet, which is the preliminary hearing to fix pleas and dates for trial, our lawyers, mine in particular, complained to the Sheriff about his difficulty in seeing the witnesses for the Crown. There was a debate on this, which all seemed very sinister to me sitting in the dock. Newspaper headlines blazoned "Missing Witnesses", so that on returning to prison from court everyone was gossiping, assuming that we had done something with the witnesses when in fact we couldn't even get hold of them.

Fears were expressed by some friends from the outside that we were destined to go down, come what may, and some of them decided that enough was enough and blew up the house of the main witnesses against us with a gelignite bomb. No one was hurt, but by the time we went for trial it was open confrontation with the police. When the trial commenced it became pretty clear that in spite of the fears of those outside, there just wasn't a decent case against us. Halfway through the case there was a recess, during which we were taken downstairs to the cells and locked up. Our lawyers came down and spoke to us, asking us to accept a plea of guilty to a simple charge of "Pushing and Jostling". I wasn't too keen on accepting this deal and neither were the others as we knew that we had nothing to do with this. Eventually we did agree to it and were taken upstairs, where Lord Strachan accepted the change of pleas and we were given a further three months' imprisonment. We put on a happy face, but that was only for the cops who were sitting in the benches behind us, as we did beat them and prevented them from putting us away for good.

In the cells below it was a different matter. Willie Smith and I were put in the same cell in the High Court Buildings and were taken in the same van to Barlinnie Prison. In the back of the van on the journey a uniformed cop in the back with us remarked how lucky we were only getting three months. Simultaneously Willie and I remarked that we weren't lucky as we had had nothing to do with it. The cop then said that if that was the case then why didn't we turn Queen's Evidence? We didn't answer simply because the last thing one does is sit in a Black Maria and chat to the cops. But the answer to it was that Willie wasn't even there at the scene of the crime yet he had come closest to being found guilty. I was there but had been with the girl Irene at the time so there was no way that either of us could have attempted to clear ourselves with turning Queen's Evidence even if we had wanted to.

Everyone was now saying that we were really lucky and some bunch of "fixers". No one wanted to see that we may have been innocent. That would have gone against the grain as we were gangsters and no one wanted to believe otherwise. Who actually killed the guy? For me to say I could pin it on anyone definitely would be a downright lie though I had my suspicions. There were a lot of people in the house who made off and really it could have been any one of them. People in Glasgow identified our names with trouble so that if we were near it then they automatically assumed that we had done it. Most of the times we had, but other times – very few – hadn't. But even then we didn't discourage the wrong assumptions as they all added to the myth which continued to grow around us. Because we all came from different districts and within these districts each of us had reputations, there had never been this sort of gathering by guys in the criminal element in Glasgow ever before. Although we were inside this was still the great motivating force – our reputation.

Back to prison we went and on entering the hall I had been celled in I saw that the place was being turned upside down with police all over the place and prisoners' cells being emptied of possessions. It so happened that someone had made a "hit" on a guy and he had died. This was the first murder to take place in a Scottish prison. All I could say was thank God I had the perfect alibi – I was in court.

But Willie Smith had another murder charge to appear on. Within three weeks he was sent to trial in the same court for the murder. All of us were rooting for him. The two brothers had attacked him in the Govan area, cutting his throat in the middle of the street, but Willie managed to get the knife from one of them and in self-defence struck back, killing the guy. He had plenty of evidence to support his case but the whole thing was very uncertain, especially with his name still fresh in the minds of people after the trial three weeks previously. But all went well for him and he was cleared. He walked out of the dock to complete his three months' sentence along with the rest of us. The overall feeling amongst us was that of victory. All these incidents had been very dramatic not only for us but for the legal profession and the police. Nothing like this had ever happened in Scotland before. In fact it was unusual by any standards.

Within a few months, that would be January 1966, I was to become a father and when the time came I received a telegram saying that Margaret had given birth to a boy. I really was very happy. It was something I could never have imagined myself being – a father. I never felt I was that type but I was very pleased. But the happiness of this was brought to an abrupt halt one Sunday morning when I was informed by word of mouth through the prison grapevine that my younger brother Harry had been arrested and charged with murder. I was shattered and couldn't really believe it. The thought of him facing a life sentence was too awful to think about. It was one thing for me to be in that position but not my younger brother. I really felt this more than I did any of the charges that I had been on. My mother was absolutely heart-broken and must have been wondering where it was all going to end. All of my family were deeply shocked. Harry was the baby of the family and held the affection of us all. At this moment, the prison authorities took it upon themselves to transfer me to Peterhead Prison to complete my sentence. This was the long-term prison in Scotland and I was being put out of the way so that I couldn't help Harry in any way or give him advice. I was sick and disgusted with this as there had been this feeling that so long as I was near at hand he would be okay.

Peterhead is in the far north of Scotland, far away from Glasgow and in an isolated spot. On reaching there I was taken into the reception area which also happens to be the Punishment Block holding sixteen cells, eight on one floor and eight on the second floor. The procedure from there is the very same as that of any prison. I was put in a cell that was a third the size of a normal one, where I could barely spread my arms. Every second cell was this size for some reason and though the authorities maintain that a prisoner was never kept in them very long, overcrowding soon blew that one and guys were doing very long sentences in them. There wasn't very much space for moving so that when he was locked in the prisoner would have no option but to lie on his bed. I got on very well and I knew everyone that mattered, as there were lots of familiar faces from the early days. Most of them were doing very long-term sentences. There was an atmosphere between the screws and the prisoners that hadn't existed in any other place I'd been in. It was extremely hostile, with the feeling of constant tension. The two factions didn't speak to each other unless it was absolutely necessary. In other prisons one would frequently see the odd prisoner talking to the screws. It seemed that the Peterhead screws had a particular dislike for the Glasgow guys and though it was put down to the city-slicker and hayseed thing, it was sometimes very personal.

For some obscure reason I was put on Rule 36. I was called in front of the Governor and told by him that I was being placed on Rule 36 for subversive activities. I asked him what the reason was and he said again that it was for subversive activities and would say no more than that. I was locked up in the punishment block which was in an isolated part of the prison with all its own facilities. There were sixteen cells in the small two-storey block and outside the back door block was an area with three small concrete boxes with a catwalk running above them. The boxes were meant to be solitary exercise yards and the catwalk for the screw to walk along and observe. Beside these yards was a large concrete sort of shelter called the "silent cell". This is a cell within a cell which means that you walk in one heavy door then into another smaller cell and the place is completely bare.

I was pretty mad at them locking me up, so when I was inside the cell in the punishment block I decided on a course of action. The cells are bare just like the punishment cells in any prison, but there was a ventilating system in the far corner of the wall to let air in. I heard voices coming from it and discovered that this was how the guys communicated with each other, by speaking through the vents. I spoke through and found I was speaking to Ben Conroy, who was doing a five-year sentence and was now in solitary. Within a few minutes I was to find that out of all the guys in the solitary block, three were old St John's Approved School kids and one was from the Gorbals.

At night-time, when all the screws had gone home, leaving the night patrol, I went up to the cell door, took my chamber pot by the handle and started banging on the door continuously. The screws came and asked me what was wrong but I refused to answer and kept banging. The continuous noise became unbearable to those about as they couldn't sleep, so they automatically got up and started banging, which meant that all the guys in the punishment block started up and the noise went to the outside halls and all the prisoners in those cells started banging, which meant that the screws' families, who lived outside the wall, would also hear and have to bear with it. The Prison Chief was called in and they opened my cell asking me what I was causing all this bother for and I told them that I was in solitary and wanted them to take me off. They left and from there started putting old mattresses up in front of my door to muffle the sounds but it was no good. The reinforcements then came in banging their sticks but I continued as I was being bloody-minded and wanted to get out of there.

This went on for some time and eventually they opened the door and took me through the back into this "silent cell". On the way I was waiting for the boots and batons to start flying but I was pulled along and as I entered the second door of the cell a figure was standing against the wall to the side of it and both of us stared at each other. It was Ben Conroy, who was waiting for the screws to come in, only to find me entering. They locked us up together, going back to quell the rest as they felt we were the persistent ones. We had an idea that they would be back, so we thought about preparing for this although there was nothing much we could do. It was surprising for the two of us to be thrown into the one cell; unheard of as far as I knew. We were concerned about what to do when the screws came back, and we felt pretty helpless. I did a shit in the middle of the floor and started rubbing it all over my arms and body and face. I thought that if they were going to come in then I was going to jump on them and grab them so that they would get shit all over them. They did come back and saw what I had done and backed out as I positioned myself to throw my whole body amongst them. At first Ben was reluctant to do this but he did so after vomiting. When the screws left we sat looking at each other throughout the night and every so often would break out in fits of laughter.

The screws obviously thought I was insane but I wasn't going to lie there naked and helpless while they beat me up and I was only doing a two-year sentence and didn't want to get involved in any violence with them and add extra time onto my two years. There was too much going for me on the outside and I wanted out, but at the same time I didn't want the authorities to start doing what they wanted with me. I was prepared to go to certain lengths to combat this, and what we had just done was an extremity that was on the borderline of violence. It was strange sitting there in this very silent atmosphere, hearing nothing on the outside; so silent that there was a slight whistle in the ears. The shit that was clinging to me was beginning to harden and flake off and fall on the floor. In the morning the screws came in wearing overalls over their uniforms and took Ben away, leaving, me alone and I knew they would be coming back to attack me. I did another crap and spread it over me and wrote "screw bastards" on the whitewashed walls with the crap that was remaining. I also tore up the two blankets that I had and made leggings and a flap to cover my penis, in the style of the Apache Indian. I refused to do anything and when food was put in the door I threw it all over the floor, and urinated there. By this time I knew that my punishment would be severe so I wasn't giving a damn. Later the screws carried me out into the small exercise yard adjoining and left me as I had refused to move from the foul-looking and foul-smelling cell. While in the yard they paid an old cleaner guy to go in and hose it out then they lifted me back in.

I lay there for days in complete silence putting more shit all over the walls, and lying on the floor covered in slops and urine. I was remanded by the Governor for the Visiting Committee – a body of civilians who visit prisons to inspect and take complaints, or punish cases that are too severe for the Governor to deal with. I just didn't care about anything at this stage, nothing mattered. One morning the Governor came round and beckoned me out into the fresh air and told me that it might be to my benefit to appear before him the following morning. I thought this over and the following morning I went into Governor's Orderly room where he holds his "court" and many charges were read out against me. I was fined in money from my prison earnings, so in many ways this was a let-off and I did appreciate it.

I resumed normal solitary in the ordinary strong cell and I looked on it now with the attitude that at least I had caused bloody hell. But they weren't going to budge and let me out of solitary completely, so although I felt that I had been able to even the score somewhat I still felt very resentful. It was while lying in these conditions that I was called to the vent by an unknown voice and told that my brother Harry had been found not guilty of the murder charge against him. The charge had arisen out of a fight that had taken place when some gang of kids attacked him while he was out with his girlfriend. Harry had taken the weapon off the boy and the unfortunate incident resulted in the kid's death. It was only when the verdict came through that I realised how much this had been weighing me down. I felt so light and easy and although I wasn't aware of it consciously, it took his acquittal to show what an effect it had had on me.

Solitary in Peterhead was different from that in Barlinnie as the solitary block was on its own – purpose-built. I would lie through-out the days and nights listening to the sounds being made and identifying people by the way they jangled their keys, the sound of their footsteps, or other noises they made. The thing about

Peterhead is that it's very seldom that one gets to know the screws' names but I did get to know their sounds. Some would whistle, others would hum, there was always some idiosyncrasy by which I could identify them. It was the same for the time of day, as certain sounds heard at certain times gave me a rough idea of what time it was. I was a very ignorant sort of person in the sense that, although very much alone, I could never think of looking at myself and trying to understand what I was all about. Instead I blamed everything on the screws and the authorities. I really hated the bastards for what they were doing and thought the screws the lowest of the low. Even to the most inveterate prisoner there is something incomprehensible, even slightly unreal, about being locked in a concrete box listening to the sounds around the place. Often it was the screws talking outside the cell door about what they were going to do that night or had done the night before. They talked about going to the Screws' Social Club and boozing or a party or something like that. After three months on solitary I was put back into the mainstream of things to get on with my time.

It was while in Peterhead that the importance of letters to prisoners struck me. Guys would look on letters as the only unrestricted means of keeping contact with the outside. Prisoners are only allowed to write home once a week but the incoming mail was unrestricted though it was heavily censored. To send out an extra letter meant fabricating all sorts of excuses such as a member of the family dying or something equally dramatic. Most times guys were denied an extra letter. It was a good feeling to come in from work and see the screws standing handing out the mail to prisoners but it wasn't too good if there wasn't one for the guy who was expecting one. Having or not having a letter can be what puts a guy into a bad depression.

Visits also put a strain on guys, as they looked forward to them and all of us expecting a visit would get all cleaned up, exaggerating the cleaning-up process and the clean shirt bit. The strain shows most as the visit time approaches. Sometimes the visit doesn't materialise for some reason or other and the prisoners dread this sort of thing as preparations have usually been taking place all week, whereas the people on the outside have other things to do and don't attach the same importance to it. Most of the long-termers in Peterhead accumulate their year's visits so that they can go down to the local prison nearest their homes to see their families once a year. This means that he is allowed to save the three visits every two months that he is due, amounting to one and a half hours. This gives him nine hours per year, but for some reason he is only allowed four and a half during his spell in the local prison. Lots of guys do this as it means saving their families money in making the journey; also it gives them a sort of break from the one prison. The atmosphere in Peterhead is always verging on the explosive so this break is needed. There are other guys who don't go down for visits and just stay in the long-term prison as they feel that there is too much pain in going down to a local prison and seeing their families. Then there are those guys who have no one at all to visit them. One of the unpleasant things in prison is the "Dear John" letter that guys get from their girls, or guys hearing that their wives are messing around with another guy. When this happens they don't go to the official side to get assistance, though there is the odd guy who will go to the Welfare Officer, but most guys have no confidence in him and see him as a screw without a uniform. Bad news from outside is a painful experience and torturing in some ways as it brings home to the prisoner just what prison is all about – loss of freedom. There is no substitute for freedom. So when faced with problems from the outside guys have to keep them to themselves though they will usually talk them over with a close friend.

During the period that I was completing my sentence, there were lots of other things happening. John McCue was appearing for trial for stabbing a guy in a fight and was charged with attempted murder. The fight took place in Peterhead and he appeared at the High Court in Aberdeen and was acquitted. Willie Smith and Frank Wilson, on the outside, were appearing in Glasgow High Court for charges of attempted murder by stabbing and shooting in the Govan district. Willie Smith was given three years, and Frank was acquitted. This meant that myself, Willie Smith and John McCue were now all together in Peterhead. There were also lots of guys from our district and other places that we had been in before. All the old familiar faces with lots of new kids coming in, and I was still only twenty-two years old.

On the outside things were pretty hectic as friends were getting involved in some trouble in London with the top "firms" down there. But in Scotland – Glasgow – things were building up, with my friends getting a measure of control in the moneylending. Things were beginning to grow and the basis for more organised crime was entering into our ways. There was a loose but growing connection with the Kray twins in London. Some of my pals had been down to see them, at the twins' invitation, and thought very highly of them. At the same time, on the Glasgow scene, there was some trouble between my friends in the Gorbals and another couple of guys, who had walked up to a friend of mine firing a shot, intending to hit him in the arse, but some loose silver in his back pocket stopped the bullet from penetrating. There had been yet another clash resulting in one of the other guys being given sixty stitches in a face wound, so things were looking difficult but interesting as I waited for my release.

9

I was released from Barlinnie Prison on 13th January 1967, and was met at the the gate by Frank Wilson and some others. We all went to my house, where breakfast and drinks were organised, and for the first time I was able to hold my child who would shortly be having his first birthday. After breakfast they all left and I was alone with my son and his mother. This was crazy and very unfair to her as I knew then definitely that this should never have been, but I felt that the child was a commitment. However, that aside, it was good to be with a woman again.

I wanted to see what was happening in the district so as to get the feel of the events now taking place. That same afternoon the guys picked me up and we went round looking at everyone and seeing things. It was a time of elation as it's great to have one of your own out from prison. We had all been brought up together so we were very close. Certainly we fell out now and again but usually this amounted to nothing and even when it was serious the opinion of the group would dictate the way it went. There was one particular incident when two of my pals fell out around this time and had a quarrel, resulting in one of them coming to my door covered in bloodstains and the other guy – Tam Comerford – coming very near to death. I helped him into fresh clothes, getting rid of the bloodstained ones. After that I went to the house where the fight had taken place and found it covered in blood. I told the two girls who were there to say nothing to the police. Tam was unconscious at the bottom of the stairs with blood pouring out of him. An ambulance was called for him and we left him to be found alone when it came. The following day I was up to the intensive care unit to visit Tam. The whole thing had been over girls and he was in the wrong, so Frank and I acted as mediators and advised Tam and the other guy to leave it there and forget it and this was done. These things went on but they were our way of life and the actions and the part that I played were normal to us. I wasn't showing any disloyalty to Tam by helping the other guy get rid of his bloody gear, nor by telling the two girls to say nothing, nor for that matter by visiting Tam in hospital. These were just done things and the fact that one of them nearly died was the way things go.

Anyway, with me just out of prison, I was given a piece of the action to get me on my feet. With this came some money to start my own moneylending book and I wanted to start my own shebeen. The money and assistance to start this was crime working at its best from my point of view. There was a feeling of strength within our group and we were sailing high.

Things with my ma weren't so good as she was in hospital suffering from cancer of the breast. When I went to see her, she looked so tired and worn and seemed to be shrinking into herself. The pain that she had suffered through having me as a son must have been tremendous, never mind the physical pain of her illness. She sat in hospital looking very frail. We talked and Ma warned me, as though I were ten years old, telling me not to get into trouble and I responded as though I were ten years old by telling her that I was finished with crime. I knew I couldn't tear myself away from the life I was leading and really I didn't want to. At the same time, I wasn't lying to Ma for lying's sake. She was such a good, kind, gentle person that it would have been very difficult to even begin to tell her the truth. In fact the thought didn't bear thinking about. The nearest I got was to tell her that I wouldn't be taking a job. The reason for this was that she would see me at different times of the day, so it was best to admit that much. Anyway, she wasn't stupid and knew the score by now and we both tried to avoid the subject. Things in the house were very quiet with Pat working, my brother Tommy married with a baby daughter and Harry working away from home.

We were now the top mob, so with a little luck we would expand and develop things and make plenty of money. The only other strong opposition was one other guy who at this time had been put away for four years, so this left a completely open field. We were going from strength to strength and the financial side was blooming. Moneylending was a lucrative business and the policy was to give it to anyone who asked, because experience had told us that most people would pay back what they borrowed. There was a bad debt list but that was inevitable, and it was small in comparison to the number of people who paid. It wasn't a case of those who borrowed the money being assaulted or having money extorted from them every week of the year. Certainly this was the picture presented by the imaginative minds of the press, and they presented this picture because it was illegal. Why then did the moneylender need heavies? Usually it was because the moneylenders themselves needed some form of protection, otherwise the money would be taken from them; but in our case it was different, with the heavies doing the business side for themselves. I suppose that it was the first hint of organised crime in Scotland.

Moneylending was traditional in most areas of Glasgow, but the majority of moneylenders were illegal, as they were usually ordinary working guys or housewives who had money to lend. They did this at work or in their homes, giving the cash to their neighbours or workmates. The interest was now five shillings in the pound (25 new pence) and if the borrower couldn't pay it back the following week then another five shillings went on top. This was pretty widespread and lots of people used this method for cash rather than go to a legal moneylender where some sort of security had to be given and time had to elapse before the borrower could get the cash. At the end of the day if they couldn't pay, the legal moneylender would impound goods in the borrower's house and take them to court. Also people didn't want to go through all the formalities, just to get a few pounds. The illegal moneylender however, had no such formality; as a known borrower could just vouch for someone else and cash would change hands. They also knew they could never be taken to court. There was very little problem with people refusing to pay back, as it meant that if they didn't, they couldn't go back again. Moneylending was very much supplying a public demand. It was a good way to earn money for nothing and so some guys on release from prison began to get involved and, though it was run on the same lines, it did attract other criminals who wanted to borrow. It was usually them who would give the problems in refusing to pay back and so the Heavies were brought in to act as "minders". Eventually it became a mixed bag with lots of straight people still doing it and also lots of guys who had criminal records. But on the whole it was accepted as a semi-legitimate game by everyone, and it was very difficult for the cops ever to get convictions for it.

Within our group of friends there were many of us with our own "Books" (moneylending businesses) and as far as finance, profit and losses went these were separate. If any heavy trouble came along then we shared it and everybody came to the assistance of the book having the trouble.

After a few weeks I set up a shebeen selling booze after hours, and the one rule was that no credit be given unless the client was known. This also meant that guys could borrow money from some of the others and buy the booze from me. As I got into the swing of things, life became pretty comfortable and all of us were doing well, some much better than others but it was growing. Slowly but surely we started spreading our tentacles into the docks and other districts where we began leaning on other moneylenders, taking a share in their profits.

The strange thing about the criminal scene is that it attracts lots of weirdos, and this includes people who live decent lives and had no reason for hanging around us. There was an antique dealer, who had no connections with the criminal world whatsoever, who paid me money just for being around him. There was another character who paid me an incredible amount of money for sitting in a car outside his house waiting for some guy who he thought was intending to do him an injury. All of us knew that the story was fictitious and that no one wanted to harm a hair on his head. This was the whole crazy set-up, but unfortunately life wasn't all that sweet. There was the odd guy who would refuse to pay money and would be thumped on the jaw, but this would only happen occasionally as no business run on fear could survive. If people were frightened about what would happen to them for missing a few weeks then they wouldn't have come in the first place. When given cash, the punters were told that if for some reason they couldn't pay, then they were always to show face and tell us that the money wasn't there and we would come to some agreement or even forget it altogether, so this is what usually happened. The guys who did get thumped were those who had deliberately gone out of their way to get money with no intention of repaying it. If they were to get away with it then the wolves who were all about would be in trying to take it off me. Lots of thieves would come to borrow and they were safe bets as we knew that as soon as they got a hoist then they would pay back.

I got a new house in Rutherglen Road a few closes from my ma's new house there. As the Gorbals redevelopment scheme expanded, with the old tenements being torn down and replaced with new ones, all of us wanting to stay in the district would move into the next set of tenements. These would usually have a two-year reprieve before being pulled down. My new house was on the top flat with a room and kitchen, but I had the place changed a bit and had the ceiling lowered and a bar put in. I also got myself a very large and powerful dog, a Dobermann Pinscher, to guard the house and look after my son. They were both about the same age. It was a very frightening animal. I would take my son into the park opposite the house and some days I'd sit there for hours in the sun. These were the peaceful moments that interrupted the tumultuous life that I was leading. Even during these very happy times I could never question my criminal way of life. I seemed to forget about all the bad things that had happened to me. The beatings, the humiliations of prison, the degradation of instances like the shit over me, I just didn't think of them, and maybe that's because I was still living in it. I had accepted this life and in many ways knew no better, nor wanted to. I didn't look on this life as being horrific, nor did the other guys. The cops pretended that they did, but then I knew so much about their way of life that it didn't matter what they thought. Some of the things that they did were evil and if that was what the "good" side meant they could keep it.

The time I came nearest to thinking a bit more deeply was after having a fight with two guys in the middle of the street one day. A car pulled up and the driver told me to get in. It was an old school pal with his brother, and he had been a member of the Skull gang way back. It was good to see him but he started saying that he couldn't understand why I led this sort of life and talked in great depth, with me just laughing him off and getting out at home. Once out of the car I felt very uncomfortable about what he had been saying. I don't know if it was because I recognised the truth in what he said, or that I knew he had done some very crazy things while in my gang and here he was talking to me like this. I do know that what he was saying stayed with me and gave me food for thought, but this was washed away as the memory of him faded.

Running a shebeen was quite a funny experience with never a dull moment. It was amazing to see the desperate measures some people would go to for a drink. Old men and women would spin the most fantastic tales to get it and the hard-luck stories would be plentiful. There was this old lady who was a hawker and she would come up with anything and everything to barter for booze. There were others who would come up with handfuls of single shillings or sixpences from the meters on their gas, T.V. or electrical appliances. There were the few that one couldn't resist – you'd have to be superhuman to be able to refuse them.

I was going away one particular day and I left this guy in charge, going through the whole scene so as to let him know what to expect. But since he had seen it all, having been around quite a bit, I left feeling confident and thinking that he would be able to handle it. The punters of course, hearing that I was away, came flooding to the door and made the most of it. On my return, when we tallied everything up, there was a bit of booze short but I was assured by this guy that it was okay as my aunt had had it. I really blew a fuse as I knew that it must have been a punter trying her hand – successfully. He told me that there had been lots of them up trying to con him and he had rejected them, but this homely woman had come up with no coat demanding to see me and had walked straight into the house, taking over, and he had fallen for it and given her what she wanted. The point is that lots of these people didn't give a shit how tough you were. If they needed drink and you happened to have it and there was some way it could be taken from you, then they would do so.

By now we had a strong friendship with the Kray twins in London, and we would go down there to big fights or to get a few days away from the Glasgow scene. Whenever we went to London we were made most welcome by the friends that we had there. I have always noticed an innate disdain by lots of Scottish guys for the English criminals – most of them thought they were a bit soft. This is certainly far from the truth, as the majority lived very tough lives but concentrated on cash, whereas we in Scotland were more inclined to weigh things up from the physical side. The English guys realise this of course and recognise that Scotland produces good heavies and that is why they have so many in their firms.

In the summer of '67 we were having a pretty heavy time, as this other gang from the opposite end of the Gorbals had caught one of our mob in Gorbals Cross and had shot him through the chest at point-blank range. This was a declaration of war and meant that we would have to take full precautions. When a person is shot like this the cops swarm all over the place for a few days. We spent those first few days hanging around the hospital waiting to hear how he was making out, and speaking to him when he was capable of it, to get the whole picture. Of course the police had spoken to him and had got nothing out of him, but we soon had the full score though most of it we knew already. This meant that guns had to be always near at hand, but with the cops hanging around and liable to search us we would arrange for someone who wasn't known, and had an inoffensive appearance, to carry the guns and walk well behind us. He would be positioned close enough for us to reach him quickly but far enough away so as not to be associated with us. Any cops giving us a pull and searching us would find nothing.

The strange thing was that at times like this, after the initial blow-up the cops would keep out of the way. I don't know if this was coincidence or whether they wanted us to do their jobs for them, by shooting it out and killing each other. There was plenty of action during this period as once or twice this mob came round taking shots at us which led to daylight shoot-outs. On one occasion we recognised their car coming at high speed up a particular street. In front of the car was a beer delivery lorry about to stop at a pub. The driver and his mate didn't see the car behind them – only us running towards the lorry with guns pointing in their direction. The two guys in the beer lorry stared in disbelief and stopped dead as we used the lorry for a shield while those in the speeding car and us behind the lorry let off shots at each other. The car stopped and tried to run as we poured shots into it, but they finally made off. Guys standing at the corner loitering all panicked and ran like hell. By this time everyone was leaning out of their windows watching and we made off. I know that the cops heard about this and in fact pulled one guy in and he was warned that if it wasn't so serious it would be funny. It was very much like a Wild West show.

The cops were now putting pressure on us and it showed in the form of raids on the pubs where we were collecting in our money. Due to the business side of our activities this meant that we were tied down to certain places at specific times, usually bars. This was why we were an easy target for the other gangs as they always knew where we were. They didn't have the same commitments, which made it difficult for us to get them. It was the same for the cops, they knew where we were so they could make raids, but we had various safeguards. Around this time, I was getting notes pushed through my door by the cops telling me to attend the Police Headquarters, which I had no intention of doing. I would hear them knocking at the door but I wouldn't answer. However, curiosity was getting the better of me so I consulted Jimmy Latta, who was a lawyer, and asked him to make some inquiries for me. Apparently some cop was identifying me for passing a rubber cheque that had been given to a nearby cafe owner. It seems that some guy went into the cafe, saying he had just returned from London and was short of cash and with the banks closed he couldn't cash a cheque and asked the cafe owner to do so. The owner was very wary so the guy told him that he knew me, and at that moment in walked one of the uniformed beat cops. The owner turned to him and explained everything, including the fact that the guy was a pal of mine. For some unknown reason, the cop told the owner that it was safe enough and to go ahead, the result being that the cheque bounced back in the owner's face. This left the cop in an embarrassing situation and he had to justify himself, so the next thing we know, I was Chief Suspect. Without wasting any time, I went round to the cafe owner and spoke to him. He talked quite openly about it and was surprised to hear that I was being involved. I told him to get in touch with the cops and straighten them out otherwise they would be hauling me in. I spoke to the Fraud Squad by phone and they retracted the whole thing.

As I have said the internal politics of our mob were very smooth on the whole and we got on well together, but occasionally nasty things would crop up. Willie Bennett was on the fringe of our group. He had been very close but due to a series of dirty strokes he was by now the outcast, though not completely rejected. No one told him that he was finished as it didn't work that way, but there would be a cold front presented to him and he knew the score. However, Willie Bennett and this other guy, Babs Rooney, another fringe man who floated around the various districts but mostly in the city centre, had teamed up on an extended drinking spree. When they ran out of cash for booze they would go to the moneylenders and replenish their purses. Now this particular moneylender they were going to was one from whom I was taking a weekly wage, so, if they got away with this then every Tom, Dick or Harry would do the same. The politics of the situation were that Willie Bennett wasn't likely to be hit, simply because his brother Malky, who was doing a ten-year sentence, was very much one of us and a person we all thought the world of. If anything happened to Willie, it would be like going against Malky.

One night in July '67 I was drinking with my friends while they collected their money. Along with me was Frank's brother William Wilson, who was the same age as me; we left and went to a quiet pub that I liked, for a drink on our own. At time up I asked him to come to Kinning Park with me. The rain was pelting down and we ran through the backs in Crown Street to go to William's house for his coat, but on the way we bumped into two guys. I was carrying a bag of beer, but in the darkness of the night a fight started between us. I had a knife but it was in the instep of my boot and so was

William's. I tried to get it out but by this time the guys got a couple of hits in with beer cans, William receiving the bulk of these. Eventually I got my knife out and cut one of the guys and another kid who happened to be passing through the back at the time, who was only sixteen years old. They all made off and we carried on to get William's coat. He had a small cut from the beer can blows and a few bumps.

On reaching Kinning Park we went to the house of Babs Rooney and the door was opened by an attractive girl who lived with Babs. I also knew her from the city centre where the prostitutes hung around. Babs was in bed, but he got up, putting on his trousers, remaining bare-chested. We were on amiable terms as he had returned the money that both Willie Bennett and he had taken from the moneylender guy and so all of us sat around drinking. Babs had been in prison with me a few times and I had known him on the outside but I had only been with him a couple of times. He was known for being around the prostitutes a lot of the time; he was not a bad-looking guy with greying hair. We discussed the money situation, about him going at the demand, and he agreed that what they had done was out of order, so we decided to forget it.

After a while he brought up an old score about a pal of mine who went to his house, or his sister's house, with a revolver, intending to shoot him, and we argued about this very heatedly. His girl, Sadie, was in the other room attending to the child that she had, so I took my knife out and ran it down his chest and cut him with a slashing motion. Both of us were standing and Babs just stood there and said nothing. I went into the next room and assured Sadie that Babs wasn't very badly hurt and she should say nothing to anyone and she went along with this. She had been around and knew the score. William stood there in the kitchen with Babs while I did this. I walked outside the house with Sadie, calming her and speaking to her. I stood at the close front with her, waiting on William coming, but after some time when he hadn't appeared, I left Sadie and went back up to the house to get him. The door was locked and when I looked through the letterbox the lights were out and no one answered. I took it that Babs had closed the door so as not to get any more. With no sign of William, I could only guess that he had come down behind me and left through the back way, so I rejoined Sadie and spoke to her again until a taxi drew up and a couple that I knew got out and I replaced them. I told the driver to take me home, then I went to bed.

The following morning the noise from the dog barking and someone banging at the door awakened me. It was two friends and they told me that Babs Rooney was dead and that William Wilson had been charged with his murder. I was completely stunned as I had been so casual about the whole thing, knowing that I had only slashed him. What could have gone wrong? No one knew. I knew it would only be a matter of time till the cops came, so I gave all my clothes and the knife that I had to my friends and one of them took them away. They were burned. I was taken to a house out of town and kept there to await further news. William was charged on his own as it seems he had been caught in the house with the dead body of Babs. I couldn't believe this. To add to it he was charged with theft and found with money of Sadie's from her purse. He was also covered in bloodstains, so things looked very bad for him. However, as is practice in such cases, the cops went over the place with fingerprint experts and my fingerprints were found on a beer can. This did it, they were going crazy to get me when I was labelled as having been there. The search was unprecedented and the cops were pulling everyone in to find me. The information started coming in thick and fast, with word that William had been offered a deal and was told that he would be given means to start somewhere afresh if he would sign a statement against me. William, of course, declined the offer. Bandit Rooney, no relation of Babs, was offered money to reveal my whereabouts. He too declined. Because such offers are general practice in an important case, we kept my hiding place a secret amongst the very few, thus cutting the risk of betrayal. Police were following guys who were known associates of mine, offering deals to others in the criminal world if they would try to find out where I was. All of this came back to me. The Glasgow police were showing boundless enthusiasm. Their resources were vast and they were moving in on me.

My house in the Gorbals was occupied by a friend and his girl, so that while I was in hiding the cops moved in, taking crates of booze and tearing the house apart in their search for evidence. They questioned the people in the house and were taking photographs of things but they never took the photos in the presence of my friends and would move them from one room to the next as they did so. My Dobermann Pinscher was taken into custody. Eventually all the people in my house were taken into custody and held for some hours and questioned. Lots of articles were taken from the house; they were giving it the works. My mind was racing all over the place. What were they up to?

The house where I was in hiding was very nice. It was in a small town with all the comforts of a home. What were my thoughts at that moment? Utter confusion. I was so sick at the whole turn of events that I became physically ill. I lay there knowing that things looked very dark indeed. The house was now very much my prison. I lay inside it for three solid weeks. Occasionally I would peep out of the window to get some fresh air. I lay in bed and stared at the ceiling, trying to forget, and then trying to remember what it was all about. The media broadcast that William was charged with murder, four assaults and theft, and this made me even sicker. The rumours going round were that William was bang in trouble but that the cops were determined to get me in. I was already aware of this and needed no confirmation from anyone. William felt that with me staying away he would be in with a chance. I didn't need to be told this either as I had no intention of going to the cops. Meanwhile the police were sitting in my house in the Gorbals and the uniformed cop detailed to do this was P.C. Howard Wilson, a name to bear in mind. From time to time, I would get visitors who kept me up to date on events. Rumour had it that the heat had cooled somewhat as they thought that I was in a hundred different places. Arrangements were made for me to go to London and within a few days I was down there. The Kray brothers looked after me for some of the time but I preferred to be very much on my own as I was always wary of bringing too much trouble to others. They looked after me very well while I was with them. They had plenty of respect in Scotland from the guys who knew them, and I thought highly of them.

10

I stayed in a nice flat in London and kept very much to myself, with the occasional visitor coming to see me. The Glasgow police were making trips down and raiding houses in London looking for me. Of course they hadn't a clue that I was getting word of their every move as the London scene was incredible for bent cops. One day I was with a friend in a London district and a police inspector offered to put me up in his house. There was no way that I would have taken him up on it, but this was how the scene there was. I walked about London freely as the place is so big and if you aren't known then it's as safe as you'll get anywhere.

I had been away over two months and it was now September, with me moving from the gangster scene to that of the Flower Power one in Hyde Park simply by changing into jeans and a sweater. I loved the London scene at this time and for the first time was finding a sort of peace even though I was on the run. It was probably the mood of the times, the general atmosphere, that was responsible. Being amongst strange people in a strange place made me forget the past and its troubles. It was almost as though the real me was emerging and I've often thought that if this trouble hadn't been hanging over my head I might have made a new life. But it has to be remembered that the dominating factor for me now was loyalty. It would have been unthinkable if I had just vanished and left the others with the trouble in hand. Anyway, it was nice for a time to go with girls who hadn't a clue who I was and who were shouting for everyone to make love not war.

All of this came to a halt when one day some guys came down to London to meet me and talk over the situation. Careful arrangements had been made for them to take precautions. They met me in the British Lion pub in the East End. Amongst them were Frank Wilson, Bandit Rooney, and Pat Gilgunn, who had just completed a sentence for culpable homicide, along with another guy. We were discussing things in the bar and around lunchtime the place began to fill with workers from the factories nearby, most of them dressed in overalls. We were sitting at the bar, and lots of small movements made by the barman seemed rather odd and began to attract my attention. He went over and loosened the bolts of the door leading to the bar from the side street. From the reflection in the bar mirror I could see an enormous furniture van backing up to the pub door. I remember wondering how such a big van was going to manage in that small street, when the door burst open and lots of workers jumped up from their tables, some with revolvers. This was very frightening as I thought they were a gang but they shouted that they were police. I was overwhelmed by them and so were the others, the bar was packed full with cops. It was so bad that we couldn't move, either the cops or us. I was pinned by the arms and crushed, so on seeing this I took advantage and caught the eye of the bar manager and asked him in very clear tones to bear witness that I had nothing to say to these men till I saw my solicitor. He said that he would witness what I had said which enraged the cops, who pulled me by the hair and finally extracted me from the pub. In the car were two Scottish cops along with the London ones. I was asked if I had dyed my hair as it seemed lighter due to the sun, but I kept still, saying nothing.

Frank and the others were taken into custody expecting charges to be placed against them. Their car had been impounded and was in the cop-shop being searched. Eventually they let them go but they refused to take the car as they were afraid that something may have been planted in it. Later I heard one of the cops remark that they, Frank and the others were a suspicious shower of bastards. At no time was I cautioned or charged. I had no idea how they had got onto us and caught me, but the obvious answer is that they had followed the others in spite of the full precautions that had been taken. I was flown home with the two cops, who asked if I could be trusted without handcuffs. I said yes and that was the only exchange we had. An escort of cops was waiting at Glasgow airport for us. They were glad to have me and congratulated each other when they met, but they knew that only half the battle was over.

Once in Glasgow I was taken to the Govan district police station and there I was charged with murder and four assaults. The book was being slung at me and this time there was a feeling of doom within me. I was put into an observation cell on the bottom flat, which had one wall made out of steel bars with a young cop sitting there on the opposite side watching me. It resembled a zoo, with cops coming in all the time to have a look at me, comparing me with the photos that they each had. The young cop was giving a commentary on me to the others, although two hours before he had sat with his mouth wide open in awe at being given the job. Some of the cops coming in and out were at the old game of calling me names. I lay in a corner pretending to sleep just so as I could blot them out. This enraged them and they said I was a callous animal and such like. I must confess that I hated every one of those bastards as they talked. At one point I rose from my bed and told those standing there to take a good fuck at themselves. The small commotion brought in an inspector; he was one of the cops who had escorted me from school all those years ago, and he put them out. Others would come in and I lay in that cell, thinking that these bastards matched everything they called me but they just couldn't see it. It was as though they were making the most of my being in their custody before handing me over to the prison authorities. I was given an Identification Parade and was identified by a few people for the assault charges but the girl Sadie didn't identify me, and this had the cops on edge. A police guard was kept on all witnesses connected to the case.

Things weren't looking too good for me when I was put into Barlinnie Prison, where I was kept under strict observation. I had visits from my lawyer, friends and family and was being kept closely in touch with what was going on. Some interesting things were coming back to me. Sadie had gone down to Manchester with a new boyfriend and another guy. They had all been arrested as her boyfriend was wanted on some charges and while in the police station she told the third person that I didn't murder Babs, and by coincidence he came into Barlinnie, which was how I found out. I cited him as a witness. Sadie was eventually arrested again in Scotland and put into Greenock woman's prison under "protective custody".

As the trial period approached, I was able to get an idea of the evidence against me. The most damaging of this was the blood-stained knife that was found under the linoleum at the entrance inside the doorway of my room in the Gorbals house owned by me. The second piece of evidence was that when cautioned and charged I replied, "I was nowhere near the fucking house." The sixteen-year-old kid who had been assaulted came from a family that I had had a dispute with in the past. I hadn't known who he was but did very much regret cutting him. Shortly before the trial, a bomb exploded outside the window of his house and the cops threw even tighter security round the witnesses.

I went for trial on 2nd November 1967, and sat in the same dock and court as on two previous occasions for murder charges. I knew that I wouldn't walk out this third time. The trial judge was Lord Cameron, the same judge who had presided over my first murder trial. During the trial my Q. C. contested the question of the knife being found in my house, asking why it should be hidden in a place where the first flat-footed policeman entering the house would stand on it. He also questioned the reply to the caution and charge, but not too severely. For some reason unknown to me, the police took a photograph of Willie Smith from my house and this too was an exhibit. When asked by the prosecuting Q. C. about it, the policeman giving evidence said that they'd had an interest in Smith at the time. This was puzzling as Willie Smith was in fact serving three years' imprisonment. I wondered why they should mention this to the jury? William Wilson was sitting in the dock with me but as far as everyone was concerned he didn't exist.

The big moment came when Sadie entered the dock and exonerated William and me from the murder of Babs. The silence from the benches seating the police behind me was deafening. She had been in prison under "protective custody" but came into court saying that two other men had come into the house and killed Babs. The court was adjourned when Sadie left the dock. William and I were taken downstairs to the cell area below, where I heard a woman crying and voices shouting.

Later, after the recess, the prosecution asked the court to allow Sadie to go back into the witness box, but both our Q. C.s objected and the judge refused as this was unheard of. I noticed Sadie sitting crying between two policewomen in the benches behind me. Lord Cameron directed the jury to find William not guilty of the murder but that it should stand against me. One of William's Q. C.s remarked to him later that he should think himself lucky to have been in the dock with Jimmy Boyle. During the trial it was brought out that the house of one of the witnesses had been blown up with a gelignite bomb, so it was all pretty horrifying.

I was sitting there and I knew that I was doomed, that under no circumstances would I walk out of that court; it would have to collapse first. I knew from the first minute I entered the dock that the only thing I could take out of it was my person, not my freedom. I felt that was gone. The lawyers and judge gave the jury eloquent speeches before they left to decide their verdict. They stayed out for barely two hours then returned to a court packed with cops and civil dignitaries. The benches immediately behind me were crammed with police. I was found guilty of murder – unanimously, also of some of the other charges. William was found not guilty of everything except the theft charges which were against him alone and he was given twenty-one months' imprisonment.

The reality of doom hit me there in the dock. All was lost but the battle would continue so it was vital for me to show no emotion. This seemed to be the last form of defence left to me in that very lonely, exposed place. When the verdict was given, the small court usher turned round to the cops filling the front benches and the cops were laughing and grinning. I stood for some time while the verdict was recorded, seeing only the civil dignitaries to my left grinning like wolves, leering at me. The sounds of glee surrounding me were bad enough but the gesture by the small court usher tore my guts out. I looked straight ahead. All the time I wanted to scream out to them all sitting in there that they were a dirty stinking shower of shit. How I ever managed to suppress the violence within me while in that dock I shall never know, but it was vital to me to make sure that I remained erect, very much in control. I know that they wanted me to collapse and cower, but there was no way. Lord Cameron went on to tell me that I was a menace to society and would go to prison for Life and he recommended that I serve no less than fifteen years. As I stood there waiting to be let out of the dock, I watched the cops leaving, looking straight at me with big grins and all shaking each other's hands in congratulations. I took a long look at what was going on. I was escorted downstairs to the cells below and was confronted by more cops in uniform, one of whom was actually doing a sort of dance saying to me that I was convicted, I was guilty. He pulled the tie off my neck and took the sheaf of defence papers from my hands and I was put into a cell. All of these people were happy at my being put away and seeing it shook me as nothing ever had in my life before, to the very core. They didn't know me, they didn't even know.*

I lay in the cell at the High Court Building and was stunned by it all. However, I was soon taken under heavy guard to Barlinnie Prison. The journey was spent with me continuing to look straight ahead and with the cops all very silent. I was put into the punishment cell, which was meant to be the observation cell in case I cracked up during the night due to the effects of the sentence. I said nothing throughout, knowing that if I did then the violence would pour forth. I was thrown into this cell with the mattress on the floor and dark shadows dominating the place, as the small light bulb was plastered into the side of the wall. I lay on the mattress not moving, just staring into nothingness. My thoughts at that

* I haven't been as forthcoming with the circumstances of Babs Rooney's death as I have been on earlier incidents in the book. The reason for this is that though I maintain I never killed him, I did slash him, therefore, by law I am technically guilty of murder. The point is that while I am writing this I am into the tenth year of a life sentence for it and that is that. I am now familiar with all the facts leading to his death and what happened but I don't feel that they have anything to do with this story. So rather than create problems for someone else I have just given the details as I knew them then and my own part in it.

time were ones of tremendous violence and rage: rage at myself for not killing every bastard that they had accused me of killing, rage for not walking into a police station with a gun and blasting every cop in the place. My inner self was broken, torn into small pieces, shattered. The pain was and still is tremendous, penetrating as it does to a depth that no physical pain ever reaches. My whole being was dead, my life was no longer. I was state-owned – forever. I was very much aware of my situation, and how my past history, guilty or not, would be instrumental in keeping me away for the rest of my life. Never would I experience freedom again; it was something that was gone forever, never to be re-tasted. The shock of losing my life is something that I can't express in words as they are so inadequate. My life was now to be lived on memories of home, of my family, of friends, of the Gorbals, and of every other small detail that had made it up – things that everyone on the outside takes for granted.

I lay on the dark floor in a terrible state. I cried that first night, my heart and my eyes cried. I was so angry at myself and the world that I just couldn't think straight. Internally I was a raging storm, but to anyone peering through the judas hole of the cell door I would look calm, as though I was just dozing. Without that facade I would have broken into a million little pieces. For some reason it was very important that I cling to this and make it see me through till I recovered from this inner blitz. I was a walking time-bomb, primed and ready for exploding: all it needed was one wrong word and there would have been such a holocaust that they wouldn't have believed it. That inner something that seemed to take over the minute the verdict was given stayed with me. By some miraculous means or other I managed to get through the first night and the next few days, though they were very hazy and I can only remember pieces of them. The press were giving it big licks and I covered the pages with the same old crap of being the super baddie. It seemed to keep up for the first week or so and guys showed me what they were saying, but by now I was sick of it. For the first time in my life I became revolted at the sight of my name in the papers whereas all the other times it had been a prestigious thing and I had enjoyed it. The press were keeping on about the moneylending rackets and saying that they would have to be clamped down on, so the cops reacted and went round the pubs in the Gorbals, lecturing to the customers and telling them to come forward and give evidence and they would be guarded. There were stories printed saying that some of us had "crucified" a non-paying customer to the wooden floor of a house. This was a statement reported to have been issued by the police. Most of what they printed was nonsense.

My hopes during the first few days automatically lay with the Appeal Court and I applied to the prison authorities, saying I wanted to appeal against the conviction. I began to think it out very carefully as this was my last chance in life and I had no intention of putting it into the hands of anyone else. This time when I went to court I wanted to speak for myself. If I failed then I would be the one to blame, no one else. I had made my mind up on this and set about gathering the necessary evidence and data to help me at the Appeal Court.

Prison being what it is, one has to go to the Governor for permission to obtain what are known as Appellant visits. These are special visits over and above the normal quota for an appellant to gather material for his case. I went to my hall Governor to get a special visit from a Mr Davidson. I told him the circumstances about wanting to speak on my own behalf and the need for a visit to get certain information. He began to hum and haw and stretch the whole thing out, telling me he would give me an answer later in the day. That was it. I could take no more. Didn't he realise what this meant to me? The anger came up from my toes and I swung a blow that knocked him from his chair and put him on the floor. I lifted a wooden inkwell but was pounced on from behind and put into the cell next door. I tore a piece of wood from the book shelving and stood with it in my hand, as they carried the Governor out. They waited some time allowing me to cool off and then cautiously opened the door; there was a mob of them. The screws said that everything was all right and I would be okay, that there would be no brutality handed out. I told them to remember that if there was brutality it wouldn't end here, as I was now in for the rest of my life and would remember anyone who laid a finger on me.

I was put into a solitary confinement cell and left alone without any harm done to me.

A short time later I heard the sound of heavy boots and the cell door opened. There stood the heavy mob all wearing coloured overalls and they told me to take off my clothes. I refused, saying that if they wanted to fight, why didn't they get on with it? I was told that there would be no brutality, all they wanted was my clothes for the cops. I thought this over and accepted that they were telling the truth as there were enough of them to beat me up with my clothes on. No sooner had I stripped off than some of them moved in, punching and kicking me. I tried to hit back, calling them cowardly lumps of shit. These were shouts of anger, but they beat me to the floor, leaving me in a pool of blood. There is something totally humiliating about being brutalised when naked. Nakedness leaves a feeling of helplessness, and even though I was returning blows it felt as though they couldn't hurt the person they landed on. There was this feeling of impotence. I lay on the floor in an absolute rage, hating myself for being such a bloody fool as to trust them.

Being a Life prisoner meant looking at prison in a totally different perspective. This experience resulting from my assault on the Governor meant that I had to rethink everything. It was obvious to me that my lifestyle would have to change in order to survive in this jungle. Certainly I had lost my life, but not my will to live, to fight. The whole of my thought processes were undergoing a dramatic change. It dawned on me for the first time that my life sentence had actually started the day I left my mother's womb. Strangely enough I now found a new sense of freedom, which I had never experienced before; it was important to me. I decided that I would now live by my laws, not giving one fuck for society or the laws of society. Their very representatives, the media, were labelling me "Animal", "Maniac" and lots of other names. From now on I would totally reject everything and everyone and label them the "Dangerous Majority" and the "Perpetuators of Fascism". Who was society? I described them as being like every para-military organisation on the government payroll, and all those silly ignorant bastards who would be brainwashed by the media, accepting their every word as being gospel. From now on the world could go to fuck. I hated everyone and distrusted everyone. They made it plain that they felt the same about me, so we all knew where we stood.

I lay with my thoughts on the cell floor in the early hours of the morning, thoroughly frustrated and angry at all that had gone on and I cracked. I ran at the metal door and banged it all that I could, which brought the night patrol in. The noises wakened the rest of the prisoners and they too joined in, calling the screws all the names under the sun. The night screws called for reinforcements and opened my cell door. They had a straitjacket with them and after a struggle I was locked into it, getting some bruises in the process. I was thrown into a padded cell, which was an ordinary cell covered in rough canvas pads. I lay on the cushioned floor, struggling with the straitjacket. It's a very strange experience being locked into one of these as the upper part of the body is completely helpless, even to the extent that one has to do the toilet in it. The rest of the prisoners had ceased their noise but I continued to struggle and by some miraculous means or other managed to break free of the jacket.

This was victory and it restored some power to my much damaged morale; I was elated at freeing myself from this degrading contraption. But it wasn't enough for me to be free, I had to prove it to everyone, so I systematically set about destroying the padded cell. I tore the padding, which was very difficult, and pulled the red-coloured coir matting from it. I worked all through the night, destroying as much as I could, so that by the morning I was able to stand gleefully in the centre of the one-time padded cell floor amidst piles of canvas and woolly coir waiting for the door to open. I was covered in blood and filthy as I stood amidst the wreckage, but I felt so proud. They might beat me by sheer force of numbers, but by fuck they would never beat my spirit into submission. I was fully rewarded when the screws finally opened the door seeing me with a big smile on my face amidst the one-time pads. The door was quickly shut and in a short time I was taken from the padded cell by a team of screws with my hands cuffed behind my back.

They took me to the prison reception area, bundled me into my civilian clothes and handcuffed me to two detectives. There were two others with revolvers showing plainly under their arms. I was put into one of two squad cars and whisked off through the main streets of Glasgow to the Sheriff Court in the city centre. The sirens were blaring as we reached the old fruit market, which was so busy that it stopped the police cars. For fleeting minutes we were held up with the congestion. I savoured these moments in the knowledge that I would never see them again. I had walked along these streets many times in my life and felt very close to them. My heart ached as I sat wedged between two cops in this mobile prison. The things that moved me were the workers walking about their business, just ordinary guys craning their necks to look into the police cars and me on the inside craning my neck to look out and drink in with my eyes their every move. I was so envious of these guys that I would have given anything to be one of them, carrying a heavy load of fruit and putting it onto the lorries or barrows. They looked in at me, but never could they see my thoughts. I, the monster, the hard man, sat there in chains between two cops, and was pining my heart out for everything which surrounded the police car. The message came home to me, the penny dropped – too late, because now I could see what it was all about, this freedom. In the past I had experienced being transported from place to place while handcuffed but always with the knowledge that I would get out. This time it was different as I felt I would never walk these streets again, ever. There was no substitute for this.

Once the congested area had been cleared, we made quick time to the court with me feeling in a desperately emotional state, my heart very heavy with pain. I was locked in a cell and when it was opened again, in walked two cops followed by the Sheriff in robes then more cops. What was this all about? It was very odd. They held the court appearance in the cell; I couldn't believe that this melodramatic scene was taking place here. This game was becoming ludicrous, what with armed cops and a court hearing in a cell. The ironic part was that the Sheriff had been the prosecuting Q. C. at the first two murder trials and here I was in front of him again at this preliminary hearing. It was the first time that this had ever happened, the bringing of a court to a cell. Later the press said that it was due to a plot by friends to get me out of prison.

After the court appearance, I was taken back to prison and to the cell that I came from, next door to the padded cell which they were busily repairing. However, they decided that something had to be done about me as I was becoming too much, so the next morning the door crashed open first thing, and a mob of screws handcuffed my hands behind my back and pulled me along the long dark corridors across a yard and locked me into a cell in what was once the Women's Wing of the prison. There was a specially selected group of screws to look after me and they were with me night and day. They sat outside my door and would talk in whispers so I couldn't hear them. I lay on the cell floor looking up to the ceiling as there was no window that I could look out of. I would lie there and think, think, think. I was on strict solitary and wasn't allowed to see anyone. I didn't speak to the screws nor they to me so it was utter silence except for the essentials. I would be taken out for exercise for an hour to walk at the side of the building with my hands cuffed behind my back between the two screws. We would pace up and down in complete silence with them not speaking to each other and the sound of our footsteps ringing in the cold morning. It was eerie as here were three human beings all touching each other with the closeness of a sandwich and not a word, only hate flowing between us with me waiting, watching for the first chance to have a go at them. The Deputy Governor and the Chief made their rounds and when he came into sight I would try to run at him and attack him with my hands behind my back but they would just hold me and I could do nothing. I would try to spit at him as I hated every single bastard. In the cell I became enmeshed in my appeal and fantasised about getting released. The appeal took me over completely and I would spend my day walking up and down the cell floor teaching myself how to speak fluently and clearly to make sure my points were getting across. This was it; I would put up a fight for them to remember. There were times when I would have doubts and think that I'd make an arse of myself, but there were others when I thought I'd get free and walk out.

Meanwhile, outside the walls, the press were making a big deal of the case and still calling for police action. They were looking for witnesses but, as the "Crucifixion" statement was doing them no good at all and was frightening the witnesses off, they retracted it. The press were told that no one had been crucified. Arrests were made for suborning witnesses at my trial and the cops arrested Frank Wilson, Bandit Rooney and Jimmy Latta, who was William's lawyer during the trial. A lawyer being arrested was big news. I lay in my solitary cell oblivious to all of this. All my concentration was on the forthcoming appeal. I pretended to have a passive period in the hope that the Deputy Governor would come nearer because I wanted to butt him right on the face as he was the one I identified with the order to handcuff me. I was so full of hatred and bitterness and would shout curses and obscenities. I always felt much better after I did something like that. It was my way of letting them know that they could chain me forever and I'd still fight them. Although the screws and I said the minimum of words there was a non-verbal communication of hatred. By this time they did as little as possible to annoy me and had me labelled as a complete nut-case. The same ones were looking after me all the time, so they weren't going to create a situation where they would be terrified that I was going to pounce on them each time they opened the door. This happened at the beginning, with them trying me out now that I was in a place all alone, but then I walked out with a chamber pot full of shit and told them that if they treated me like shit I would throw it over them every time I was out. These were the tense moments that marked the thin line between violence and words. The threat was effective, and there is no doubt about it that I owed a lot to shit.

One night as I lay in the far corner of the cell with my eyes shut, thinking, the door opened quickly and a small paper bag was thrown towards me, then the door shut immediately. I was startled and opened the bag to find two small chocolate biscuits. This almost broke my heart. It seemed that two of the screws had left to go and do something and the third when seeing this had opened the door and thrown in the biscuits, even though the strict ruling is that no less than three screws must be present when the door is opened. Although it was obviously the human in him, why did he do this? It confused the picture, as it brought something human back into me and I would have preferred to think of us all as animals in the one jungle. This guy had no idea what he had done, he would never imagine how this small action caused me so much inner conflict. I didn't ever say anything to him nor him to me, but he had got to me.

Another night I was lying on the cell floor when I heard the judas hole slide back and instead of closing again as is usual, I was told very briefly that my girlfriend had had a baby girl. It was in this way that I found out that my daughter Patricia had been born. Margaret had been pregnant before I was arrested so now I was father to a boy and a girl. I felt very sad and very happy, so with this mixture I took great hope, as this birth took place a few days before I was due to appear before my appeal, on 19th December 1967, and I took it as an omen that by some fluke I would win.

On the morning of the 19th there was a great hustle and bustle and sounds of activity outside my door. It opened and I was given my suit of civilian clothing to wear and was made ready for court. Leaving my cell, I was confronted with a large number of Glasgow detectives in the bottom flat of the prison hall. They were to be my escort and some of them were wearing guns. There were no words between us, all we did was stare. Some of them I knew from the past, some I didn't. I was handcuffed between two screws using special handcuffs, and put into a squad car. There were four cars on the escort in all and I was bang in the centre but every so often they would change positions like the pea under the nutshells. The journey passed in silence with us overtaking the commuters travelling along the Edinburgh Road oblivious to what was happening. On entering Edinburgh the cops there met us and escorted us to the High Court.

I had never been in an appeal court before, though I know that three judges sat instead of one. I do know that the general feeling of prisoners who had been to one was that it was an exercise in futility, but try telling that to someone like me who saw it as his last chance for freedom. I had to believe in it. On entering the court I caught sight of the small white-haired macer who had been there when I was found guilty. I told myself that given the chance I would lay one on him. The three judges, all very old men, entered the court, sat down and told me to proceed. I reminded them that I was only a layman, and might bring out points that had no legal substance in their eyes but that they ought to bear with me. From there I went on to give my points, of which I had many, but as quickly as I put them they threw them out, without so much as an explanation. This procedure really stunned me as I thought they would go over each point that I put to them and discuss it, but I was wrong. It was as though I was the only man in that room who was alive, who had enthusiasm. I stood there for over fifty minutes speaking and putting point after point. To make matters worse I dropped some papers and the court macer picked them up for me, a kind gesture which got through to me. After I had finished speaking the three judges rose from their chairs, put their heads together for the briefest of moments and sat down, telling me how they had listened to my case and had given it their full consideration but could find no grounds for altering the conviction.

I was dragged from the court feeling hate, hate, hate. I was carved up, set out and finally doomed to live out my days in a tomb. I found myself back in the cop car manacled, not really seeing anything, just hating everyone and everything. My life was gone, as that had been my last chance, no more would I have a sense of hope. Who could ever measure the total despair that I felt at that moment? Was this dreadful pain never going to cease? All this while the fleet of cars were making a swift exit from Edinburgh and it was some miles on before I was to realise that we weren't heading in the direction of Barlinnie. We were going through beautiful countryside. I would never have asked the bastards where I was going. I was too shattered and wasn't really caring, but I kept wishing that the car would crash or something and kill us all. I had never experienced the countryside before and here I was passing through picturesque scenery in my mobile prison, seeing things that I had never seen before. It was nigh on Christmas and there was snow on the ground. As we passed small cottages I could see the warmth emanating from the lights in the houses and the Christmas trees in the windows. There were occasions when we passed a house and would catch sight of families sitting at a table eating. Fleeting glances that showed me the beauty of home life.

Seeing these things really twisted my guts causing me terrible nostalgia. The countryside showed me total freedom, with deer running in the distance, and here was I travelling in this prison, manacled, squashed between two screws and three other cars. From the roadway signposts I could see that we were heading in the direction of Inverness.

PART THREE

PART THREE

11

The prison in Inverness holds about seventy prisoners serving local sentences but there is a block reserved for the troublemakers, so that Inverness is the Siberia for prisoners in the Scottish penal system. There are special rules laid down for treatment in this prison. No prisoner is to stay for a period less than two months or more than six months. Each prisoner's case is reviewed every two months by a Board of Governors to decide if he should return to the prison that he came from. If a prisoner gets into trouble while there, he automatically gets held for another two months. The conditions are spartan with a minimum of recreation, and the whole programme is structured to encourage boredom so that the prisoner will behave accordingly and be glad to get back to his normal prison. I was put through the usual procedure of being stripped of my clothing and having everything taken from me. I was taken into a hall by a large group of screws and it was so silent that the ring of our footsteps echoed. There were perhaps sixty cells in the hall but there were only three prisoners. The cell was the standard size, eight feet by twelve. There was a bed, a chamber pot, and on the inside of the window there was heavy wire mesh to prevent access to the glass, with the usual heavy bars on the outside. In the morning, the cells were opened one at a time for the prisoners to slop out and after each one had finished another was let out, with guards by his side at all times. After the six o'clock slop out and breakfast, they allowed the prisoners out to a workshed at ten o'clock.

Soon I was able to see who was here. There was John McCue, my pal from the district, and Ben Conroy, who had been in various institutions with me. The worktask was making fishing nets, which hung over a steel bar attached to the wall. These were a distance apart to discourage conversation. It was very nice to see people I knew. They had obviously known what I had been through, or were able to identify with a part of it, so that was something. Ben was serving his five-year sentence and was taken away almost immediately to another prison for release. John had been in the block for six months and reckoned they would be putting him away soon. Another guy was brought up to replace Ben. John was worn away by the boredom of the place so was glad to see me and get some home news. Being in Inverness like this was almost worse than solitary as we tended to get everything out of perspective and would speculate on what was for lunch, even though we knew what it would be. In order to change the subject someone would talk about a letter he received so that before long we were discussing intimate things about each other and our family lives, saying things that we would never normally say. I always hated this when I returned to my cell, thinking that I shouldn't have said this or that, but I would always say similar things again. I was fortunate in that John and I knew each other's families very well, but the personalities changed every few months in the block, and this was a problem.

I had been in the block only a week when I was issued with an Indictment for the charge of assaulting the Barlinnie Governor which stated that I would return to Glasgow High Court on the first week of January. This brought fresh life into our conversation, dominating it for a spell. The other two were looking forward to the latest news I would get while back in Barlinnie. The same escort that had brought me up came to take me down to Barlinnie and it was the same procedure of armed guards and squad cars. I was returned to the same solitary cell and waited there till the trial date. On the day of the trial two cops came into my cell and were handcuffed to me. From there I was taken to the High Court and the three of us were locked into a cell in the courthouse. Here I was back in the same court, going into the same dock where I had been sentenced to Life Imprisonment nine weeks previously.

There were the same old faces, the small court macer, the cops, and then of course the civil dignitaries. In a way I felt good because every bastard in the place had thought they had seen the last of me, but here I was as large as life only this time I had nothing to lose. I pleaded guilty to the charge of punching the Governor on the face and breaking his cheekbone, and was given eighteen months. Afterwards I was to hear that certain people present in the court had been inquiring whether the eighteen months was concurrent or consecutive. This was the ultimate in getting or trying to get blood from a stone as it was surely obvious to everyone that having already lost my life there was nothing more that could be taken from me. I was hurriedly taken back to Inverness and could only relate my own experiences to the guys there, as I had been kept on solitary. I'd had no way of obtaining news that would be a point for discussion. While I was away, John McCue had been transferred to his old prison.

I had only been back a few days when I realised that this place and its regime were bent on turning me into a vegetable, so I went on request to see the Governor. As I entered his office, I picked up a chair lying nearby and threw it through the windows and set about trying to ransack the place. Due to my last assault on the Governor at Barlinnie, they had been taking precautions and had screws waiting in readiness. They came rushing in the door and we all fell about the floor in a fierce struggle. I was dragged along the corridor with some blows and kicks landing on me. I was then thrown into the "Silent Cell" and the door was closed.

This silent cell was the same as the one in Peterhead, and being in one was very much like being in the other. The silence was all the same no matter where one was. I urinated all over the floor and threw my food all over the walls and floor and just lay there. I just wasn't giving a damn. The following morning I was taken to the Governor's room to be punished for smashing his office up, and I went there naked with my hands cuffed behind my back, and a heavy escort. Entering the room I shouted repeatedly "Bastard,

bastard, bastard, bastard . . .", which meant that they couldn't read out the charge, so they dragged me out and back to the hole.

We did small things to annoy each other, or punish each other. The screws would give me my food when it was stone cold or with spit in it. In return, cold or not cold, spit or no spit, I would eat it up and put the plates at the far end of the cell. The screws needed them for the next meal so would have to enter the cell stinking of shit and slops to get the plates. I felt that they were humiliating and degrading me, so in my way I was doing it to them. As the filth mounted up to outrageous proportions they would send in a screw who was recognised as being not a bad fellow and he would speak in a low confidential voice, showing every sympathy with me. He agreed that the Governor and most of his fellow screws were fucking idiots, and how I was usually a very hygienic sort of guy and that this was not my usual way of behaving. I knew that this was all part of the game and that this was how the "tough screws" use the screw least interested in brutality, but I didn't want to compromise in any way. Certainly I didn't hate him like the rest but there was no way I would let him know that, for then he would be used by the others to sweep up their dirty work when it got too hot for them to handle. I realised that this guy would repeat everything that I said to the Governor so I told him that I intended attacking the Governor and every other Governor that I could lay my hands on. They were causing the trouble so it would be brought directly to them. The stench was foul but I lay there and after a time got used to it and it didn't bother me at all. The place was absolutely freezing so I would leave a patch of floor free of contamination so that I could run on the spot without slipping. There was very little air getting into the place but I ceased to think too much about that. I really hated the screws so much that I wished they would put a small hatch on the cell door to pass my food through so that I didn't have to see them. They would all take part in the brutality as "one of the boys" but it was this constant and protracted continuance of the trouble that they didn't like. For over a week they had to come in and feed me, and take in the stench as they did so, and afterwards go home to their families and be with them.

Eventually I went back to the segregation block to find that the guys who had been there when I left were now gone and replaced by others. This was the way it went – new faces would come and go, yet I would remain. There were times in Inverness when I would go into terrible depressions and be in the depths of despair. The sheer enormity of having to live with the fact that I was in my tomb was weighing heavily upon me. I lay in my cell one night realising that I just couldn't go on. I had managed to conceal a small piece of razor blade and lay with it in my hand pressed to my wrist, willing myself to end it all now. There was nothing ahead for me except moments of relief during periods in solitary. My heart was terribly heavy and my insides were tearing me to pieces, emotionally I was in an awful state. I could feel the sharp edge of the razor against my veins and knew that all of it could be over in seconds – I being the decider. This was the first time in my life that suicide had entered my head. In the past I would have looked on it as something only a weakling would do. I would never have admitted that I couldn't face up to anything, but now that part of me was crumbling as I lay with the razor against my wrist, my eyes tightly closed.

I didn't do it, and the deciding factor was the images and thoughts that flashed in my mind's eye. All the people with their shark-like grins in the court that day, the court macer, the dignitaries and the cops in the past who had planted evidence on me and verballed me, they were what prevented me from doing it. They were the ones who kept me alive that night. I knew that to do away with myself was the easy way out and would give much pleasure to those who stood in the court that day. The pure hate that I had for them was what kept me from doing away with myself.

I learnt a lot from this and emerged all the stronger. It also brought home to me that it takes a very brave man to commit suicide. I knew that come what may I would carry on and let those on the outside know that I was very much alive and let those on the inside know that they had had their day. I had no intention of sitting back and letting them do what they wanted with me. I was myself and would remain that way; all it could cost me was my life and that was already gone.

During this very introspective period when I was in a state of emotional distress I was given a book that reflected what was going on within me: *Crime and Punishment* by J. Dostoevsky. It somehow matched what I was experiencing internally. I had never heard of the book or the author before and in fact it was the first serious book I'd ever read. The torment of Raskolnikov was so revealing, so accurate in my own terms, that I marvelled at the author's grasp of pain. I identified so strongly with the book that it put me off reading it for a while. It opened up a new dimension in reading and thinking for me, but I had so little knowledge of literary classics that I had to rely on luck more than anything else. Books became a very important aspect of my survival in solitary and I would always try to get ones that would be emotionally fulfilling, books that would become a partner, that I could read time and again. They were mostly by authors like Dostoevsky , Victor Hugo, Tolstoy, Charles Dickens, Solzhenitsyn and Steinbeck. I concentrated on the works of these men and whenever I got one of their books, I felt I'd discovered a new treasure, as the mere possession of it delighted me.

While I was in Inverness a big trial had taken place with Frank Wilson, Bandit Rooney, and Jimmy Latta for suborning witnesses at my trial. They had been sentenced to long terms of imprisonment, with Frank getting twelve years, Bandit four years and Jimmy Latta, the lawyer, getting eight years. The fact that a respected member of the legal profession had been found guilty aroused all sorts of suspicions and was felt in all sections of their world. None of us felt that he had done anything wrong and I believed that he had simply fought the case, using the same tactics as the cops, but evidently the jury thought differently. The cops were riding high on the crest of the wave of convictions.

I had been in Inverness four months when a riot erupted in Peterhead prison resulting in a number of the screws there being stabbed. With my feeling of hatred I loved hearing these things as it pleased me to know that other people were now having a go. I knew the guys involved, all of whom were serving heavy sentences. One of them was Larry Winters, who had been in Approved School and Borstal with me. After a few months of awaiting trial they were taken to court. Larry was given fifteen years on top of his Life sentence, the other three were cleared of all charges. They were all sent to Inverness as a further punishment, and the escort that brought them up was the one to take me back. After being there almost eight months, this was me going back into full circulation.

Going back to Peterhead after the trial verdict was a problem, as feelings were running high. The screws were sick, as they looked on the verdict as being a victory for the prisoners, three of whom had been cleared. The atmosphere in Peterhead was explosive at the best of times but this meant that the slightest spark would blow the place sky-high. I had been there some hours and was being placed amongst the top-security prisoners. The first screw escorting me upstairs was jabbing me in the back and pushing me. I waited till we got to a place at the top of the stairs shadowed by the landing above, where I would nip him quietly. The screw continued to jab me as though I were a lump of meat so, at the appropriate moment, I turned round and thumped him on the jaw, putting him on the floor, where he clung to my feet curled in a ball. This was seen by another screw, who shouted a warning, and others came running and dragged me off. Prisoners who had seen all of this came on the scene and dragged the screws from me. Two of them took the batons from the hands of the screws so that in the space of a few seconds we had a situation bordering on the explosive. Everything froze as the screws found themselves outnumbered and trying to cool everyone. The cons had taken enough shit from them and were ready to run amok at a given signal. The atmosphere at this point was intense. The ball was at my feet as I had to decide whether I wanted to involve these guys who were mostly doing determinate sentences, some with only a short while to go. The truth was that I didn't and I began to cool the situation. The guys told the screws that there would be no trouble so long as I wasn't brutalised and the screws promised this. Two of them escorted me to the solitary confinement block and there I was searched and had my shoes taken from me then the door closed. The two screws that escorted me to the cells left after I was locked in, but they came back.

That night, an hour or so later, the prison doctor was called to attend to some injuries that I had sustained. There were several scalp wounds, numerous bruises and two suspected broken arms. I refused to let the doctor treat me. The police were called and I was charged with assaulting two officers in the main prison hall, and biting one prison officer in the punishment block cell. After they had made the charges against me I told the cops that I wished to prefer charges against some prison staff for giving me the injuries that I now had. I couldn't write a statement due to the arm injuries so they had to do it for me. The cops had to strip my clothes from me in order to take them as evidence for the forthcoming trial. I didn't know the names of any of the screws that I was charging so they set up an Identification Parade for me to pick them out.

There are two versions given at the subsequent trial of how I got these injuries. The screws, about six or seven of them, testified that they had locked me up in the Punishment Block, then came in to search me and at that moment I had pounced on them and started biting one of them on the neck for no reason whatsoever. The senior screw said that he ordered batons to be used on me – to restrain me. He said all the batons were used on my arms and shoulders and the numerous cuts on the top of my head were the result of my falling on the floor when hit by the batons on the arms.

My defence in court was that after having been searched, and the shoes taken from me, I was then locked in. I had been in the cell just a minute when the door flew open and a mob of screws came in the door with batons in their hands. They were being led by the screw that I had punched in the main hall. This was what we call the "Batter Squad", out to extract their own pound of flesh. I backed to the corner of the cell as they came towards me, forming a semi-circle. My only means of protection were my arms. The batons in their hands once again gave me that impotent feeling of helplessness, but experience of similar situations was with me. They started lashing at me but my concentration was on getting hold of one of them, which I finally managed to do. I grasped him, wrapping myself around him and sinking my teeth into his neck while the others continued to hit me with their batons. I clung there as long as I could but was stunned by one heavy blow that finally prised me loose. I don't remember falling, only waking and they were still hitting me as I lay there. I got to my feet again and one of them panicked and started shouting while hitting me with his baton, "Get down, you bastard, get down". Eventually I passed out, waking to find myself alone. They sent for the doctor and when he came I stood in the corner like a wounded, frightened animal, refusing to trust anyone, but very dangerous. I refused to let him treat me telling him that he was one of them, part of them. The blood was splashed over the walls and running down my face and body.

By the time the police came I was thinking rationally and thought that I should charge the screws and reverse the whole thing. They got an Identification Parade and I went on it and tapped everyone of them on the shoulder whom I was accusing. The following morning I saw the doctor, who treated me and got me out to the hospital for X-rays to my arms. They weren't broken. The horrible part was that due to the arm injuries a screw had to write the letters to my lawyer as I couldn't do anything with them and I desperately needed photographs of my injuries for the trial. It was a terrible shame having to rely on a screw to write for me, so I limited the words to the bare essentials.

I lay in solitary for four months awaiting trial and experienced moments of downright despair listening to the screws beating up guys who were being brought into the solitary block. I would have preferred to be involved in the trouble rather than being in a concrete box hearing the sound of the thuds. At times like this the other prisoners would get up to their doors and bang them constantly, shouting for the dirty bastards to leave the guy alone. This is all one can do as one is in a completely helpless position having to listen to the blows thumping into him, his moans and occasional screams. The whole process is deeply humiliating to everyone. Most prisoners, when they are beaten up, just curl into a ball and accept what is given out as they know that to retaliate will lead to them being charged by the cops, which would only lead to an additional sentence. I felt that my position was totally different from most of the others. I was in prison for what seemed to me to be the rest of my life, and the only way I was going to be able to live with myself was not to succumb, not to allow the screws to do what they wanted with me. No, by far the best way was to fight them, even if I lost, and suffered the pain that went with it. One important thing I noticed was that I was getting stronger after each incident. If it can't kill you it can only strengthen you. If I continued to gather strength then the system would be the eventual loser.

When the guys came into the solitary block and were brutalised I would shout through a ventilator and tell them to make an official complaint. Some guys would but others wouldn't. The official channel for complaining is to request to see the Governor and ask for a Petition to write to the Secretary of State. When this is completed it goes to the Prisons department in Edinburgh, where a civil servant looks at it, then returns it to the prison Governor for his comments. The usual reply in those days was "No cause for complaint". I wrote petitions after each guy was brutalised and made formal complaints. It was important for this to be placed on record as by now I was thinking ahead and felt that all this information might come in handy at my trial. After a few such petitions, I was warned that I would be punished for making false allegations. One of the guys, who had been brutalised and had complained by petition, was charged for making false allegations and was put in front of the Visiting Committee and they took a month's remission from him. This was enough to frighten others from petitioning or complaining and I was angry at this, but fully understood their positions. These guys all had liberation dates but I didn't, so it was easy for me. In fact we were in such a futile position that it would have been nigh on impossible for us to substantiate our allegations in any court of law. Most people have preconceived ideas about prisoners, so when it comes to a direct confrontation of believing the screws or the prisoner then the latter is usually the loser.

I used to give a lot of thought as to why this sudden spurt of brutality was going on and seemed to be getting worse in the long-term prisons. I know that screws felt they had a form of protection when Capital Punishment was in force, therefore brutality didn't seem to me to be as prevalent then. Most screws are pro-hanging and at this present date are active for its re-introduction. Whenever a screw was assaulted by a prisoner, a bunch of them would get together and go down to get their own back. In the past they would hit the prisoner with their fists and boots but now they were using their batons more frequently. In many ways the baton replaced the birch. They felt that by doing this it would deter others and in some cases it did. Those that didn't lash out at screws felt that to do so was a mug's game as it meant losing both ways: getting a beating and additional time to their sentences. I've seen many instances where guys were openly humiliated by the screws in front of everyone but would refuse to retaliate. This meant that prisoners witnessing or being on the receiving end of such frequent humiliations would withdraw into themselves and make sure that no such incident came their way again. As a result, the screws became a law unto themselves and given the inch they took the mile. I have seen prisoners accept things that made me squirm with embarrassment over petty rules that had been long forgotten in the rule book but could be applied at any time by the zealous screw. The point is that these prisoners were veritable walking time-bombs by the time they got out. No sooner were they released than they were back in again after blowing up when free of the strict regime. By making this point I am not advocating a case for the screw to stop brutalising and let the prisoner thump him on the jaw every time he feels depressed: I am arguing for a system that is going to help the guy while he is in rather than make him worse, as is the case in the prison system today.

Here I was lying in solitary in Peterhead, with quite a few brutal beatings under my belt. I was preparing for another High Court trial, my second in nine months, for assaulting prison officials. As far as I was concerned, it was war and I would use all these past incidents as learning experience so that the next one would be more difficult for them. There was no doubt in my mind that there would be a next one, as by now I was fully committed to having a go at the dirty rotten system. I was still doing daily exercises while in solitary to make sure I was fit for what I was getting into. My hair, which had been long and curly, was now cut close to my scalp so that it couldn't be grabbed. I knew what the future would be but the screws hadn't got the message yet.

In October 1968 I was taken to Aberdeen High Court. I pleaded not guilty to the three charges, but included Special Pleas: on the first charge that I acted under provocation, and on the other two that they were self-defence. The screws came in and the Crown evidence led, saying that I had attacked them for no reason. The prison doctor came in and said that my wounds were consistent with being hit by batons. Other prisoners came in and said what they had heard. I went into the witness box and offered all I could, the photos of the bloodstained walls, my own injuries, my bloodstained clothing. All of this I gave to them. Lord Johnston, the presiding judge, summed up and here are some extracts from his speech to the jury:

"... Now I come to the third charge, ladies and gentlemen, and that is the charge of assault in the prison while in the solitary confinement block. Let me remind you of what may have been forgotten or, rather, hidden in parts of the evidence, and that is that it is not the Prison Service of Peterhead which is under accusation here. The person accused is the prisoner in the dock. He stated what he did, and freely admitted that he jumped upon the officer as the officer described, and that he bit him. The question is, whether that was done in self-defence or not.

"Now, a man who is attacked as the accused says he was attacked, is entitled to defend himself, to use reasonable force, and if you accept the evidence of the Accused and the other evidence that he was attacked in the way he says he was attacked, there can be little doubt – though it is a matter for you – that what the Accused says he did was no more than necessary and, indeed, he says it was sufficient to repel the attack on him. But, ladies and gentlemen, the burden of proving that an assault is done in self-defence is on the Accused and he must show you, he must satisfy you, that on the balance of probability his story that he was attacked and was doing no more than defend himself is true. Well, ladies and gentlemen, you heard the Accused in the witness box; you heard all the other evidence and what the Defence described as the real evidence. I don't intend to go over that evidence again, but there are certain questions I have no doubt you wish to ask yourselves, such questions are these – why was it necessary to search this man immediately after he was put into the cell? You ask yourselves, was it necessary for four officers to come in? It is true that the Accused had, if one accepts the evidence, shown some violence earlier, a few minutes earlier, but it seems to be accepted by all the evidence that he walked quietly from the second, or near the second flat to the solitary confinement Block, and you may ask yourselves why, in these circumstances, it was necessary for four men to go into the cell? Now there is the evidence of those in the neighbouring cells and you must consider that evidence along with that of the Accused himself. And against that evidence you must consider the evidence of the Prison Officers and their account of what happened, and it is on that evidence, ladies and gentlemen, that you must make up your minds what occurred, and you must make up your minds whether the charge is proved or not proved. . . ."

The jury was allowed to go and decide their verdict and I waited, locked in one of the cells. I had cited lots of prisoners as witnesses to the trial and for us there was a holiday atmosphere, with everyone glad of the day out and the change of food. The jury returned one hour and twenty minutes later; on the first charge I was found Guilty Under Provocation. Not Proven on the second charge. Guilty on the third charge.

The Advocate Depute moved for sentence and read out my previous convictions dating from 1957: "The initial convictions are offences of dishonesty and, in particular, in 1963 he was sentenced to two years' imprisonment for assault to severe injury and assault by stabbing; in February 1963, he was sentenced to imprisonment for assaulting the police and with attempting to resist arrest. He was sentenced to two years' imprisonment in 1965 for assault; and in October 1965 there was another sentence of imprisonment with regard to an assault; on 3rd November 1967, he was sentenced to life imprisonment for murder; and on 8th January 1968, he was sentenced to eighteen months' imprisonment for an assault – that assault was on a Prison Officer."

Defending Q. C. said: "Your lordship has heard the evidence, and I think that the only thing I would say is that the injury in the third charge was a very minor one in the nature of assault."

Lord Johnston: "James Boyle, you have been convicted of two charges of Assault – the first under provocation. You have a deplorable record and you are now serving a sentence of life imprisonment for murder. I cannot emphasise too much that if you are to serve your sentence of imprisonment in such a way as to obtain some remission from the sentence of life imprisonment, you must behave yourself. The sentence which I am about to pronounce will have some effect in that it will be taken into consideration if and when the time comes for consideration of your release. I now sentence you to four years' imprisonment."

Throughout all of this trial I had become very hopeful as the evidence came across well in my favour, or so I had thought; but now I was thoroughly deflated. Had I won then I felt it may in some way have helped my behaviour and that of the screws. It now meant that I would go back to take up where I had left off. There was no way out. I felt that I had to kill a part of me in order to go on without thinking too deeply about it. When one is in a concrete box and has bad injuries then one is constantly thinking about the next time the door opens. The further four years added to my sentence was purely an academic exercise. It didn't matter whether it had been four days or forty years, what mattered was the actual conviction. I had committed myself to having a go at the screws and the system in order to expose them for the things that they did, and with this sense of commitment I had hoped that victory would be just around the corner, but it's never that easy. I was led back down the stairs after sentence to the cells, where I was locked in. The voices outside the cell door were jubilant at their victory, but what I minded most was a reference to the injured screws being able to get new car engines with the money they would get from the Criminal Compensation Board. At this point I was on the brink of a form of insanity with emotional pain that was burning with a fierce intensity. My God, I've never hated as I did at that moment. I was not returned to Peterhead but sent to Inverness Punishment Block. I had received physical injuries, been given further imprisonment, and now they were giving me yet another punishment. As far as I could see, the whole deal was structured to make sure that my spirit was broken.

The Punishment Block at Inverness had changed its location. Previously it was a few of us in a large hall but now there had been a swapover, with the local prisoners being put into the large hall and the few on Punishment situated in the smaller of the prison's two halls, which held sixteen cells. It was a two-tier system with eight cells on the bottom flat and eight above. Next to this hall they were adding another hall that would contain the new Punishment Block and a work shed. The work for this was going on while we were there. When I arrived three guys were already there. Amongst them was Larry Winters. It was getting back to the grind and the boredom that was destroying our souls. Guys would crack up in their cells at night and smash whatever they could. Most of them were getting drugs from the doctor. Some would shout and scream and smash the small pieces of furniture which they had. Sometimes it was due to depression, other times it was to break the monotony of our daily routine. The following day they would be taken in front of the Governor and punished.

The remark about the Criminal Injuries Compensation Board was eating into me, so I made an application to claim for the injuries that I had received during the incident in Peterhead. I was refused compensation but I wrote to the Board appealing against their decision, and informing them that I wasn't really after compensation but that I wanted to inform them that prison staff were creating assaults and claiming Compensation. I heard nothing from them and don't know to this day if they received my letter.

I was now doing physical exercises in my cell with an intensity that I hadn't shown before. I came to the conclusion that from now on the confrontations would be fierce and bloody, and therefore I should be prepared both at a physical and mental level. The only way to pass time was to do exercises and reading, and thinking thoughts of hatred. My former life was far in the distance and I would try not to think of my family as it hurt too much.

My ma would come up with my son to see me on occasions but I tried to restrict these visits as much as possible. When I did send them a pass I would be very excited and looking forward to seeing them, but when the moment arrived there would be glass and wire barriers between us. My son would shout Da-Da and try to get in. We would sit looking at each other, Ma and I, trying to pretend that the barrier didn't exist, nor the screws standing behind me. We would force conversation, deep down realising that things had changed, but clinging to the childhood and growing-up memories. I would have preferred to have just sat looking in silence as the words Ma spoke as she recounted the past and the present opened up the parts that I was trying to kill; the cherished parts of me that made me feel human in an inhuman situation. These were the parts that I felt had to be submerged in order to survive but Ma could penetrate the strong barriers of hatred that had been built up and she could do it with ease. After the visit was over I would feel very depressed because the visits from my family always confronted me with almost everything that had been beautiful in my life, and the part that would never be again. I would get letters during the week from my ma and brothers and other relatives but I knew that I was becoming alien to all of them and I could sense that it was all taking place within me.

I hadn't completed a full year of my sentence and had been twice in Inverness. How many more times would I experience this? Would I spend the rest of my life being shuttled to and fro after court appearances? This period in Inverness was destined to be a long one; this was made clear from the start. The maximum length of stay was supposed to be six months, the rules were explicit in stating this. However, my first period here had gone beyond that.

I built up a daily routine of exercises and writing my thoughts on paper and this got me through the first six months of my second stay here. The only other guy to be here that length of time was Larry Winters. We put in for the Inspector of Prisons and asked to see him on his next rounds. He made a quarterly visit to each prison to take complaints. I put it to him that I had been here for six months and wanted to be moved out. He told me that they were having difficulty in finding a place to put me into. Meanwhile the daily grind was continuing and by this time there were four of us being kept for an excessively long period. We had kept out of trouble and given them no excuse to keep us there for such an extended period. We thought that things were going beyond the tolerable.

Those of us in the Block were a pretty solid bunch, so one day in the shed, while we were working on the numbing job of fish-net making, one of the guys, the youngest, who had been in institutions since he was eleven years old, walked up to one of the screws and attacked him. The alarm bell was rung and that started it, with all of us getting into a big stand-up fight. Reinforcements came running, but somehow we managed to negotiate, with me being spokesman and telling them that all of us were fucking sick of this place, and the sight of their faces, and that it had reached the stage where attacking them was one way of breaking the monotony of our daily torment. The screws said that they were sick of us in their prison, which was meant to be a quiet local one and that they wanted us out of it. We came to a compromise as all of us seemed to have that same hard-done-to feeling. The compromise was that we would be allowed out for an extra two hours' recreation that night. With this, all of us, screws and cons, crossed the yard, but some steps on another fight broke out.

All the short-term prisoners were up at their windows and shouting out at us. They would enjoy it, as rumour had it that after a spell in our place, the screws would go back to the ordinary part of the prison so tense that they would become very authoritarian with the short-termers. We were giving them a sort of grim satisfaction, as they couldn't endanger their short sentences by indulging in our sort of behaviour.

Meanwhile we were all rolling about the yard fighting, but sheer weight of numbers defeated us and we were dragged into the cell area. I was kept for special treatment and was dragged through to the silent cell and brutally attacked. This was the worst beating I had experienced to date and I knew it at the time as the screws were pounding me in their rage. I could only retaliate by punching, kicking and biting, but due to the number of screws I wasn't doing much of that. I would have given anything for a weapon at that moment. They pounded me severely and though still conscious I realised I was badly injured. I had been kicked all along the corridor into the silent cell and left there, but my hatred was so strong that I rose to the judas hole screaming at them and calling them all the cowards of the day. I was challenging them to come back and fight but they had me where they wanted. I kept feeling the injuries to my face and tried to gauge the extent of the damage as it was bleeding badly and felt very swollen. Being in this bare cell with the roughcast walls was almost like seeing an old friend. There was nothing that I could use to look through to see my injuries, but I was able to see my body and legs and they were badly bruised. The nearest anyone came to seeing me was through the judas hole but whenever I heard them I was up and shouting and banging the door, telling them to come in. No one did. Although I had been angry originally, there was a coolness within me and I occasionally laughed when I thought back to the stupidity of us all rolling about the yard. There was this feeling of having changed the day, of having made it different. It's very difficult to explain this, but the nearest I can come to it is that I felt I was becoming used to all of this, even the brutality. Yes, I had lost the fear of pain. It was a day later that the prison doctor came in and his reaction to my condition was pretty strong though he tried not to show it.

He was not a hardened prison doctor; I knew, as did the others, that what was going on in Inverness was against his own principles and he made it clear that he wanted out of it. The only thing he felt he could do to help was to give us decent medical attention and this he did. Certainly we would have liked someone to stand up and shout out loud and cause a scene about these things, but we knew that this was expecting too much But certainly the doctor was the nearest thing to a neutral in the camp. There was no doubt in my mind that a riot charge would be made against us all so I was glad that this man had treated my wounds. I was looking forward to another court trial as I would use it as a platfrom to let people know what was going on in there.

Two days later I was allowed to slop out. By this time I had again thrown all my filth over the floor and was preparing for a long stay in this cell. I went to slop out as curiosity was getting the better of me and I wanted to see the extent of the damage to my face. I could see some of it from my reflection on the chrome tap of the sink. There was a lot of discoloration and swelling but decorating all of this was the imprint of a foot covering my face. The print was clearly made from the tacks that were on the guy's boot. If one was in the business of handing out sore faces then there is little doubt in my mind that here was one to be proud of. I was standing there trying to see it in the sink tap without a stitch of clothing on, surrounded by screws who were waiting for a reaction. I turned to look into their faces and told them that as long as I was alive I'd remember every bastard who had laid a finger on me. They said nothing to me, in fact they were very apprehensive as judging by all previous incidents I should have been grovelling at their feet. They were no longer angry or full of emotion as they had been at the time, but I was letting them see that nothing short of killing me would stop me continuing on my merry way. The only other way they could rationalise my behaviour was to assume that I was mad. To think this and to be left with me was frightening for them. I would never let them know any different.

Later that morning I was taken to the Governor's room to be charged and went there naked. Using all my old tactics when entering I shouted repeatedly, "Bastard, bastard, bastard . . ." till they took me out again. I had decided to myself that I was never going to speak to them again, never to any of the bastards even though this meant not being able to ask for a toothbrush or any essential. I hated them so much that I found it revolting to even see them, never mind speak to them. Moments of succour were when I was locked in the silent cell alone with the silence. Later that day someone shouted through the judas hole that I was remanded pending a decision from the Prisons Department. This was because my continual chanting had stopped them from being able to speak. To me this meant that the cops were coming in, but as far as I was concerned it didn't matter a shit.

I began to dabble in yoga as I had read about it some months previously and had looked at some of the exercises. So I began to try them. I found them very difficult and avoided doing them at the beginning, but finally I felt that if I didn't I was left with only one alternative, staring into space, and one can have too much of that in the kind of situation I was in. The mind dictates the mood and I knew that if I was to sit or lie about all day then black periods would be the inevitable result. I was oblivious to the filth and smell that permeated the place, but I had my clean strip where I could lie, and sleep and do my exercises without slipping. I knew that the shit and the slops were necessary weapons, the only weapons at my disposal and an important part of my survival. It was strange to notice how screws who had seen blood pouring down my face could be quite insensitive to it, yet they would be very upset at having to feed me and face the smell. I was in the silent cell for over a month before being taken in front of the Visiting Committee and charged with attempting to assault a Prison Officer. There was a very middle-class but quite beautiful woman taking notes on the proceedings and the Committee sentenced me to twenty-eight days solitary and twenty-eight days remission; someone should have told them a lifer has no remission. But with this I was back in the silent cell. The prison authorities had about-turned on this issue that it was pretty serious and kept it an internal matter. Little did I know that the other guys had been sentenced to fourteen days solitary by the Governor. I heard later that due to the injuries received by the prisoners there had been a lot of hushing up of the police charges. By any standards, it was a riot, but due to the cloak of secrecy that hangs over prisons the authorities managed to keep it all quiet. It was the first serious charge that I had been involved in that was smothered up.

It was around this time when I was slopping out one day that two of the screws standing watching me were talking, and one of them mentioned his sister, who worked in a store in town. This matter-of-fact conversation stopped me dead as I had become so alienated from society that I somehow couldn't imagine this guy having a sister, or even being human. My whole way of thinking had become so introspective and introverted that I was practically cut off from all that had gone on in my past life. I was becoming animalised. This simple conversation between two people has stayed with me; it was the only means for me to measure the change that was taking place. But I wasn't too worried about it as I felt it was necessary in order to survive. This world that I was living in was so empty of human feeling that it was difficult to be aware of the inner transformation taking place.

By this time, the screws were saying that I must be transferred to another prison, but the hard fact was that no other prison would take me. I had seen the Inspector of Prisons a number of times about my lengthy period here and he told me this, time and again. The Governor of Inverness prison who was due to retire was in a dilemma, as he was faced with hostile staff who wanted me removed, and a hostile prisoner who wanted to be transferred. So for the first time the screws and I wanted the same thing. A compromise was reached by which the Governor, having made it clear that no one would take me, offered me a painting job. This meant painting the cells on my own, so I was agreeable. It was to isolate me from the rest of the guys, and we knew it, so all of us were let out of solitary to go back to the few hours' work that the prison could provide. There had been some movement amongst the prisoners as a few had gone. Larry Winters and I remained and Ben Conroy had returned. Ben had been out only days after the end of his five-year sentence when he was arrested and given a further seven years. He had lost most of his remission for offences during his five years' sentence and it looked as though the pattern would be repeating itself in this recent seven-year sentence. In his place two other guys had come on the scene. One of them was being given electric shock treatment after which he would come wandering into the hall area looking like a lost soul. The other was an elderly guy who was getting large doses of drugs to quieten him down.

It was around this time while I was busy working on the cell-painting job that I returned after lunch one day and noticed that someone had been into my cell. A brand new hacksaw was lying on the floor and I immediately sensed that I was being "fitted up". Someone had planted it there. Hacksaws were like gold in the jail, but I didn't know what to do as I sensed that it was a trap. I would love to have hidden it, so that I could have a laugh at the screws when they came in search of it. But there was nowhere to hide it, and even if there had been it would probably have been pointless. So I barged into the shed where the other guys were working and told them. The screws knew something was in the air and we walked out en masse along to the cell with the screws following us, asking what the matter was. There was a direct confrontation with me asking them about the plant. The scene was explosive and tension mounting as the screws made denials all round. We were told that an investigation would be made into this, but like all things we heard no more about it.

I was in the Inverness Punishment block for nineteen months and was always on the verge of exploding. The place had been structured to encourage boredom. Most of us here had been labelled as anti-authority, which meant that the only thing left to do was to clash with each other, which didn't bother the screws. Tempers would become frayed and we would bite at each other in verbal exchanges that came close to violence but the cardinal rule that we made from the early days and always passed on to newcomers was that there would be no fighting amongst ourselves. There were exceptions to this rule and guys did have their physical fights but they were few and far between. I felt as though I was one of the living dead as I had been there three times longer than the maximum period stated in the rules. It looked as though they would keep me here forever.

In November 1969 at approximately 12.30 a.m. I pretended to feel sick. I rang the cell bell bringing the night screws and asked them for treatment. They went for the nurse screw and one other. They returned some time later. When called in at this time of night the screws usually noise the place up to make sure everyone is disturbed. My door was opened and I was given two aspirins but I threw them back, telling the screws to stick them up their arses. A fight broke out between us and we were outside in the hall area. But there were too many of them and I was held down. The rest of the prisoners were shouting for them to leave me alone. Some of the other screws went round the other cells once they saw that I was being subdued but when they went into Ben Conroy's cell he came barging out of the door and flew into the thick of us and it was a battle once more. Both of us got to our feet and attacked the screws, but finding ourselves next to Ben's cell door we jumped inside and banged the door shut, locking ourselves in.

We barricaded the door with his bed and an old wooden chair, then smashed the windows by putting a metal spar torn from the bed through the metal grill covering the window frame. Ben and I were both stark naked as our clothes had been taken from us before going into the cell that afternoon but we were drunk with pride. The screws were in a right fix now as they would have to explain how it was possible for two prisoners to get into the same cell during the early hours of the morning. The rules stated that two doors weren't to be opened at the one time, particularly at that time. Here we were, locked away from them and sharing a cell when minutes before we thought we were going to be beaten up, so it showed that nothing could be forecast. For a while the tide had turned in our favour. This was a winter's night in November and it was extremely cold. An hour or so after we had locked ourselves in, there were noises and movements outside and they began breaking the windows. They put the nozzle of a hose in the window and turned it on, soaking everything and leaving us wet and cold. They kept telling us to come out but we shouted back, slagging them. As the night wore on we got colder and colder, so that within a very short time Ben and I lay on a metal bed frame and embraced each other for body warmth, wrapping our limbs around each other. The new Governor who had taken over the prison a few weeks earlier came to the judas hole in the late morning and beckoned us to come out, but we gave him mouthfuls of abuse. Later we found out that there had been an application to the Prisons Department to use tear gas but this had been rejected. Eventually Ben and I were dragged from the cell and I was thrown into the silent cell so that once again I was in total isolation.

While Ben and I had been in the same cell, the rest of the prisoners had become involved in fights as the screws, in a state of rage and frustration due to our barricades, had gone to search them. John, the youngest guy, got involved in a fight and was dragged downstairs and was the first to experience the new solitary block that was being built nearby. Tam, the elderly guy, went to the toilet and burst all the toilet facilities, and he was the next to experience the new block. Larry Winters hadn't been involved but they put him there just in case. When Ben and I were extracted from his cell after the falling of the barricades, he too was taken to the new solitary block. I was taken to the old silent cell. I lay there ten days and then the cops came in and charged me with attempted assault with a knife. They charged Ben with assault using a hammer and we were accused of barricading ourselves in Ben's cell and destroying prison property.

On 25th November the Governor "brought me up" in front of him and told me that £10 had been sent into me from outside. I informed him that it was to enable me to buy some Christmas presents for my children. He said the money couldn't be used for this, but I told him I'd done it the year before as one of the office clerks had arranged for the buying of the gift. He denied me the request and I gathered the biggest spit I could and spat it at him then tried to hit him with the desk in front of him. There was a violent struggle and I was thrown back into the cell. All the other guys heard about it and when the Governor did his rounds they shouted abuse and one of them fired piss at him. The following day I was taken to his orderly room and repeated the previous day's actions and was dragged away again.

Later that day a mob of screws came to my door and took me from the silent cell to the new solitary block. There were eight cells in this new block, all in a row on the one floor. I was thrown into the first one, then John, blank, blank, Tam, blank, blank, Ben Conroy. Larry Winters had been moved to another prison so someone had scored out of it. The inside of the cell was bare and painted a clinical blue. Even so there was a novel feeling about it. There was a window that had armour-plated glass on it, double glazed, and a heavy metal grill over that. The only space for air was a small ventilator that was made of metal screwed to the wall. The windows were frosted glass so that we couldn't see out. I lay in the cell raging about the two previous encounters with the Governor and trying to think up other schemes to get back at him. For some reason or other I went to the small ventilator and messed around with it. The building was brand spanking new and the cement was still very soft so I managed to get the ventilator off, after plenty of perseverance. I scraped away at the brickwork leading to the cell next door and managed to tell John about it and the two of us hacked silently away at the brickwork from each end as he had his ventilator. Before very long we had a small hole in the wall but we were constantly listening for the night patrol coming through. We were able to look at each other through the hole in the wall and speak, so it was exciting. However, we kept at it, increasing the size till at long last we had a hole big enough for me to slip into his cell and this was great: it was beyond all possible dreams and we embraced each other and laughed silently, not believing our luck that we had managed to do it. The joy of being together and knowing that we had done it was a fantastic morale booster and what a victory. The new solitary block, the pride of their system, and it was seriously flawed.

We decided to try to get to the elderly Tam and so moved quickly to tear the next wall down. One of us listened for the night patrol while the other went to work. With dust parching our throats and hands cut from working, we finally got to the vacant cell next door to Tam. Each wall was getting harder as our energy was being expended. The sheer success of the operation was all that we needed to get started on the next wall. Who would have believed it? On reaching the wall of Tam's cell we managed to get a brick out. Tam, who was banged full of heavy drugs each night, was lying on his floor as there was no bed in the cell. He was next to the part where we were coming through and he was snoring. He was only serving a two-year sentence and had been sent to Inverness for repeatedly smashing his cells up due to severe depressions. The drugs that he got were the knockout type and as we worked to widen the hole, Tam continued to snore. We worked like beavers to get through and the fact that we were doing what we were and Tam was doing his snoring was such a direct contrast that we would stop and laugh like hell, trying not to waken him or cause the screws to come. It was so totally unreal. Here we were covered in dirt from head to toe, having destroyed the walls of four cells, only to find the guy in the fifth sound asleep.

We did it and had one helluva job waking this guy from his sweet dreams. He looked at us from the floor where all of us lay, through a haze of drugs and continued staring. This massive man looked at us as though we weren't there. He looked from us to the hole at the side of his head a few times then burst out laughing after it sank in. None of us had said a word, but he laughed and laughed so hard and loud that we had to put blankets over his head to drown out the noise. He cuddled us and laughed some more and then we talked. Inevitably we then decided to reach Ben to make the victory complete. The laugh was that while we were working on the walls to Ben's cell, Tam told us that he had once been a tunneller when he was outside. So with equal enthusiasm we managed to break through to Ben. He greeted us with wild joy and all of us hugged and embraced each other over and over. We laughed at this beautiful victory and knew that this was the ultimate dream. It was agreed that we should knock down all the walls and use the bricks to build a fortress for us to hold off the screws in the morning. We did this and built what we thought was a reasonable fort, then lay down to rest our weary selves. The rest was beautiful as we lay curled up near each other and glad of the company. It was the first time in years that I had been able to be with people without screws prying down our necks and listening to our every word. Although still very much in prison, there was this glorious sense of freedom about us sitting there together, talking quietly and able to say what we wanted. There were good-humoured remarks about what we would plead when we went to court for it, as inevitably we would: "We'll do anything for a game of Bridge, your honour" or "The Devil finds work for idle hands", etc, etc. We would have a good laugh at ourselves and make guesses at the media headlines "Hole in the Wall gang strikes again" or form a business on release "'Boyle and Company, Demolitions', See Inverness Governor for references". On a serious note, we found that each of us had already been charged for the incidents earlier and speculated on going to the next High Court at Inverness. This would be hard luck for Tam, who only had two months to go on his two-year sentence. We would just have to wait and see.

It was still dark at six in the morning when we heard the screws coming to give us breakfast and my cell door was opened first. They had a torch with them and they shouted to me to come to the door for my breakfast, but when they shone the torch in they found an empty cell. They soon realised that there were no longer any single cells and that a dormitory now stood in their place. The cell door was slammed and the sounds of running feet and shouts filled the air. We laughed, but realised that another battle was near at hand. The cold dark morning was long in clearing and it would be almost ten o'clock before full daylight came to this part of the country. We decided to do an Alamo and fight to the last. Making sure that our fortress was strong, we prepared for them coming back, which of course they did. We could see out of the slits in the brickwork and they had heavy metal crowbars and extra-long riot batons. There were plenty of them, all in brown overalls; one had a large 14lb hammer. At first they called to me asking if we were coming out and I told them to go fuck themselves, that the fight was for real. High-powered hoses were turned on us, causing us to duck below the brick wall. We, of course, were under the impression that our little fortress was impregnable, however, to our amazement we saw the high-powered jet from the hoses partly destroy the wall, and with the other mob attacking it with crowbars and 14lb hammers, we were standing exposed in next to no time. Without wasting any time the large riot sticks were used and we were dragged along the corridors into the cells in the old hall that we had originally been brought from. The doctor came to see me and give me treatment.

I now began a six-month period of solitary, never leaving the cell once during this period. It began quite well, with me very proud of our achievement in knocking down the walls of the solitary confinement block. The cops came and charged me with attacking the prison Governor and destroying the solitary block along with the others. All of us now had a long list of charges against us and knew that it would be another High Court appearance.

I took up yoga again during this period and became very involved in it, to the extent that it took over my whole existence. At first I dabbled in it and then went into the meditative side and became quite confident in my involvement in it. I restricted my diet and tried to eat as little as possible. Food was the only thing that I had to look forward to so I would test my willpower and self-discipline by eating less. This was a period in my life when I reflected on my whole being. Self-analysis became a daily habit as I was trying to find out more about myself and to come to some understanding of where I had come from and where I was going. I looked at myself critically and thoroughly till the pain was at times unbearable, and shook my very soul. What was I doing in this place? Was this my life? What was my life all about? The pain from the realisation of my position and its futility was so powerful that I would just curl up in a corner and try to endure it. I went through a period of deep shame about the life I had led. All of this I was finding very difficult to cope with and I sat in this cell suffering as I had never done before. I would think of the kids who were doing the same things as I had done and who would follow my pattern to eventually reach this point of torment only to realise the futility of it, and these thoughts would make me feel sick. Is this what it was all about? I had suffered every year since I was a child but hadn't a clue about anything as I was so dumb and inarticulate and here I was, now an adult, feeling pain like I had never done before.

But now I was beginning to put it all together, probably for the first time in my life. Day after day I lay in this cell thinking, thinking, thinking. I didn't speak to the screws and never saw anyone else. At night I could see the moon when it was out and I would long to see it without having to look through bars and heavy metal frames. I could hear the occasional noises outside my window as the short-term prisoners walked past with the screws and I would have given anything to be in their shoes. During this period of self-analysis, I heard the sound of civilian workers erecting a new security system on the wire fence that was inside the wall and the sounds of their voices travelled across to me and I would listen to them in great pain. I would hear them checking the alarm system and would latch onto their every word. I would look at the differences in our ways of life and feel the futility of mine. At night they would pack up their tools and I would feel envy running through my whole body as they left, chatting together, oblivious to the fact that a guy was lying on a floor, sick at their parting sounds. If only they knew what misery was going on around them. It was very difficult for me to cope with the fact that I had this big blank in my life with nothing to look forward to. The only alternative was to be an arse-licker to the screws, losing my own personality and individuality, and being their pet lion. The one they had tamed. The rewards being the occasional pat on the head.

The only change would be a modification in my behaviour, but the future outlook for me could never change. The one thing that I could hold onto was the fact that I was me. I felt that I mustn't give this up or all would be lost. I tried to look at myself and see what was happening to me at that moment. Was I cracking? Was my spirit breaking? Was this me just in a pathetic state and feeling sorry for myself? No, for the first time in my life I was looking at myself and seeing clearly what was happening to me. Seeing just what I was doing to myself. The important thing was that I had journeyed inside myself, got right under the skin and into the soul. The pain of finding out more about myself was terrible for I had been living a life of self-delusion ever since I was a kid. I now realised that some of the things I had done were very bad and I was probably paying for it now, not by being sentenced but by the real payment which comes with the realisation of what it's all about. Now that I had all this awareness, what could I do with it? As I said, by this time I was fully into yoga – in fact it had dominated me and purified me, having a calming effect. With all this clarity of thought came a realistic appraisal of the present and the future. I had come through this painful period and was now aware of all that had gone wrong in the past, but having reached that point I also realised that I would have to live in the jungle-like existence that reigned supreme within the walls of prison. In other words, I had to pull myself together and prepare myself for the future. I had come out of this experience stronger and felt the power surging through my body.

It was around this time that I heard scuffling outside my door and later I heard that Ben Conroy was in the local hospital with his jaw broken in three places. Shortly after this, with barely a few weeks to go of his two-year sentence, Tam, the elderly guy, was certified insane and put into the State Mental Hospital. I had not been alone in coming through a terrible journey. I was living in a jungle and there seemed to me to be no alternative but to live like an animal in order to survive in that jungle.

In the middle of May 1970, I was handed a charge sheet informing me of my trial date and preliminary hearing. We had all been charged with maliciously damaging seven ventilators, fifteen panes of glass, seven light fittings and six brick-dividing walls. I was further charged with attempting to strike the Governor by overturning a desk against him. In all, there were about eight or nine charges including the attempted assaults with weapons. The puzzling feature for me was that all of us had charges that would normally have taken us to the High Court yet we had been summoned to appear before the Sheriff court. This didn't smell right to me. It was also on the summons that Tam had been certified insane and was now in the State Hospital and this was how I found that out.

Around this time I had a visit from my ma, the first in a long, long time, and it was beautiful to see her and the two children. She was looking terribly old and I knew that bringing the kids all this way was too much for her on her own as they were full of life and running all over the place. We had a very emotional and heart-breaking discussion. I loved her as I'd always done and she was my world; her loyalty to me never faltered, never wavered. She wrote to me each week and kept me in touch with all of the family and the growth of my children. In order to keep me firmly in the minds of the children she would conjure up little tricks for them, like opening an envelope saying that I had sent their wages – pocket money, and would extract the money from the envelope and give it to them. If the kids were in her house when she was posting a letter she would lift them up to the postbox and they could say they had sent a letter to their daddy. After this visit I went back to my cell and thought, and thought, and thought.

John, Ben and myself were taken to court on a beautiful summer's morning and it was magnificent to see them even though we were all in handcuffs and surrounded by cops and screws. The fresh air and the clear day were a joy to breathe and see. To smell the grass and most important of all, to see the people as we passed in the prison van. The three of us had a brief chance to discuss the situation. We were facing a great many charges and it was a puzzler for us all to be at this court, very much a disappointment in fact, as there would be no publicity and this was important as we wanted everyone to know what was going on and there is nothing like the High Court for giving a platform. This chance had been thwarted and I felt that I should take the blame for most of the charges as I was the one who started most of it off anyway. By the time we got to court it was decided that I would plead guilty. In the court I was given a further six months' imprisonment. Ben and John had pleaded not guilty so they were further remanded. Eventually Ben was given six months and John four months. Tam was named in the charge sheet, but wasn't allowed to appear.

12

Ben and I were sent to Peterhead, John to Perth prison. Once in Peterhead I made it clear to both prisoners and screws that I wanted no trouble. I had personal reasons for saying this and was wanting a quiet period. I told all the guys that if there was something on, to leave me out and this was understood. At first, the screws refused to believe this, and the fact that I had such a bad reputation kept them away from me for a while. I was kept amongst the top-security prisoners and we worked in the tailors' shop.

Before I arrived at Peterhead there had been three cops shot in Glasgow, two of them were killed. The accused had been to court and the one who shot them was sentenced to Life Imprisonment with a recommendation that he serve no less than twenty-five years. This guy was himself a one-time cop; his name was Howard Wilson. He was one of the cops who had sat in my house while the police were searching for me for the murder charge. I thought it very funny that the cop guarding my house should now be locked up a few doors away. Most of the guys sent him to Coventry and were sniping at him for being an ex-cop. I didn't like this because I knew why he had been put in this prison: so that the prisoners would do the dirty work. When any white-collar workers are arrested and convicted and finally sent to prison the last place the authorities put them is a prison like Peterhead, which is very hostile. It's the land of the lost and is known as this throughout the system. Cops found guilty, and even screws, are sent to the soft option prisons automatically as they are looked upon as being different from the ordinary scruff like us from the working-class districts. This is blatant discrimination. So placing Howard Wilson in beside us was something extraordinary and unprecedented.

There was a lot of bad feeling about Howard amongst the prisoners as they felt that once a cop that was it. I would never have argued with them because some guys have suffered greatly through dealings with the police, such as fabrication of evidence and "planted" evidence and I felt they were entitled to keep their hatred. I went out of my way to speak to Howard. He had done the unthinkable by killing his own kind. His nerves were shattered by everything that was going on around him. Being thrown into a jungle like Peterhead for the first time must have been a terrible experience. His problem wasn't only the prisoners, the screws were messing him around constantly. They would be more arrogant with him than anyone else because they recognised that he was an outcast so was open game as far as they were concerned. This is the worst part of it, because prisoners will go to a certain point then stop, as they can identify with how the guy is feeling, but the screws were oblivious to this and wouldn't know when to stop. As a result, Howard was confronted with some humiliating experiences that went beyond those of the others. He was always walking about like a guy who was waiting for something to be stuck into his back.

Being in the top-security group with him meant that he was part of about twelve prisoners who had a line of cells on the second flat of the main hall. We were kept together and taken in a group to work with extra screws assigned to watch us at all times. We were "A" category prisoners and this included those prisoners with exceptionally long sentences who were liable to escape, or guys who had previously tried to escape, which meant they had to be kept under special supervision. At night, our clothing had to be put outside the door of the cell. Our lights were left on all night and the screws would scrutinise us when we were in our cells. We were being watched all the time at night. For two hours during the recreation period under the constant scrutiny of the screws, the "A" category men were allowed to mix with the guys in the main hall. Other prisoners could go to night classes and for football in the yard outside, but such activities were denied us.

After a few months of me keeping out of trouble, the screws began to put subtle pressures on me. There were a lot of them who hated me and others who feared me. There was this constant feeling of them wanting me to crawl. It was obvious that as far as they were concerned I was a symbol of something – the enmity lay barely beneath the surface. At night they would come into my cell and take the cell searches to the extreme by stripping me naked and telling me to bend over and pull my cheeks apart, so that they could look up my arse to see if I was hiding anything. In many ways I felt that the more pressure they put on me and got away with then the more they would try on the other prisoners who had caused them no bother. It reached the stage where I was so determined to keep out of trouble that I was searching my own cell for as much as a sewing needle as this was punishable. I was overreacting to them and in a sense retreating. The reason for this was that it was vital for me to keep out of trouble. The screws were making it blatantly obvious that they were very much in control. Amongst the prisoners there was lots of talk, petty meaningless talk, directed against the screws. There was an underlying current of total hostility against them. There was also the brutality, which seemed to be reaching a peak, some of which had taken place in full view of a large number of prisoners in the hall next to the one I was in. There was gossip about it during the work period and there would be lots of big talk, with guys trying to retain some sort of self-respect even though they had stood there and seen a prisoner being slapped about by screws.

On the prisoners' side there was a group of guys who were part of a clique; they were the prison bullies. They were led by a guy nicknamed "The Poof". He was doing fifteen years for offences concerning rape and prostitution, but while serving this sentence he was found guilty of murdering another prisoner and received a life sentence, so on top of his fifteen years this left him very much a hopeless case. The way he coped with his sentence was to prey on weaker guys and there were instances where some younger prisoners, or young-looking ones, were raped by this group. It became widely known and he had quite a reputation for it, so much so that screws in their uncouth way would pass remarks to the young guys on the transfer bus telling them that "The Poof" would get them when they arrived in the prison. As a result they would be terrified when they arrived, and some of them would ask for "Protection". The screws of course thought this all very funny, but personally I felt deeply humiliated that another prisoner could allow himself to be "used" in this way by them. In his own way he was policing the prison for them and the fact that he was causing conflict amongst the prisoners meant that pressure was taken off the screws. He didn't get away with it completely as some individual prisoners would have a go at him, including some of his group. But he had a frightening effect on prisoners in the main and this gave him some measure of control.

The interesting thing here is that before getting his life sentence, The Poof was a non-entity in the prison, although he was recognised as a guy always in trouble with other prisoners. But since receiving his life sentence he was quick to exploit the situation and use the power it gave him over others. He had no future, very much like me, therefore he had nothing to lose. He worked on the same principle as most screws did, which was that the majority of prisoners don't want to lose any of the remission from their sentences and this fact can be used as a weapon against them. I have seen frequent cases of guys that could fight exceptionally well in the streets outside backing down to guys in prison that they knew they could knock the shit out of. The Poof was an ideal example of an ordinary guy with no exceptional fighting abilities, although he had been beaten up and stabbed a number of times. For me the sad fact was that this guy and his group of sycophants were unaware of what they were doing to those alongside them. They didn't like the screws either, though they didn't have much trouble with them. They had experienced some of the treatment the screws had been giving to all of us, but for some unknown reason they just couldn't begin to see that what they were doing was an awful lot worse due to the fact that they were prisoners. They continued on their way with the raping of young guys, putting knives to their throats and doing so with impunity.

In most prisons there is a place reserved for prisoners on "protection". This takes the form of isolated cells for guys who for their own reasons don't want to mix with the main body of prisoners. Some of them are police informers. Some have debts that they owe to the Barons. Some of them have committed sex offences against children, and others just give the name of a prisoner with a bad reputation, saying he is going to attack them. This may not always be true, but whatever the reason, the guy just doesn't want to mix as he is frightened of prison and the jungle life. The Protection wing is a hall of its own with sometimes forty to fifty prisoners in it. Guys going on protection don't tell the Governor that they are doing so because they are afraid of being raped. They give some other reason, or name someone, so as to save face. While there, they are kept in semi-solitary conditions and even within the prison it is a place where they are looked on as the lowest of the low. The guys there look and feel that way, and they are treated like shit by all of us, screws and prisoners alike.

In October 1971, The Poof had some trouble with a quiet guy who kicked him around a cell, causing him to have his eye treated for a cut. The following week, after the movie, when all the prisoners were leaving, The Poof was walking down the prison corridor with a group of his sycophants when he was stabbed three times. It was obvious that something like this would happen and there was rejoicing amongst the prisoners. The strange thing was that the screws didn't take it too well, even causing one prisoner to remark, "You'd think he was one of their own." But these stabbings and the intrigues were all part of the prison jungle that we lived with.

Two days later I was eating lunch in my cell when the door opened and a gang of screws stood there. I was taken to the Solitary Confinement Block. Later that day I found out through the ventilating system that Ben Conroy had also been locked up on solitary. The following morning I was taken in front of the Governor and told that I was being put on Rule 36 for a month. When I asked the reason I was told it was for subversive activities, but unofficially I was told it was for stabbing The Poof. Ben had been put in for the same thing. When The Poof returned from hospital and was put into the prison hospital, the rumours were that I was locked up for it. A guy like him who had trodden over lots of prisoners can never afford to show weakness as there were too many people waiting to trample him into the ground. He was in a sticky situation, for though he knew who had actually stabbed him, there was still this rumour that I had done it. Some knew that this wasn't true but others wanted to believe that it was. He had no option other than to say that he was going to get me. Apparently he was lying in hospital making this pretty clear, saying that he intended killing me the first chance he got. There is no doubt that he was saying this so as to get out of the situation he felt he was now in. The next thing I knew he had been transferred to Inverness Prison.

Meanwhile I was lying in solitary thinking that my trying to keep out of trouble had been a waste of time. I really hadn't wanted trouble for personal reasons but it was obvious that there was no way this would be allowed. Whether I liked it or not, I felt I would be put on solitary at the slightest whim of my keepers. I was now thinking along the lines of how when prisoners enter prison they experience a loss of their rights as a citizen and how from there everyone assumes you have no feelings – that these automatically turn off. The authorities are quick to tell you that you have no rights the minute you question anything that is being done to you and through this process you are made to feel less than human. You shouldn't question or complain. Of course this was nothing new to me as I had felt very much like this on the outside when staying in the Gorbals and so what was happening in prison was only an extension of that. The difference now was that I was beginning to waken up to the fact that this was wrong. It may be that under the circumstances that I was now living in I would have to accept the forfeiture of my rights as a citizen but definitely not my rights as a human being and this is really what it was all about. This was the whole area of conflict throughout my life and when I thought about it, my past behaviour was that of an inarticulate rebel against what was being done to us in places like the Gorbals, and now in prison. Even at this stage I was very uncertain about this and felt that I may have been making excuses for myself and my past. This was an area of confusion within, one that was to become very clear and strong as time went on.

After two months I was allowed out of solitary and back into the prison mainstream. It was approaching Christmas, a time of great tension in prison. The message was by now coming on pretty clear that the screws would prefer me to be out of their prison. By this time, with The Poof out of the way, I was advising guys to form a group called P. S. M. (Prisoners Solidarity Movement). We got some pamphlets printed, stating that anyone willing to join the group would face the possibility of losing all his remission or facing court action as there would, no doubt, be fights with the screws. It went on to state that anyone of the group who was assaulted by the screws would concentrate on his attackers, passing the names of the brutalisers to those of us in circulation and we would attack them, and this would go on and on until such times as the subsequent court trials brought the whole thing out. While we were getting this off the ground and the pamphlet was circulating, I was given a cell search and taken to the Punishment wing for having an extra mirror. I had been given permission to have it, but no one would admit to this. I gave the screws a mouthful of abuse as I was escorted away, with the realisation that things were moving and that by the time I came out of the solitary block the pamphlet would have been distributed and the guys would have had time to think it over. I knew that the authorities were very much afraid of this Solidarity Movement and its possible consequences.

I was taken in front of the Governor for abusing his staff over the mirror and was sentenced to ten days' solitary. I did this ten days doing exercises and keeping very fit. One night the Deputy Governor entered the gloomily lit cell, saying he had bad news for me. My immediate thoughts were, ah, they are going to pile on the solitary confinement. I lay back on the floor and he continued, "Your Mother died tonight at 6.10 p.m." – it was the 10th December 1971. The force of this statement caused me to stand, sit, stand then sit on the floor. It was almost as though I was being lifted and pushed down by some giant invisible hand. I just didn't know what had hit me. Anything but this. All that I had recognised as good in the world was gone. . . . I sat alone in that cell, crying my eyes out. I felt vulnerable, exposed and very much alone. I loved her so very, very much. It shook me to the core, it was the last thing I had expected. She had written to me her usual letter that very week. What the hell was going on? I paced the floor all night thinking of her and how she was an angel to me, to all of us. The most beautiful person in the world, and now she was gone . . . I felt a terrible guilt at having given her such a terrible life. Even these past months when I had tried to avoid trouble, I had failed. Being told of her death while serving punishment made it all seem so futile. There is no use me trying to put in print what I felt that night and even ever since, as nothing could possibly describe it.

The following morning I was whisked away to Barlinnie Prison, where arrangements were made for me to attend the funeral. Because I had been in solitary in Peterhead the Governor continued to keep me in solitary while in Barlinnie. I was allowed to see my brothers through the glass and wire partition and we wanted to hold each other as all of us were badly broken. Ma had died of cancer.

Two days later I was taken to the prison reception area to change into my civilian clothes. I was going to try and tell the escort to trust me not to do anything at my mother's funeral and ask them to leave the handcuffs off. While changing in the dog box I heard the escort being instructed by what sounded like a superior, saying that he was in charge of the escort security and that they were taking every precaution, that though my mother had died I was still a very dangerous man and should be treated as such. They made it clear that they had weapons. Any idea that I had of asking them to trust me on this occasion was thrown from my head. I was heavily escorted in handcuffs, with patrol cars lining the route and elaborate precautions taking place. I was taken to the graveyard. Sitting in the middle of the cemetery was a van filled with cops and police dogs. All around the graveyard were cops with walkie-talkies. I was filled with rage. I was left to feel that by coming to the graveside I had desecrated it. I was deeply hurt by the fact that no one considered me human enough to attend Ma's funeral and be able to give her the respect she deserved. Instead I was taken there hand-cuffed to the screws. My brother approached, asking if I could be allowed to help carry the coffin. After a lengthy discussion they decided to go ahead so with one handcuff being released I was allowed to carry it with my other hand chained to the screw. Amongst the mourners were relatives and friends who I hadn't seen since I was sentenced. My son was amongst them and I was touched when he came over and stood beside me, taking my hand as we said prayers over the grave. Afterwards I was taken swiftly back to Barlinnie.

There was no delay in taking me back to Peterhead under armed escort and before very long I was back in the thick of things. It was very near to Christmas with the atmosphere hostile and tense. There was the feeling that things were going to happen very soon. The hall that I was in was full of screws that were the recognised hardliners. This meant that we were sitting on a time bomb. Within myself I felt as though death would be welcome. I didn't give a fuck about my life and somehow felt this more now than at any time during my sentence. I kept thinking that I would be dead within a year as though I had set myself a time limit. Christmas passed and it was just like any other day, though the press rubbed it in by stating how beautifully we were being fed and how the pensioners weren't half so lucky. I thought that the fucking pensioners would be welcome to the shit that I was eating. They seemed to scrimp and scrape all the year round to give us a meal that was really nothing. What does a meal matter in circumstances such as this? I dare say press garbage does something to salve the nation's conscience as to how well even the bad prisoners are treated. New Year's day, the highlight of the festive period for the Scottish people, was the same, with us being built up for this meal. Like Christmas, it too passed.

The bomb exploded on 4th January 1972, when a prisoner convicted for something he didn't do went into the recreation part of the hall and destroyed the two television sets and smashed everything he could get his hands on. He did all of this on his own and told the screws the reason why he had done it. He was taken to the solitary block. Everyone else was locked up and the following day there was no work, so we knew that a full cell search was on. The screws came round and searched every prisoner and every cell. The prison was very tense. Around lunchtime when the search was over, there were sounds of shouts and scuffles coming from the far end of the hall and it was obvious that something violent was happening. Within minutes of hearing this my cell door flew open and there stood a mob of screws, who took me with them. At moments such as this I know what is going to happen. As I walked along, surrounded by them, I was planning what I would do when the violence did come. I was as ready for it as I would ever be. As I entered the solitary block there were loud noises as prisoners banged their doors. Ben Conroy was spread-eagled on the floor, covered in blood and seemed to be unconscious. He was in the process of being dragged into a cell.

Before I could begin to do anything I was clubbed on the head from behind and a fight started. There was a furious struggle and I distinctly remember someone trying to pull my hair but it was so short they couldn't grip it and I remember feeling pleased about this while I fought. I heard them shouting for a straitjacket and saw it in the hands of one of them. I strongly resisted this, knowing full well that if they got it on I was finished as these bastards would kill me. I struggled with all I had, but realised that it would be in vain. The blood was pouring down my face as the batons battered down on top of my head. They were holding me at waist level, some with my upper body and others with my legs and yet others battering into me. The jacket was being put onto me and tightened up. "BASTARDS, BASTARDS, BASTARDS, BASTARDS," I screamed in utter frustration. During this fierce struggle we ended up next to a sink full of dirty water and by this time I was well strapped into the straitjacket but still struggling and cursing them. They lifted me and my head was pushed into the sink full of water to the sounds of someone calling out to drown the bastard. I was aware of a struggle between the screws, some of whom were frightened, trying to pull me out, while others were for drowning me. During all this time I was coughing and swallowing water for what seemed an eternity. I was pulled out, though some, having lost control of themselves, were still trying to push me under. I vividly remember mental flashes saying that it was all over, that I was dead. I was still coughing and spluttering when I was pulled out, all the while being kicked. When I was able to, I used the only weapon that I had, my tongue: "I'm going to kill you bastards the first chance I get." I repeated this over and over and over again, making sure that it sank in. I was being carried with my head near the ground and my legs up in the air, all the while being hit with sticks and boots. I could see the trail of blood I was leaving on the ground. My last memory of the affair was seeing a shiny boot bounce onto my face and strike me. I lost consciousness.

I came to lying on a stone floor surrounded by hazy figures, notably a man in a white coat. As my vision cleared I could see that the walls were painted an asylum blue and that I was inside a cage, the likes of which I had never seen before. My heart sank as I knew I was in an asylum. I had always dreaded this sort of thing, always suspicious that it would happen, and now it had. The straitjacket was saturated in blood. I drifted off again and when I came to, I was cleaned and smelling of disinfectant. The place I was in looked weird from where I lay. It was an ordinary cell with a large cage front, which cut the cell to half its normal size. I was locked in the cage. Outside the cage front was the ordinary metal and wooden door. This meant that to reach me the screws would have to enter the one door then the cage door. On the wall at the other side of the cell there was a notice and I crawled over to it. In large writing it said "Rules and Regulations for Prisoners in Inverness Special Unit". It dawned on me then that I was in Inverness Prison and not in an asylum.

Relieved beyond belief, I then looked over the place and noticed how the windows were familiar. I should have recognised them before. A doctor had been called into the prison to attend my injuries, not the regular prison doctor but another one. I heard two screws discussing me and one said that I had arrived like a parcel of butcher's meat. I tried to make out to the doctor that I was all right but my face and body were cut and badly bruised. My head was full of very large lumps. My face was in one helluva mess and I wasn't allowed to send for a visit because of the injuries that were showing.

I didn't make any official complaint about my condition and played it down until I was allowed a visit from my brother Harry and he went to our local M. P., who in turn wrote to the Prisons Department in Edinburgh complaining that I had been assaulted. He was told that I had tried to attack a Prison Officer with, a metal tray and any injuries I had received were while I was being restrained. They gave my M. P. a description of the incidents and violence that I had previously been involved in. This list was formidable and my M. P. shrugged his shoulders saying that there was nothing he could do. Had he investigated this supposed "assault", he would have found that I had never been charged for it by the police or through the prison disciplinary system. Had their statement been true, why was I not charged for it? Harry by this time knew that the situation was desperate and took it to the *Daily Express* in the hope that they would bring some attention to bear on the brutality. They printed it but it did no good, except to let the Prisons Department see that I was continuing to fight them. I was now in a position where the people in charge could literally do what they wanted with me. They could justify it by stating that I was "Scotland's Most Violent Man".

Inverness was in many ways a different prison as there had been a change of staff. We were given one book per week and the food was thrown under the bars, just like an animal in a cage. The screws hated me back here as I had been the source of so much trouble in the past. This time they had a feeling of control as the new set-up was to their specification with me in the cage. This was the building where I had helped destroy the cells. They had renovated it and strengthened it by halving the number of cells and putting in four with very strong cages inside them. They had also built in another silent cell. While I was there two other guys were brought up and placed in the cages next to me. One was John, who had been involved in the cell wrecking here in Inverness. He was now awaiting charges of serious assault on screws in Perth prison. He was sporting a bad scar on his forehead which had resulted from his fight with them. The other guy was serving a six-month sentence with only weeks to go. Unfortunately he had got involved in a clash with the screws in Edinburgh Prison so was sent here. He was brutally assaulted while in Inverness and complained to the Governor and the doctor. The Governor took him aside that afternoon and asked him if I had put him up to this. I told the guy to go to the press when he was released as I could see things coming to a head here and wanted as much evidence as possible about what was going on in these places. He sent me a postcard on his release saying that he had done this.

Governors from various prisons met every two months to decide if those of us in the cages were eligible to be returned to our original prisons. Around March 1972, I was told that the Deputy Governor of Peterhead was coming to see me the following day. I was intrigued by this as it was a very unusual thing to happen. He came and I was put into an office with him. He told me that The Poof was back in Peterhead and he asked me about any trouble I may have had with him. I told him that as far as I was concerned there was no trouble, but that I had the feeling that certain people in responsible positions were trying to create a problem where there was none. He then told me that after I was taken from Peterhead, the screws had searched my cell and found two keys. One of these fitted the cell door and the other the main door leading to the cell block. We argued over this and I told him that this was rubbish. Finally he broached the threats that I had made concerning his staff. He was referring to the threats that I had made while being brutalised in the straitjacket. Apparently the staff were apprehensive. He then went on to tell me how staff were only ordinary working chaps with families who really didn't want trouble. I was really raging at this sort of shit. This was the same old story of screws attacking someone unmercifully in the heat of the moment and now that it was time to pay the penalty, they were squirming. I pointed out that the same people that he was talking about had nearly killed me. There was a sinister aspect to this meeting that I didn't like and quite frankly it had me worried. He told me to think it over, then he said that he would be coming back to Inverness Prison in two weeks to discuss with the Board of Governors the possibilities of my returning to Peterhead.

That night I lay thinking about what he had said. What were they up to? He told me as I entered the room that he had been given official approval to come and see me. He had mentioned The Poof trouble, keys that had been found and the impending clash that seemed most likely with the screws. He had said a number of times that I was a continual embarrassment to the Prisons Department. I saw the prime motive for his visit being that the screws were putting pressure on him because they were worried about my returning to Peterhead. I had very grave suspicions about what game was being played here and I wanted to make sure that I had everything recorded, because there was only one thing I was certain of and that was that I would soon either be attending another court trial or be dead. I wrote a full account of what had been said at that meeting and gave it to John, who was in the cage next door. He was due to return to Perth Prison for a trial involving the serious assaults on screws. I told him to keep it with him at all times and to give it to my lawyer if I went for trial but to make sure it got into the right hands at all costs.

Two weeks later the Board of Governors met to decide which of us would return to our normal prisons. They met on their own to talk it over then came into the prison hall, where they set up office in a prison cell and the prisoners marched in one at a time. I was taken in to be faced with two Governors and the Inspector of Prisons, who was there as the representative of the Prisons Department. He told me that it had been agreed that I should be returned to Peterhead Prison, and I thought to myself that this was the first time that I had ever been sent back at the correct time. Why were the rules functioning properly for the first time? It left me feeling more suspicious than ever. I spoke to the Deputy Governor and he was a sort of deathly pale colour and seemed rather nervous as distinct from his usual casual self. The Inspector of Prisons introduced himself saying that we hadn't met but that he had heard plenty about me and that I was an embarrassment to the Department. This was a phrase that was coming up far too often for my liking. I knew I had been, and I certainly hoped to continue to be, but the repetitiveness of the phrase was banging home some message to me. I was well aware of the fact that on returning to Peterhead I was going into a very hot fire. This was very well known throughout the prison system and was the main topic of conversation on the grapevine.

For starters I knew that The Poof and his gang were broadcasting the fact loud and clear that they were going to kill me. But as far as I was concerned, the main problem was the screws as they had given me a rough going over the last time so now I was in the position where I would have to back up my threats otherwise they would make a thorough job of me next time. The other fact was that Ben Conroy was in the solitary block awaiting trial for the assaults that had taken place on 4th January when I was put into the straitjacket; so getting witnesses for this was also a priority. There was much to be done but the odds against me were overwhelming.

I was taken under heavy escort to Peterhead Prison. As the van stopped outside the reception area I could see all the prisoners waiting outside the Governor's room to be "brought up" in front of him. Handcuffed to two screws I was taken through them and into the reception area. It didn't surprise me to find The Poof amongst them. What a coincidence! I put a calm face on it as I moved through the crowd with both hands cuffed to the screws, but I was watching everything. I passed within inches of The Poof but he didn't take his chance, only passing a snide remark for all to hear. As the reception area was part of the solitary block it meant that I could take a look at the list giving the names of the guys on solitary. There was Ben Conroy, and another kid just up from the Young Offenders Institution awaiting trial for stabbing The Poof, though the injuries were only scratches. I was changed into prison uniform and taken to the top security hall and was only there some minutes when a guy came up to tell me to watch out as The Poof was going about shouting that I was getting "done in" as soon as I entered the jail. Within half an hour of entering the prison at least six people had told me the same thing and I reckoned that even the seagulls must have known. Shortly after I arrived I was handed a lump of iron that had the point sharpened and this was to be my knife, but as knives go it was a poor substitute. The Poof was allowing himself to be the prime mover, diverting me from the fundamental issue, the clash between me and the screws. The sad fact is that I entered into it because of this silly prestige thing and loss-of-face aspect. But I vividly remembered what they had done that day. They themselves knew it and I could see the fear in their eyes. They were only too glad of the diversion being created by The Poof. I was aware of all this but became drawn into it just the same.

On Saturdays and Sundays the whole prison population is allowed to mix together. One particular Sunday it was beautiful, with the sun shining brightly. On reaching the yard, I noticed The Poof and his questionable crew in deep discussion, looking rather sinister. My tactics were going to be that I'd allow him to come to me and thrust, so that any move made after would be in self-defence. I felt enough confidence in my own reflexes to allow him that first thrust. I knew a court case would come out of it and I had my defence for the trial prepared in advance. The ironic thing was that for years now I had been trying to expose the authorities, and now I saw that a fight between two prisoners could possibly be the way to do this. We were in the yard, in full view of everyone, as there were lots of screws on the scene and most prisoners out to see the big fight. It was a carnival atmosphere for some. The Poof made a run towards me and thrust with his knife, giving me two slight cuts. I took a swipe at him missing, but he quickly ran back to his gang, urging them to join him. They refused to do so. The screws were coming over to split it up and they pounced on me first. I knew that I could have stuck the knife I had right into them but I didn't. It was one thing punching a screw or a cop in the heat of the moment but it was another stabbing them. And really when one is conditioned, as most criminals are, not to stab or shoot cops or screws, then it is very hard to overcome this. So there I was, in the middle of the crowded yard being held by screws, when a fight broke out with two guys attacking some of the other screws, and this caused a very heavy scene and lots of us were dragged into the solitary block. The funny thing was that there were cops in the solitary block taking photographs of a cell with a tripod camera. One of the guys being dragged in before me managed to get his foot free and kicked it so that the tripod went into the air and fell, smashing the camera into pieces. Later when we were all locked up, I lay and roared with laughter at the camera and the face on the cop when he saw it.

The cops came in the following day and made charges against all of us – four in all: The Poof, myself and two other guys. The charges were that The Poof had been cut on the chest and that we took part in a riot in the prison yard where screws were assaulted.

This of course meant me back on solitary awaiting trial. I spent my time doing physical exercises every day and followed a routine that would keep me fit and active. I thought a lot about defence tactics for the trial. Every morning, either the Governor or his Deputy with the prison chief would do their rounds and pass my door and I would be there with a big smile to greet them. They would ask if I was all right and I would tell them I was, often inquiring if they were. Mentally and physically I felt in tip-top condition as at long last the struggle was getting somewhere. I had grand illusions of an "expose" of the penal system. I intended citing every top prison official that I could think of, also the Governors and Chiefs of Peterhead and Inverness. The Deputy Governor of Peterhead who made the fateful trip to interview me, and the note that I had given John in Inverness, were also cited so I felt that I had enough evidence to put up a case.

I was able to speak to my next-door neighbour by getting down on my hands and knees and shouting through the archaic ventilation system. He was Paddy Meehan, who was on voluntary confinement to protest against his conviction and sentence of Life imprisonment. There was a very large movement by eminent people to get him free as they supported his protest. I became very familiar with his case as it was all he would ever talk about. I already knew he was innocent, as did the whole of the underworld. Paddy was never a popular guy with the other prisoners but that aside, there was total unanimity about his innocence. It was interesting for me to note how he survived; he did this by always assuming that he would be released the following month, and in this way he would live from month to month. Although everyone in the prison system had some sort of belief that he was innocent, for years there was no budging and so Paddy had to lie there and rot. The only hope that he really had was what his own family and the other interested people were doing to help him. There is no doubt that it was a torturing experience for him, and now he is finally cleared, who can assess or give him back what he has already lost? The rest of the solitary cells were filled with guys awaiting trial for various offences and others doing short solitary periods for disciplinary offences.

One beautiful August morning I was allowed out to the small exercise yard. There are three of these attached to the solitary block and the prisoners are taken outside one at a time and put into them for fresh air. They are about fifteen feet square and when in here I would run round in circles to keep my lungs exercised. On this particular morning when my time was up I was taken back into my cell as usual by two screws, with a third one walking on a catwalk above the exercise boxes. I was locked in my cell and shortly afterwards I asked if I could get out to use the toilet. The toilet was in a recess next to the top of the stairs on the second flat, where my cell was. The screw escorted me and stood opposite the door. Now the doors of the toilets are cut in half so that the screws standing outside can see up to the knees and from the chest upwards if anyone was standing inside. The middle part is what the door covers to give the guy sitting on the seat some privacy. After I had been to the toilet I went to wash my hands at the sink and noticed that there were no screws there, which was very unusual, very unusual indeed. I walked out to the top of the stairs and was confronted by The Poof coming up the stairs. On seeing me he pulled out a very long shiny knife from his waistband underneath his shirt. There was a screw a good six paces behind him but he ran downstairs as though going for reinforcements. The Poof came for me with the knife and I backed into the recess. There was no escape, but by a piece of luck I kicked him in the balls and we got into a clinch and I knew that I was fighting for my life as I had never done before. While in this clinch I managed to get the knife from him. Getting it firmly in my grasp I stuck it into him time and again, causing him to fall to the ground. Screws came running upstairs and separated us by pulling me off him, but I managed to give him a kick which caused him to roll downstairs onto the bottom flat. I gave the screws the knife and was locked into my cell, pretty shaken as it had been a total surprise.

The Poof was taken to the prison hospital then rushed to the hospital in Aberdeen thirty miles away with a collapsed lung and other injuries. Voices were coming from the ventilator with guys asking what had happened as they had heard screams from The Poof. I was now absolutely delighted that I had managed to take the knife off him and reverse the situation. Minutes after coming close to killing this guy I was delighted with what I had done. I had had no alternative as one minute I was facing death and the next it was the opposite, but that is how close one comes to being either the murderer or the murdered in this jungle that I was living in. My mind was running in circles trying to fathom what had happened. After the latest charge of the riot in the yard the prison authorities had been given explicit instructions to keep The Poof and me separated. What I couldn't understand was that here I was in the Solitary Confinement Block and he just happens to meet me and just happens to have a knife with him. This was very sinister to me, especially as I was an "A" category prisoner. With all of this racing through my head I went to the ventilator to tell the guys in the other cells what had happened. It was difficult for them to believe it, but when they heard they cheered with delight as we all knew that this was a victory against the establishment. Later that afternoon the cops came in and they charged me with attempting to murder The Poof. I made no reply.

The following morning I was taken in front of the prison Governor, who was looking very stern and worried. He told me that the matter was in the hands of the police and that was all. The position I was in meant that nothing more could be done with me. By the laws of this land I had reached the ultimate: I had become that being who had no life or anything at all to lose. Once a person has reached this stage then he can never lose. There is no doubt that it was a state of mind because there were other guys doing very long sentences and they were plodding along, getting internally ill. I had come through too much and by this time was committed to fighting back with all that I had. Death was all that would stop me. I knew that and so did everyone else. The Prison Authorities had this feeling of impotence with me simply because I had endured all that they could throw at me and come out all the stronger for it. I had always been told by the prison officials that I was banging my head against a brick wall. From where I stood the wall was beginning to move. As far as I was concerned I honestly would have preferred no trouble with The Poof because I knew that this would give ammunition to the prison authorities, who could then say we were always fighting with each other. I had tried as much as I could during the five years before this to avoid clashing with prisoners though at times this was very hard as being so close together one was always liable to bite the one nearest. The Poof was also doing a long sentence and had to endure the same humiliations as I, therefore it maddened me to think that he hadn't been able to see what he was doing to himself, never mind to me. In the end, he became a symbol of all that the screws stood for, so that when I took the knife from him it was symbolic of a victory over the screws. It had a profound effect on them in relation to me as all of us could see the day of reckoning being not too far away. This meant that I was now facing two court trials as I had the riot charge in the prison yard and the latest attempted murder charge.

I wasn't worried at all as I had long since given up caring, but I still kept up my yoga exercises and did a lot of reading. Although my mother had gone, I still remembered her and though I am not a religious person, I showed loyalty by saying a few prayers each week on the day and time of her death. This was the least I could do. My Aunt Peggy replaced my ma by writing to me often, as well as my brother Harry, who kept in constant touch; so through these two I had contact with my family and news of the latest happenings.

There was a lot of unrest in prisons throughout Britain in the summer of 1972 and it was at this period that a group of ex-prisoners in England started a movement called Preservation of the Rights of Prisoners (PROP). They were calling for better treatment for all those inside Britain's prisons. This was needed and long overdue. This small group gave hope to lots of guys serving sentences, but the important thing was that it was coming from the outside, from people who had experienced what it means to serve a prison sentence. Lots of guys talk about what they are going to do when they get released, I mean in terms of writing to people or similar things to get the conditions improved, but they very rarely ever do it. The fact that these guys had organised PROP was great. It came into being in a blaze of publicity by asking prisoners to protest against conditions. Throughout Britain large groups of prisoners were taking part in sit-down strikes and climbing onto rooftops in massive demonstrations to show support for PROP. The time was right and it had to be seized and they did so in Peterhead. Even as I lay in solitary I could feel the excitement of what was going to happen; it seemed to penetrate the thick walls of the solitary block.

One beautiful afternoon, as the main body of prisoners were being assembled in the prison yard for work after lunch, there was a loud cheer. One hundred and sixty-eight prisoners had climbed onto the prison hospital roof and were standing up there, shouting and cheering. I lay in the solitary cell very jealous of them and thinking I would give my eye teeth to be with them. The adrenalin was pumping through my body as I jumped up to the small window to shout encouragement. Some prisoners were caught in the act while trying to get up there and were brought into the solitary block, being beaten up on the way in. I was at the small cell window, trying to shout to those on the roof that guys were being brutalised, but their cheers drowned out my voice. It was a pity they couldn't hear for what an ideal opportunity they had for making it public as they were on top of a roof in full view of the world. They were all up there singing and cheering for all they were worth. The screws were all called in to stay overnight and were issued with riot batons. The mood of the prisoners was one of solidarity. Light aircraft and helicopters were circling overhead, carrying newsmen and others from the media. The prisoners stayed up there all night and into the following afternoon. Before they finally came down, a spokesman for the prisoners spoke to the Chief Officer of the jail, saying that it had been a peaceful demo and that they wanted assurances that if and when they got off the roof there would be no brutality. The Chief gave his word to all the prisoners who were listening to this exchange and so they all descended. All of this was done in a lighthearted fashion, the atmosphere was reasonable. During these negotiations the Deputy Governor was doing his rounds of the solitary block. He asked me if I was okay and went on to say that there was one thing to be grateful for which was that I was locked in the solitary block. I told him that had I been out there the demo would have been far from peaceful, and that was very true.

A couple of hours after they descended, the solitary block doors were thrown open, which was an indication of new admissions and things to come. One can always tell when something is on as the sounds outside one's cell go very quiet and the screws talk in whispers and a sort of electricity permeates the air. The fact that both doors to the entrance of the block were opened meant that a large number of admissions would be UNWILLINGLY admitted. The sounds outside the cell become a sort of language. The preparations were being made for the forthcoming brutalisation and the doors opened so that no one could grab onto them when being dragged in. The passageway leading to the block was cleared so that nothing would stand in the way of the ritual. I lay waiting for the first sounds with butterflies in my stomach. Instead of the usual blows which I was expecting, I heard footsteps coming up the flight of stairs as though under a weight and the sounds of heavy laboured breathing and occasional groans as though someone was unconscious. The sounds led to a cell then a door was closed. This sort of thing was repeated four times and then three others were brought in accompanied by the usual sounds of pain as blows banged off them. Those of us on solitary responded with the only means available to us, which was banging on the steel-backed doors and shouting for the dirty bastards to leave them alone.

Later that night, I shouted through the ventilation system and asked for details of what had happened and who had joined us. The few who were not unconscious answered, identified themselves and told me what had happened. Some had been walking down the corridor, had a blanket thrown over their heads and were beaten up all the way into the cells. Others had been on their way to the solitary block and had been set upon while coming through. Out of the one hundred and sixty-eight prisoners who had rioted, these had been selected by the screws for the treatment for reasons that they alone knew. When they had all regained consciousness and identified themselves, I found that one of the guys brutally attacked was Howard Wilson. Another was Willie McPherson, who was serving twenty-six years for bank robbery and political offences. Willie was from the Gorbals and had gone around with me when we were young. He left our gang in order to do more for his political beliefs. His robberies were to boost the funds of an extremist group. These two and the five others were identified by the screws as being the leaders of the demo. Once again I was left with the impotent feeling of having to listen to stories of guys being brutalised. It constantly reminded me of my true position of being totally helpless and completely at the mercy of those in charge of me. I have had to endure many times the humiliation of having to listen to these sounds thus causing me to relive them, and it was a form of torture. During such periods one was faced with the fact that this was all that the future held. All through the night most of us sat at the ventilators and tried to think of ways of destroying every one of the bastards. There had to be some way.

By an amazing coincidence, on the morning following the brutalisations, the screws entered my cell with my civilian clothes and told me to get dressed. I did so, wondering where I was going and thinking that it would be Inverness. When I got into the police car the cops told me I was going for a preliminary hearing for the attempted murder of The Poof. I was delighted at this stroke of luck and began formulating a plan in my head as we drove there. I was handcuffed to a screw and when we reached the court I was taken upstairs to the Sheriff's Private Chambers. On the way we passed a group of people sitting on a bench outside the Chambers; they were all civilians waiting for appearances or just to watch.

The brief charge was read out and the Sheriff went about putting the necessary signatures to the charge papers. I interrupted him, saying that I would like to bring something to his notice. He looked at me and asked what it was. I told him about the recent peaceful demonstration at Peterhead Prison the day before and told him that I wanted to report a crime to him. I said that at least seven prisoners were lying in the solitary confinement block with bad injuries due to being brutally assaulted and as the law's representative I would like to ask him to do something about it. I told him that I could give him the names and injuries of those victims. The Sheriff leaned back in his chair, fiddling with his pen, and thought for a minute. He asked me if I had brought this to the attention of the Prison Governor. I told him that I hadn't as I had no confidence in the internal investigative procedure. I went on to tell him that by bringing it to him I was seeing that everything was being done fairly. Again he thought for a short time then leaned forward in his chair in a decisive manner and told me that his duty was to the law of Scotland and with this in mind he suggested that I report the matter to the Prison Governor when I returned to the prison. I pointed to the Procurator Fiscal and implored the Sheriff to instruct the Fiscal to look into the matter. The Sheriff looked at me sternly, saying that he had said all he had to say on the matter and would hear no more from me. The screws and cops began to usher me out but I tried to jump on the Sheriff's desk, screaming at him, calling him a whitewashing old bastard. There was pure panic in the court and I was dragged out.

As I was led by the bench full of civilians I held onto the banister at the top of the stairs and shouted to them to go to the press and tell them that prisoners were lying in the solitary confinement block after being attacked by screws for peacefully demonstrating. If anyone ever spoke to a stone wall it was me that day. The people on that bench just sat like lumps of wood, staring at me as though I was off my head. It was so bloody pathetic and I was so angry at myself for failing to get through to anyone. The cops and the screws were in pure panic and I was taken downstairs and locked into a room along with the screw who was still handcuffed to me. I turned on the screw asking if he was one of the bastards who attacked the guys the previous night but he kept his head to the floor and wouldn't look up. I challenged him now that we were alone and reminded him that I could kick him up and down this room and would never be found guilty as we were on our own. I told him that I'd probably regret not having done so as he would most likely be into my cell with the rest to batter my head in. All the time I spoke, he sat with his free hand holding his head as he looked at the floor, not daring to look at me in case I did give him a going over. Eventually when the cops did return, he sprang up on his feet and told the cops to get us back to the prison. I then learned that I would be brought back for contempt of court.

This really lit up my heart; it had not all been in vain. These were the words I was wanting to hear. The cops drove us back to the prison and the screw didn't mention a word to anyone but I knew he was raging, not so much at me but at the cops for leaving him alone with a madman like me. When locked back into my solitary cell I went straight to the ventilator and shouted to the guys, telling them what had happened. My plan, which I had formulated on the way to court, was that I would speak to the Sheriff in the nicest way possible, asking for him to investigate my allegations, and if he didn't accept this then I would attack him so that the subsequent trial would be in the open court, where I would be able to state my reasons for doing this. However, I wasn't able to actually hit the judge but had done enough to warrant a contempt appearance. All of us again sat at the ventilator and speculated on how the appearance would go. The fact that it was to be a form of punishment for me didn't alter it at all as I was looking upon it as a place where I could bring out what was happening in these tombs of secrecy called prisons.

The following morning, the Governor and the Chief Officer entered my cell, half-closing the door behind them, leaving the accompanying screws outside. The Governor said he wanted to thank me for not taking advantage of the officer with me at court the previous day while he was locked into the room with me. He went on to say that I could have taken advantage of the situation with impunity but hadn't. I told him that it was his mob who were the liberty takers. I said he had given his word that none of these guys would be punished but here they were lying in these very cells with bad injuries from having been brutalised. Pointing to the chief officer, I told him he had given his word to the demonstrating prisoners on the roof that there would be no physical reprisals if they came down in an orderly fashion. What happened after that was without his knowledge. The Governor went on to tell me that what he suspected had happened the previous night would not happen again. He then went on to explain that when a prisoner received injuries, the staff put in written reports to him as to how these injuries came about, and if all the reports that injuries were received while being "restrained" or because the prisoner "fell" then he, the Governor, was not in a position to dispute this. When he sees the prisoner, he may accuse the staff of brutalising him, but the Governor has to weigh up the evidence of the one prisoner and his accusation against the reports and verbal evidence of his staff. He said that although he may sometimes doubt it, he has to go by the evidence in front of him. Having had first-hand experience of what actually happens in situations like this, emotionally I was totally rejecting what he was saying but intellectually I knew he was correct. In spite of all the anger within me, I did feel the Governor was concerned and intent on doing something. The following day I was also told that the Sheriff had been in touch with the prison and that the Contempt appearance would not be going on. I was very sick indeed at this and explained that I wanted to be taken to court. They left and I sank to the floor utterly deflated and miserable. It was the first time in my life I had been sick at not being taken to court and charged. There is no doubt about it that "justice" moves in mysterious ways.

For the next week we concentrated on getting the story out to the press. We had this obsessive belief that getting it into the papers would be the panacea, although earlier experience had shown us differently. The feeling amongst us was that the screws could kill us and no one would turn a hair. There was this desperate feeling within me that there was only one person I could depend on and that was myself. The other guys were taking the matter through official channels and had requested Petitions to write to the Secretary of State complaining of brutality. I had been through all of that scene before and recognised its uselessness. The solitary confinement block was full of brutalised prisoners and the place was yet again a very tense and fragile time-bomb just waiting to explode. All of the guys who took part in the demo were taken in front of the Visiting Committee and given from six months' to a full year's loss of remission and a spell on solitary. I was lying in my cell early one morning when the door burst open and a mob of screws came in and told me to change into my civilian clothing. Once again I started on the long road to Inverness.

13

This was my fourth spell in Inverness so I was getting very familiar with the roads. I was put through the normal reception procedure and taken by another group of Inverness screws to a cage and locked in. I had spent most of my five years in solitary conditions and by now was used to it and looking on it as my way of life. In the cages next to me were two other guys, Ben Conroy and Larry Winters. Ben sounded as fit as ever but Larry didn't. He shouted to me that he had wounds in his head from a beating in his previous prison. Both of them were allowed out to make fish nets in a small, newly built workshed, though only for a couple of hours each day. The screws were sick at the thought of having us three in together again as it meant that they could expect anything in the way of trouble. Just the fact that we were under the one roof was enough to send the shit running down their legs. Therefore, it came as no surprise when the Governor of the prison told me that I wasn't to be let out with the others as I was awaiting two court trials and the Prisons Department had instructed him to keep me locked up. We argued all the way on this but they wouldn't budge and the reasons were obvious to us all.

I would lie in my cell cage all day doing exercises and reading the one book I was allowed each week. I came to know the cage well during this period. It had a large cage front which cut the cell in half and it had the effect of making one feel very small. This was a comment made by most guys who had experienced the cages. The only way the cage door could be opened was by someone who was outside the cell altogether. There was a locking system there that had special keys to open it then a bolt-locking device that ran through the centre of the cage door, which had to be drawn before anyone could open the door. This ensured that no one person could open the door on his own. I was pretty angry at not being allowed out to see the others as I should have been and was frustrated at being so totally helpless under the circumstances.

A week after my arrival in Inverness, I heard noises of others being admitted into the two vacant cages. They were Howard Wilson and Willie McPherson, both of whom had been sent here the day before their punishment ended in Peterhead. This was a form of further punishment. Both said that their introduction to Inverness had been a bit hectic but neither would elaborate on this as they thought the place was bugged with listening devices. They told me that a few days after I had left Peterhead, two young guys, just into the prison, had climbed onto the Tailor's workshed roof as a protest and had been pulled off and brutalised by the screws. Both Howard and Willie were kept on solitary in Inverness along with me, though after a couple of weeks both of them were allowed into the workshed for a few hours each day. Two nights a week all four of them were given recreation in a very small room above the cages.

After four or five weeks, I was allowed out to work beside the others. The building was self-contained and the workshed was purpose-built with red brick walls and no windows. We were made to work on fish nets about ten feet apart. I was taken into the shed while the others were working and for the first time I saw them in the flesh. Although we had spoken to each other regularly it had been over a year since I had set eyes on Ben, three since I had seen Larry, a year since I had seen Howard and fourteen years since I had seen Willie. All of them had changed but none more than Larry, who had long black hair and a big beard. He had sores on his face and around his eyes and he was heavily drugged. The other three were reasonably fit-looking. Out of the five of us, four were serving the longest sentences in Scotland. The screws at Inverness were angry at us being put together under the one roof. The atmosphere in the place was very hostile. We badgered the

Governor each day to get us out of these cages and into the routine the same as the rest.

On 19th December I was given an Indictment that said I was to appear at Aberdeen Court to face charges for the prison yard riot. There was a feeling of excitement amongst us; I had cited all the prison officials as witnesses. The trial was to be a Sheriff and Jury, and though I would have preferred a High Court, I decided that I would make the best of this one. There was panic in the ranks as prisoners would be quizzed and asked why I was citing so many top prison officials. I also cited lots of prisoners so that on the morning of the 19th, all of us were locked into cells at Aberdeen Courthouse. There was bedlam, with the prisoners making the most of their day out. Elaborate security precautions had been taken in getting us there and these were maintained during the actual hearing. The Poof was put to one side of the courtroom and I to the other, with the two other guys charged beside me. The normal dock was dispensed with and we were put on the front bench surrounded by cops and screws. I had both hands cuffed. Legal arguments were made on the actual charges and they lasted for a period of two hours after which the Sheriff stated that he was dismissing the charges as the Indictment was irrelevant. A screw sitting next to me on the journey back said to one of his colleagues that he felt it was a fix. I was ambivalent about the acquittal as I would have preferred to have seen the officials in the witness box. The two guys next to me were delighted about getting off as they could see themselves getting out at a future date. No time was lost in getting us back to Inverness.

I had to appear at one more trial for the Attempted Murder in the Solitary Confinement Block and I was looking forward to this as I would definitely be going to the High Court for it. In Inverness, rumours were circulating about a new prison being opened in Barlinnie Prison, Glasgow, for potentially violent prisoners and I was left in no doubt that this was where I was going. Speculation was rife and wild as to what it would be like. It was to be psychiatrically orientated and supposedly a halfway house to the State Mental Hospital for those prisoners that were not certifiable. Rumour had it that prisoners would be injected with drugs and kept down, that there would be television monitors throughout the place and that everything in it would be electronically worked. The impression I had of it was the same as that of the State Mental Hospital. I was scared of being certified insane and looked on this new place as being the means for the authorities to do this. I had never had anything to do with the rare psychiatrist that came into the prisons as I just didn't trust them. The screws in Inverness and in the whole of the Scottish penal system were looking forward to this new establishment opening in Barlinnie, purely as a means to get us out of their way. The Prison Officers Association had been calling for such a place for years now and it couldn't come soon enough, particularly for the screws in Inverness at that moment, who made it plain that they just didn't want any one of us in their prison, never mind all of us together.

Inverness was the prison that I felt most helpless in. It was structured to be that way and built for boredom. Being inside a cage, inside a cell in the solitary block which was only a part of the prison as a whole, made me feel that I was at the very core of isolation. I realised just how alienated I had become. Every day a screw would come round the Segregation unit and check everything, such as toilets, worksheds and cells, to see if anything could be used as a weapon. The only thing that we were allowed was plastic, such as cutlery and a mug. I was constantly on the lookout for anything that could be used as a weapon. I saw one or two things that could be used in an extreme emergency and would watch this screw doing his rounds each day. He would walk by the objects that I had already decided could be used, but how could he see such things as he wasn't in the desperate situation that I was in? How was it possible for someone to render a place "safe"? There was a feeling of confidence amongst the screws as they felt that they had it all under control. Even the safety razors they supplied in the morning had locking devices on them. Each night we were given a cell search. My whole life was tuned into making the most of any flaw in the system.

Two nights each week we were taken to the small room above the cages for an hour or so and we would sit there and listen to an old battered radio. On the day of the 27th we were into our usual routine, though Ben Conroy was locked in his cage as he was sick. Although we all appeared to be working on our nets, I was in fact constantly keeping an eye on the screws and listening to every move. There seemed to be a change in their behaviour pattern. These changes would be hard to explain but one comes to know or sense things, and being very perceptive I knew that something was going on as there was plenty of coming and going. I thought maybe they were transferring Ben, as a guy is usually ghosted out without warning. The screws were supposed to stand at each corner of the shed observing us but for some reason this day they seemed to be speaking more together. There was a jittery feeling running throughout the place.

It was two days after Christmas but it was like any other day as far as I was concerned as I had forgotten what the Christmas feeling was like. This particular night of 27th December 1972 the four of us were taken to the recreation room and by the end of the evening six screws had been taken to hospital and three of us prisoners with them. A fortnight later, four of us were charged with attempting to murder six prison officers and attempting to escape. At the court trial the screws said that when we went to the recreation room we attacked them, pulling out knives and stabbing them and a fight erupted with the alarm bell going off, bringing more screws, all of whom denied using their batons on the prisoners. One of the prison officers lost his eye during the fight and others were stabbed a number of times on the body.

My defence was that while working that afternoon I noticed a lot of activity amongst the screws and there seemed to be a lot of coming and going in the cell area where Ben was. On going in after the work hour, I looked into Ben's cage through the judas hole and he was bending over a plastic basin with blood running from his nose and baton bruises on his back. Ben gestured that he had been beaten up. I told the others about it as we were getting water to wash ourselves and we came to a quick decision to make a protest that night in the recreation room. We were then locked into our cages. I weighed all the pros and cons up and at first came to the decision that we should cool the whole thing till the next morning and get the Governor and Chief Officer on their rounds. I was of the opinion that to take it to the top might have the desired effect. I wasn't interested in taking part in a peaceful demo as I could vividly remember the last one, and this was even more dangerous as being in Inverness we were that much more vulnerable and remote. I knew that it would only end in violence but if we were to go ahead then the emphasis should be on us doing as much damage to the enemy as possible. Earlier that month I had managed to pick up the heel plate of a boot that I had sharpened up and when my cage was searched that night I hid it in my mouth as I did whenever searches were given. There was little chance of this being discovered as the talk was minimal between screws and prisoners.

We were taken to the small recreation room and I made my views plain to the others and tried to push my past experiences onto them by telling them that violence was necessary. Both Howard and Willie weren't interested in getting in too heavy and so were pushing for a peaceful demo. Larry was for going along with me so that we were evenly split but this is where the unwritten code enters into it. In this case it would have been out of order for me to go in heavy with the violence when in fact two of them didn't want to know. It would have been okay had I been able to do my own thing but that wasn't the case here as we were all in on it. I compromised by telling them that I would go along with the "Peaceful Demo" but that if any violence was used I would be cutting as many screws as possible. They knew what I had been through in the past and agreed that they had no intention of letting others have a go at them. Feeling like a bloody fool, I took part in the demo and linked arms with the other three and sat down on the floor.

I told the court that the screws rang the bell for reinforcements and when they came Howard started by saying that this was a peaceful demo and then a baton was battered down on my head. I grabbed the old radio and crashed it into the face of one of the screws. I got my piece of metal and started sticking it into as many as possible. The whole place was like a battlefield. The first baton that landed on me had splintered and as I fought I could feel the blood running down my head and the blows still landing. Finally we were subdued, but I was thinking of the next move and that would be their coming into the cages afterwards so I managed to hide the small piece of metal in the vague hope that I would get away with it. At the top of the stairs I was made to run a gauntlet of screws with batons and someone repeating over and over again to kill that bastard Boyle. I fell onto the landing below on top of Larry and Willie. I rose to my feet and another baton was broken over my head. Finally they managed to get me into my cage, and there was so much of a panic that they didn't search me so I still had my piece of metal. Once locked in I knew that I was badly injured. I felt no pain, only a numbness. I heard them going from cage to cage and beating the others systematically. This time I was listening to it not feeling too bad as I knew they were coming back to me and I was prepared for them.

Eventually it was my turn, and the cage door was opened. They came in and I pulled my metal and struck out as much as I could. I lost the metal in the process as the batons came banging down on me. It felt no different from many gang fights that I've been through in my life. As the batons continued to crash down on my head I remember thinking that this was it. I didn't feel fear or anything – just that this seemed to be it. I remember coming to and I was lying naked on the floor and a screw took a rush towards me and kicked me but I don't remember feeling it. This was the night of 27th December.

My next recollection of anything was coming to on 2nd January 1973. I was in a cage, and I couldn't move as the pain was racking my whole head and body. Later I was told that I had been in hospital though I can't remember a thing about it. All I do know is that I was badly hurt. I couldn't stand up. My food was thrown under the cage door, the first few meals having to lie there till I could crawl over and reach the plate with my face lying beside it while my hand scooped it into my mouth. I felt terrible during this period as I knew that they could do what they wanted as I was helpless. It was essential that I get back to health. The doctor told the court that I was in such a bad way he didn't expect me to last the night.

I was lucky to be alive. Although I realised I wasn't well I had this obsession to get back to being fit and on my feet. I was naked in my cell with four blankets, but once they saw me on my feet they gave me pyjama trousers and took the blankets. There had been lots of damage on both sides but to what extent I just didn't know. One night I heard a voice calling and it was Ben. The ventilator system was useful in the cages too. We knew that the screws were sitting outside listening to everything we were saying so we had to talk generalities. He told me that three of us had been taken to hospital with injuries and that Howard was the only one who hadn't gone though he had had bad injuries too. He told me that I was supposed to be at death's door, that out of everyone injured I was probably the worst.

A week later the cops came in and charged me with attempting to murder six screws and attempting to escape. I honestly couldn't have given a shit about the injuries to the screws. It was the first time I'd been involved in a clash with them where I had been able to do some real damage. I looked on this as a consolation. I was now awaiting two High Court trials and from where I sat, I began to think that this was how life would go on, with me getting into one piece of trouble before another had been cleared up. I wasn't worried as I felt that this is how it goes and that death was all that lay ahead. I was handed an Indictment to appear at Aberdeen High Court for the attempted murder of The Poof on 30th January 1973.

I consulted my solicitor and decided to let the evidence unfold as it was. I called about thirty witnesses. Ben and Howard were amongst them. I was taken from my cage to the High Court in Aberdeen. On previous occasions when travelling I envied the people that I saw walking the streets but this time I didn't. Something had died within me. I was now animalised and felt nothing, only a complete numbness. During the trial, the screws gave evidence saying that I had not asked to go out to the toilet but had, by some means, escaped from my cell and into The Poof's cell. The screws gave their account of how this could be done and there is no doubt that it was unacceptable. The Poof came in and reluctantly gave evidence saying that he couldn't remember much about anything. I had lodged a special plea of self-defence. Other prisoners gave evidence to the fact that The Poof was a bully-boy and how the screws hated me. Evidence had come out that a young guy had committed suicide because of The Poof's interest in him. I was acquitted and immediately sent back to Inverness and my cage. This was a great morale boost to me.

On returning to the cage, I was able to distinguish by the noises that Willie was no longer with us. Within a few days, Larry and Ben vanished and the only possible place they could have gone to was the new place in Barlinnie Prison. A couple of weeks later, Howard was moved so this left me alone. There had been lots of hostility from the screws with the four of us there so it became more intense now that I was alone. There were open confrontations between us. I began to lose sleep due to noises being made in the corridor. Loud banging would resound through the block and these noises would go on throughout the night. I knew that my best defence was to take the offensive. I started calling them all the names I could whenever we came in contact to show them I wasn't worried, although I was.

The result of not getting any sleep was having a tremendous effect on me. The screws would come in mob-handed and search me. I would be told to pull the cheeks of my arse apart and bend over while they inspected it, and open my mouth while they looked in. All I had was a pair of pyjama trousers and I had cast them off as it felt humiliating to be told to take them off before the searches. These searches took place three times each day even though I hadn't stepped out of the cage for one minute. This was all part of the psychological campaign that was taking place. I thought that just by knowing that it was all against me it wouldn't affect me. How wrong I was. As things were, I was very suspicious of being left alone in this place so I was constantly on guard in case the screws came into my cage. The noises continued unabated and I would jump awake whenever they happened so that before very long I was under tremendous strain and very much aware of it. While the noises went on I used to walk up and down my cage singing at the top of my voice. This was to let them think that it wasn't bothering me. After three weeks of this I was cracking up. I knew I was on the verge of insanity. It got so that I challenged the screws to fight and would ask them where all the mice were that were making the noise.

After a month of this I was taken from my cage one day to an upstairs room, where I met a psychiatrist, Peter Whatmore. He told me that he was a representative from The Special Unit, Barlinnie Prison. He interviewed me with the purpose of my going there, but I can't remember too much about it as I felt quite far gone and my insides were in a turmoil, though I managed to put up some sort of façade.

PART FOUR

PART FOUR

14

My torture continued till ten days later my cage was opened and I was taken to another cell along a corridor. This was a brand new silent cell that must have been newly built. I was put in here and they brought in my civilian clothing for me to change into. Not a word was spoken between any of us. I was then told that I was being transferred to the Special Unit. I didn't believe them as I felt this was still part of the campaign. I was heavily cuffed then taken to a prison van with police car escorts, but even then I thought they would go round the prison and back in. I didn't dare let myself believe that they were telling the truth because I knew that to accept this and find myself back in the cage would be the last straw. Even when we were well on the road I refused to believe it as the distrust was ingrained in me.

I was too numbed to feel anything about the Special Unit, after all I didn't know what to expect. All I could compare it with was the places I had been in during the past. I was totally alienated from many things. I knew that I was a stranger even to myself, so many things had changed within me that utter chaos and confusion dominated by very primitive survival instincts were what I lived on. On my entrance to the Special Unit I was greeted by Ben Conroy and Larry Winters, who came over to meet me. They immediately saw the very strange look on my face and felt the alienation within me and were visibly shocked. All of us recognised this but nothing could be done about it. These were inner barriers that I had built to help me survive the last weeks alone and they would not come down easily. I felt extremely weird and thought that I was quite mad.

The screws were very friendly towards me, calling me Jimmy, but I wasn't being taken in by that. I did find it very hard to accept but through keeping up my façade I managed to pull through this first stage without causing any bad feelings. I felt like someone lost in a wilderness. Ben made me a coffee and took me aside to whisper in my ear that the place might be bugged. He explained to me how the screws were very friendly but they had to be watched – he didn't have to tell me. He also told me that there were a couple of screws who had reputations for brutalising prisoners in the place but that there were one or two others who seemed okay. I was then asked by the screw if I would come round and sort out my personal property with him. I went, and while we opened the parcels containing old clothing, he did something that to him was so natural but to me was something that had never been done before. He turned to me and handed me a pair of scissors and asked me to cut open some of them. He then went about his business. I was absolutely stunned. That was the first thing that made me begin to feel human again. It was the completely natural way that it was done. This simple gesture made me think. In my other world, the penal system in general, such a thing would never happen.

With the abolition of capital punishment, the Scottish Prison Officers' Association expressed concern about the vulnerability of its members particularly with regard to those of us serving life sentences who were being violent. A Working Party was set up and they took oral evidence from officials in the Prison Service and senior medical officers throughout Britain. The recommendations of the Working Party were accepted by the Secretary of State and it was decided to provide a Unit as quickly as possible, and after looking into one or two locations it was decided that the former woman's wing of Barlinnie Prison should be adapted for this purpose. It was obvious to everyone within the system that Inverness, even with its cages and strong disciplinarian regime, was an absolute failure and as the level of trouble there was much higher than in other prisons, it seemed there was nothing else they could do for virtually everything had been tried.

But here I was now in this other extreme – the Special Unit – and my first afternoon and evening in the place were confusing and utterly bewildering. In order to survive the cages I had had to use "craziness" as a defence mechanism and it had become so much a part of me that I now felt very much like a crazy animal in this new atmosphere. The one thing that struck me immediately was that I was able to walk more than ten paces without screws standing at my side, but although I knew I could do this I felt too uncomfortable. I kept waiting for the hands to come down on my shoulder and push me into a cage. I was conscious of the fact that I wasn't acting or feeling normal and at times felt that the people moving around me were very frightened as they too recognised this crazy animal part that was dominant in me. I felt so much alone. I didn't feel at ease with people moving around and occasionally speaking to me, or with having so much space to move in and I couldn't understand it when two of the prisoners who had come from relaxed prisons showed anger at the claustrophobic atmosphere of the place.

I try to recall standing there that day watching the movements of everyone and one screw coming to me with a cup of coffee and asking how I was feeling and me so bound up and watchful not answering him, just asking myself, what the fuck is this place? That evening a screw came in wearing civvies and took me into a small room and gave me the usual line of patter. Instead of stopping there he went on to talk about the philosophy of the Unit as he would like to see it. His name was Ken Murray. I sat listening to what he had to say but remained silent. What he was saying was fine and along the right lines but as far as I was concerned he was just another lying bastard who was looking for a quiet time while he tightened the screw on me. There was no danger of me falling for the load of crap that he was spouting.

That night I was locked in my cell at 9 p.m. along with all the others. The cells had prison furniture: a locker, a chair, a mirror nailed to the wall, and a chamber pot with a lid on it. The bed had a mattress and a pillow and these were all very novel to me. The first thing I did was to throw the mattress off the bed and lie on the hard board with a blanket, staring at the ceiling. I had my transistor but couldn't play it. My inner self was in a turmoil and though I was terribly weary through lack of sleep my mind was so active I couldn't sleep. I kept waiting for loud banging on the cell door. I lay there hating myself for taking the cup of coffee from the screw, and reprimanding myself for being so weak in even acknowledging them. I thought I was an idiot for letting their tactics get me into such a state. Some of what Ken Murray had said was going round in my head but even if every word of it had been true, it was no good. "It's too late, far too late. My life is finished. Don't give in, Jimmy, don't give in. . . ." I didn't sleep one wink all that night.

The following morning I was on my feet when I heard them coming to open the doors at six o'clock. One thing that I noticed about myself, both in the extremity of the cages and on this first day or so in the unit, was that my senses were "heightened". I could actually smell people, especially the leather from their boots or shoes, from a good distance away. When I ran my fingers over the rough walls of the cell or over the skin on my face it felt different somehow. I could also hear sounds from a great distance, but I am digressing. Like other "A" category prisoners in normal prisons, I had to strip off my clothes and leave them outside the door the night before, so when the door opened I pulled them in, dressed (this was a luxury as clothes hadn't been allowed in Inverness) and went along to the toilet archway to wash and shave with a razor. I was allowed to open it and change the blade myself. After that sleepless night and endless thinking, I found myself mentally much more settled and more able to face the day.

The unit is an "L" shaped building with a small hall area, where the cells are. There are two floors in this part, with five cells on the second floor and five on the first. There is a small kitchen, with a cooker for making tea and coffee, and some sinks. There is an area just large enough to accommodate a small billiard table, and a small television room, then a governor's room and staff room and the psychiatrist's room. We were free to move about these areas when they were opened up. We could make tea or coffee whenever we wanted, or go into a small workshop on the second floor where the cells were. This was a joinery store but as yet it was empty. One of the ten cells had a double door and was to be used as a punishment cell, if necessary.

There were five of us in the place. Ben, Larry and I kept very much to ourselves. The other two guys, Rab and Ian, I didn't know. They had come from more relaxed prisons than Inverness and they were the ones who found the place very small and claustrophobic, whereas the three of us felt it to be very big. That first morning I felt better able to speak with Ben and Larry, but we were terrified of bugging devices and so would lean into the other's ear to speak or would get into a huddle with all our heads touching and whisper. Whenever a screw came we would jump up straight and be silent till he passed us by. I put them in the picture about my spell in the cages alone but it had been so long since I had held any conversation with anyone that my vocal chords became painful when I spoke for any length of time. Ben and Larry told me that the screws would come round and try to talk to us. They said the only time we would get any peace was at meal times, as they always left us alone to eat. We told each other to watch the bastards; this was just a move to get information out of us.

As there was no work I just stood about all day. I felt very guilty about this and it also bothered me that if I used the toilet no one would follow me. Larry and I had the Inverness trial to attend, so we spoke in whispers to each other about it. We had someone to watch out for the screws while we searched our cells for listening devices. We would come up with endless permutations as to what the game was. A screw would mention something completely innocent and we would pounce on it later when alone, dissect it and interpret it in all sorts of different ways. Each morning, after a hard night's thinking, Larry, Ben and I would meet and discuss our latest theories fantasised the night before. The whole day was ours to spend as we pleased. I could if I wanted go up to my cell and sit there away from everything and everyone. Having this time on my hands in solitary was one thing, but having it to walk freely about the place was another, and I felt utterly lost.

But being able to speak freely to one another, to see and to touch one another, was tremendous. Just being with other guys was so good for me that this alone eventually reduced the overpowering feeling of helplessness that had existed in Inverness. I hated the screws, police and the whole system so much; basically these were the topics that dominated our conversations. The unit had no electronic devices either in the locking-up system or elsewhere. In fact it was just another small prison – structurally. The screws wore white coats to distinguish them from the screws on the outside. Apparently before the unit started they had discussed civilian clothing but had decided against it, opting for the white medical coats that gave them a hospital look and went a long way to confirming my thoughts that the unit was a halfway house to the State Hospital. All the staff had volunteered for the unit and had gone on a six-week course to places like Broadmoor, Grendon Prison in England, and Carstairs State Hospital in Scotland. I had no doubt that the unit was psychiatrically orientated – I sussed this out the minute I walked in the door. Also, some of the staff had been involved in attacking prisoners in other prisons. We knew this, so to us at this stage it was the same old game of "conning" us. One screw took me aside and said in a sympathetic manner that he realised that I had had a lot of "stick" in my day but that was all finished now. They didn't use the stick here but an injection instead, to drug us if we caused any scenes. I'm sure he thought he was being very considerate and understanding but inside I was using what he had said to reinforce all my fears that they were intent on drugging us at the first chance.

I was told that there would be a staff/inmate meeting every Tuesday and at these meetings I could raise any subject I wanted to. If I had any complaint about the place or staff then I could voice it here. I could also express myself strongly in a verbal way during these meetings so long as I didn't carry the aggression out of the room and keep it up afterwards. A complete load of balls thought I, and when speaking to the others about it we would laugh our heads off, knowing that the screws thought we were nutcases. The day following the meeting, the staff would have a meeting of their own. This confirmed all my suspicions. Any meeting that they had as a group was to talk about us, and it was obvious to me that they would put a false face on during the meeting with us on the Tuesday and express their real feelings at their own meeting the following day. The general idea of the place, I was told, was to create better relationships between staff and prisoners, therefore it was a unit geared towards experimentation that would be used to improve the general penal system.

That first day the screws came over and tried to talk away as normally as possible but the whole atmosphere was extremely difficult as we were two factions – enemies – and the hostility was stark between us. I felt very strange just standing there. We were told that the day was our own to structure, so Larry went into the T. V. room and turned on the television. One of the screws came in and made a scene so this caused the first confrontation, ending with the screw admitting he was wrong as he was acting as he would in the main prison. The Governor was someone whom all of us had known. He had the nickname in other prisons of Dr No, as he always said no to anything that anyone ever asked for, even if it was only a pencil. Here in the unit he was quite different and said we could call him and the staff by their first names.

On the prisoners' side there was Rab, who had come in as a boy of fifteen to serve the sentence of Her Majesty's Pleasure. He had come from Scotland's model prison in Edinburgh, Saughton. He had been in thirteen years and was sent to the unit for causing slight management problems there. Then there was Ian, a guy with deep personal problems who was in for Life for the murder of his girlfriend after a suicide pact that had gone wrong. He had done five years of his sentence and had been sent here as being potentially violent while at Perth, which was a training prison. These guys had only heard of Ben, Larry and I, so they felt thrown into the deep end as they knew us by reputation, as did the screws, and realised that any trouble that we were involved in was likely to be very heavy.

Larry and I were considered the hopeless cases as we had these very long sentences on top of our Lifers and were now awaiting a High Court trial for six attempted murders of the Inverness screws in the riot. I had no future, so what the fuck did I want to get to know screws for? Ben was doing a seven-year sentence and had lost all his remission but at least he had a date, and was our "star" witness for the Inverness trial. This forthcoming trial was on all our minds and made any talk of building anything in the unit very difficult. Although Larry and I would discuss it in depth, we realised that there was nothing ahead anyway so it didn't really matter. The great thing about being in this sort of situation is that nothing really matters. I felt that most likely I would get anything up to twenty years on top, but it seemed irrelevant. I knew that the screws in the Special Unit had this fear in their minds that Larry and I would react violently to the sentences if they were very long. They didn't realise that once you have reached a certain depth you can go no lower.

Two days after my arrival in the unit my brother Harry, his wife and my two children came to visit me. The visiting room was the one we used for the weekly meetings and so they were able to sit down at a small table in comfortable chairs; but most important of all, we were able to touch. One of the staff sat in the background, making a genuine effort to keep well away. It was a terribly moving experience for me. How can I express what it felt like to touch my kids after a six-year absence? To sit beside my family without a physical barrier between us? To realise that all I had to do was reach out a hand and touch one of my own? In the other prisons the visiting conditions had been nine hours a year, with wire and glass barriers dividing us from the visitor, and screws standing behind listening to every word. I wasn't at ease during the visit; in fact I was terribly apprehensive for numerous reasons, most of all because I knew that I had become something of a stranger to my family due to what had gone on within me and because of the physical restrictions imposed on us as a family by my imprisonment.

The visit was to last two hours and I didn't think that I could sit with them that long. When I saw my son and daughter I was scared to attempt to give them a cuddle and kiss as I was afraid of being rejected by them, yet I wanted so much to grab them in my arms. I just didn't know what to do and both of the kids were very shy indeed. Those past few years I had tried to blank them from my mind in order to survive. I had lived too long as an animal try-ing to bury this part of my life and here I was confronted with it in the flesh; confronted by people that I deeply loved, yet whom I had tried to cast out of my thoughts because the thought of never being with them again was too painful to think about. I could see in my brother's and his wife's eyes concern for me as I was thin and a deathly grey colour. The air of detachment that I felt must have been frightening to them. I said earlier that people in Glasgow, or Scotland for that matter, very seldom express themselves to their nearest and dearest by physical embrace, but it was something that I longed for now and felt was very important after what I had come through. At the end of the visit I did embrace them all after drinking them in with my eyes like a thirsty man.

That night I lay in torment thinking about the visit. I was in a quandary. I was in a terrible state of mind as I had a tremendous amount of suspicions about the unit and everything in it, but in conflict with these thoughts was something that meant so much to me – my family. That day's visit had hit me so powerfully that I was now in a state of total confusion. My whole way of thinking was so dominated with the past experiences that it was impossible for me to think rationally about anything, but I knew what I wanted, and that was to be near my family. I felt a certain amount of comfort and ease being back in the Glasgow district. I was home. This night of tormented thinking didn't bring me any answers but I did see my family and even if that was all the unit had to offer, it was what I wanted most of all.

In the days following I had visits from other members of my family that I had not seen for over six years and it was very moving. My Aunt Peggy would organise and bring up other aunts and we would have emotional hours together. They would cry over the loss of my ma as it was the first time they had a chance to tell me about it, though it was now eighteen months ago. My cousin Margaret, who is almost a sister, would come regularly. These were the people on the outside who were bringing me alive again. They were piercing the barriers that I had put up to protect myself. I had tried to eradicate them from my mind but it was impossible and being with them proved this, as the emotion pouring from me on these visits was something special. I needed to touch them, as though to assure myself of their presence. They brought the children as well, as if knowing they were the key to bringing me back to being the Jimmy they knew.

Work was thought up for us and it took the form of painting the unit walls as they were the usual institutional battleship grey and so some fancy colours were made available to us. This was revolutionary, as was the fact that some of the staff joined in by helping us, or making the tea and coffee while we worked. It was our first collective effort and though it started and ended in a strained manner, we did it together. Tools were supposed to be coming for a small joiner's shop but we were told they were held up in the "pipeline" due to administrative reasons. Naturally I thought this was just an excuse, but I was proved wrong. A few days after my arrival, one of the staff, who was a joiner by trade, brought in a box of tools for us to use. While I was working with him I wanted to use the chisel to work on a piece of wood. I remember being very self-conscious about the way I lifted it so as not to raise his suspicions in case he thought I was going to harm him with it. This was the state of mind I was now in after living in the plastic world of Inverness. It was as though I had to relearn how to be at ease and to live again alongside other people. I had been so used to living in a world of deceit and enmity that it was difficult to have an innocent conversation with a member of staff without trying to find hidden meanings.

It was strange during this period because there was a great amount of hatred in me for all screws, yet some of the unit staff would approach me in a way that was so natural and innocent it made it difficult to tell them to fuck off. Something inside me, in spite of all the pent-up hatred, would tell me that there was something genuine within them. I knew I didn't really want to recognise this part of the screws. I preferred to see them all as bastards; this would have been so much easier for me. There were one or two of them even at that very early stage coming across as very genuine: in particular, Ken Murray. He is a political animal and was on the Executive Committee of the SPOA and had a part to play in the setting up of the unit. He was committed to improving the role of the Prison Service, and in doing so wanted to improve conditions for prisoners in a very realistic way. As full of hatred as I was, it was very difficult to reject any conversation with a person like this. It was the staff like him in the unit who gave me the moments of conflict and inner turmoil, as they were so unlike the screws that I had known in the past. At nights I would lie in my bed tearing my guts out, thinking intensely about this place and what it was all about, and often wishing I were back in solitary.

At that first Tuesday staff/inmate meeting I sat and weighed the whole thing up. I could see that Larry totally rejected the staff, calling them a load of codswallop. Ben, like me, would sit and watch the faces of the screws, seeing those who were uncomfortable in the meeting and those who were natural and at ease. The three of us would occasionally look at each other and burst out laughing at this silly game of men all sitting around feeling self-conscious and stupid. But it is true to say that even at that first meeting, I realised the potential and did make a statement to that effect. Minutes were taken at every meeting and a Chairman was elected. The process was a democratic one with each person given an equal vote, from the Governor down.

It was at these meetings that we were to put forward any ideas we had to improve the unit and help to make the rules for running the place. Any proposals we put could be adopted there and then. If it was a tricky one the staff would use the stalling technique by saying they would discuss it at their staff meeting the following day. This sort of crap we just didn't go for and we made this clear to them; however, it seemed it would have to be. The meetings would be the testing ground between us and the staff and so we would ask for more materialistic things, such as tools to work with, and weightlifting equipment, etc., etc. The other two prisoners, Ian and Rab, would sit and say nothing as the whole experience seemed to be overwhelming for them. If one of us had a go at one of the staff then the rest of us would support him all the way, conversely most of the staff would back each other all the way so the "them and us" situation continued. These early meetings consisted mainly of petty bickering and sniping at each other. Sometimes they would be flat with nothing said, but such meetings were rare.

The Prisons Department officials played a prominent role in the place, and the Controller of Scottish Prisons, Mr Alex Stephens, would come in frequently to see how the place was going. His position was pretty powerful within the Prison Service and he was probably the man most responsible for getting the place off the ground. Everyone looked on the unit as being his "baby". He was quite different from anyone I had met on the prison side; he was a creative and intelligent person. The fact that he came down and showed interest was very important as others in the department also came down, following their boss's example. For the first time in their lives these officials, who were responsible for the whole Scottish prison system, were coming inside and speaking to the inmates. All the time I was weighing this up: it was the first small but positive sign that let me see the Special Unit could be different from any other prison. Although I was able to see it, the difficulty lay in accepting it as my instincts were so opposed to integrating with the screws.

Apart from the unit and my personal difficulties within it, there were the wider issues to be taken into account. I dearly wanted to see much improved prison conditions and hated the thought of anyone else experiencing what I had been through. But even as I sit here typing this I know that there are still guys lying in these terrible conditions, being subjected to daily humiliations. I had the foresight to see the potential of the unit for introducing change into the penal system but I knew that it would take a long time and herein lay the problem: I hadn't got enough sense of security to make me believe that I would be here for any length of time. My previous six years had been spent mostly on the move from punishment cell to punishment cell in prison after prison, which is why I could never believe that I would be in the one place for very long. I had truly felt that the only way this could be achieved was by violent means: using violence and being on the receiving end of it; this had been the only way I could see myself working.

There was another problem that had been with me for a few years now, even while I was in my cage in Inverness. I'm sure those people who had seen me in my cage thought me a right bad bastard with no good thought in my mind. The unfortunate thing is that we mostly weigh others up and pass judgement on them from what we see physically, not by what we are told. The fact is that I often thought of the vicious circle of staying in places in the Gorbals and how I had always looked up to all the hard men in my street and district. Then the kids looked up to me and saw me as the game guy who would do anything and had done things which they saw as heroic, but never did any of us see or want to see the other side of it. And yet if only they could have seen me in that cage with no future nor even a cotton vest to cover me. There is nothing more painful than becoming "aware" of it all when it is too late. I could see all the traps that I had fallen into during my life and I felt passionately for those younger kids about to step into them. I would have given anything to stop them doing so.

I would hate this to sound as though I'm on the evangelistic trail for that is not my purpose and I don't give a shit for that side of it. I have simply been on a journey and experienced terrible pain of a physical, spiritual and emotional nature and I want to stop those of my ilk from doing the same. My feelings in this direction were heightened even more as I had children of my own and was fearful for their future. They are still in the Gorbals and in very much the same environment as I grew up in. It was bad enough thinking of kids in general but because of my own kids the issue became a personal one. I feel the situation is even more critical now than ever before as the kids are getting involved at an earlier age. It was all of these thoughts that were racing through my mind and I hasten to add they were not all of an altruistic nature, but the complexity and intensity of them were giving me a hard time. For the first time in my life I was having to think very deeply about violence and other methods of gaining status.

During this period I was full of indecision, it was a turning point in my life – I would have to decide one way or the other. At nights I would lie in my cell thinking of my family who were playing an increasingly important role in my life. I owed them something, and that could be staying and accepting the unit. They reopened all the old wounds that had been almost closed and I seemed to have no control over this as I lay trying to come to terms with it. The strange thing was that during this period I sometimes yearned for solitary confinement and the simplicity of it. On the other hand during the day-to-day running of the unit the staff were getting closer to us, especially Ken Murray, to whom I was getting quite close and beginning to respect.

Finally I decided that I had to get the fuck out of the place and so I went to the Governor and told him. I got a Petition to send to the Secretary of State and wrote to him saying I wanted to go away. I gave no reason why, as I was afraid to admit the problem: some of the screws were genuine. This would have been seen as a weakness not only to the others but to myself. I certainly had good vibes about the unit but felt it wasn't for me. The only way for me to get any peace of mind was to get out of it and return to the solitary situation as that was the method I could handle best. I knew where I stood there. This wasn't a complete denial of the unit, as part of me was screaming out for it, to accept it. Another part of me was saying that it had come too late, and regretted that it hadn't come along sooner. On hearing that I had put in for a transfer Ben and Larry did the same as they too were going through similar experiences. But at the next staff/inmate meeting, Ken Murray informed us that there was no way we would be allowed to leave the unit as the place was for us. He expressed this as a personal opinion, as did some other staff, and at no time did I, or the two others, get an answer to our Petitions.

15

On top of the normal difficulties, there was the question of the Inverness trial, which seemed to be always looming in the background. By this time we knew that the other two involved with us, Howard Wilson and Willie McPherson, were in solitary in Peterhead. Eventually, we were all served with our Indictments that charged us with attempting to escape by overpowering the prison officers and attempting to murder six of them. My lawyer had been visiting me regularly since I arrived in the unit and he now brought my Q. C.s and we discussed the defence. I knew that I was in a hopeless situation, so as far as I was concerned the emphasis of my defence shouldn't be on getting a not guilty but on bringing light to the conditions of Inverness Prison; the brutality, the cages and the treatment in general. I couldn't see any future at all for myself so I didn't see why I should bother one way or the other about acquittal when, win or lose, I would be going back to stay in conditions that would probably bring about another riot, if not for me then for someone else. If a client is concentrating on a not-guilty verdict, then he is putting a harness on his lawyer or Q. C. as caution becomes the tactic rather than exposure. I wanted the facts brought out, so the latter was the order of the day.

As the trial date approached, tension began to build up in the unit as we anticipated returning to the cages for the duration of the trial. We were very suspicious as I thought that once the trial was over we would be kept on there. Alex Stephen made the arrangement that half of the unit staff should travel with us to Inverness, which meant that they would look after us and do the escorting to the court. Some of the Inverness screws were cited for court as witnesses so they were all emotionally involved.

The day for transfer to the cages came and we all travelled in a large prison bus. On reaching the prison the hostility between us and the Inverness staff standing nearby was raw but we were quickly taken to the Segregation Unit. On entering the building a remarkable change took place, with Larry, Ben and I, all bunching together, the unit staff doing the same. Everything that had gone before in the previous months completely vanished. They became screws and we became prisoners in the traditional roles. It was as though a barrier had suddenly fallen between us. On entering the small dark corridor where the cages were, it all returned, with Ben going into his cage and slamming the barred door behind him and screaming out obscenities, and Larry curling up on the cage floor. I walked into my cage and looked around, feeling as though I had never been away. The interesting thing was the reaction of the unit screws, who stood staring in disbelief as they hadn't believed that such conditions existed in Scottish prisons. One or two of them had heard about them but hearing was one thing and seeing another. On the whole the cages were kept very quiet. The prison grapevine is usually fast and reliable but at no time did I hear about the cages till I actually woke up in one in a straitjacket.

At the short preliminary hearing the security precautions included massive police escorts with arms, and a helicopter flying overhead. I informed the judge on the bench that I didn't understand the Indictment and when questioned about this I stated that the screws had attempted to murder me and no Indictment had been given to them for that. I was told I would have to bring this up at the trial when it opened.

The trial started and the screws gave their version that we had attacked them without any provocation and tried to escape. All but one of them denied using their batons on us, and the one that admitted it said he hit one of us on the arms with it. During the cross-examination of the staff it was brought out that the Segregation Unit was to give a "short", sharp lesson to prisoners; describing the "sharp" as "Just strict supervision and a minimum of luxuries", and that we had to eat our food on the cage floor or on our knees and that we prisoners were searched daily. Included in the evidence were some very revealing exhibits: a long rope of knotted sheets, two knives about a foot long, a dry-cell battery and a radio.

At the conclusion of the Crown evidence, that of the Defence started and each of us went in. We told our side: that we had been fitted up by the staff after a peaceful demo. The jury were then spoken to by Counsel. The verdict was returned and the attempted murder charges were all dropped, but we were found guilty of assaults and attempting to escape. Each of us were sentenced to a further six years and that was the end of the trial. The sentence didn't bother me nor the others as most of us didn't feel we had a future anyway. Willie McPherson, doing twenty-six years, was the only one with a liberation date but it was so far away that he didn't think about it. We had satisfaction in that we managed to bring out the conditions of the place and highlight the brutality in the system. All of us had spoken of this while in the dock. We felt that we had achieved something.

Larry, Ben and I returned to the Special Unit in Barlinnie; Howard and Willie back to the jungle of Peterhead to face further hassles. For the first time in eighteen months I was without criminal proceedings hanging over me. With this weight off me and the idea of leaving the cages behind, combined with the satisfaction of having exposed the system a little, I felt better about the new experience of the Special Unit. I thought over my present position and figuratively speaking I had the Life sentence with the fifteen years recommended minimum, eighteen months, four years, six months, and six years, so it was very difficult to think of anything for my own future with this on my plate.

But I felt very much at ease and ready to give it a try. I could see that bit more clearly now, realising that the unit could have the potential to show that change was needed and could be made within the system. We were now speaking openly with the staff, and usually the discussions would focus on the penal system, and they admitted that there was a tremendous need for change; so that just by talking at this level we were able to see that something could be done. I began to accept Ken Murray – I was now able to see that he was genuine in a practical sense and not the usual "fanny" man who smiles to your face and sticks the boot in it the minute you're down. Before very long there was a small nucleus of staff and inmates interested in proving that we could do something. This was the purpose of the unit.

I realised that to talk about "commitment" to something is one thing, but to practise it day in and day out is another. I had lived the previous six years in a lifestyle that made me accountable to myself, but this was something new: it meant all of us had to be accountable to others as well as ourselves – Responsibility. Whenever I was in solitary I realised that a routine was essential in that spartan existence but though the unit was new, I did realise that the struggle for survival was still very much the name of the game and so I would have to get myself a routine. This meant a great deal of self-discipline, but as I needed it there was no problem.

Within the first few months we had managed to break down many of the barriers that were between us. This was a vital period as it could make or break us and the unit. Larry was still rejecting the unit and had been involved in two scenes that were on the verge of violence. He was also still getting his official dose of barbiturates. Ben's problem area was different. He had lost all of his remission and was full of hatred. He said he was going out in eighteen months and there was nothing the authorities could do about it. He didn't want to owe them anything as he had been brutalised and totally degraded in every way. At the same time he had tremendous loyalty and knew that the unit was something I was beginning to believe in, so although he was sceptical and dubious he kept going at a superficial level for my sake. There were times when he would get terribly angry and bitter about his past experiences and we would go away and talk about it. Ian was always locking himself up away from everyone. Rab was so much a victim of the system that he was a living indictment of them. But in spite of all these problem areas we were still making progress. A girl was allowed in to show us soft-toy making and this was quite revolutionary. Soon after this another woman was allowed in; she was an art therapist called Joyce Laing. Having women in was great for us and a big deal as it made us smarten ourselves up and watch our tongues, as one tends to use swear words every second word due to being in the coarse male environment.

The most important development taking place at this time was through the staff/inmate meetings. I suggested that we should do away with the punishment cell with the double door. There was a mixed reception to this as lots of the staff were very apprehensive and felt that it would leave them without a means to punish whenever something went really wrong. I was continually testing these meetings and this was why I threw it in. However, this was one issue the staff wanted to discuss at their own meeting. I pointed out to them that all of the inmates had been on solitary for different lengths of time, but the majority of us had been for a number of years. I said that this had done nothing for us or the prison we happened to be in. The presence of the punishment cell meant that sooner or later one of us was going to be taken in front of the Governor and given solitary and that would be the beginning of it. By doing this the real problem wasn't being faced. Whenever I had gone in front of the Governor of any other place he just gave me solitary and we parted, neither of us any the wiser as to how the thing happened in the first place. The unit was different as it had a group-meeting situation, therefore a means to get to the source of any problem that arose. The staff listened and took the matter to their own meeting, but it had to be carried over for a number of weeks.

Eventually they conceded and allowed the extra door to be taken from the cell. It was a tremendously symbolic gesture taking the door from the hinges, and a big cheer went up. By doing this it gave potence to the meetings and let us all see that change could be made through the group. It also meant that any problems we did have would have to be absorbed by the group meetings. Up until then we had had some minor problems to resolve when an inmate or a staff member had been particularly abusive to someone or something like that. They had to face what we now called the "hot seat". This meant that anyone doing anything anti-social would have to explain it in the staff/inmate meetings and he might well receive some very harsh words from everyone. If it was the opposite and someone needed support due to some problem, then everyone would reach out and touch him, and by that I mean help him over the bad patch. Either way the group meeting was a very powerful force. There was less closing of the ranks amongst us now though it still went on to an extent. There was less petty bickering and complaining and more straight talk, which in itself could be quite an experience. The hot seat is extremely effective as it is a system that gives everyone a say on the matter in hand. There is nothing magical about it as there are times when the guy will return the following day and be in the hot seat for the same reason as the day before. But when the pressure is put on by all present and the breakthrough is finally made then it's most rewarding.

The screws in the rest of the prison system had sighed with relief when the unit opened and took us out of their way. They could now get on with the job of doing things with the prisoners who presumably caused them less bother than we had. To get into the Special Unit the staff had to come through the gate and pass the other screws in the main prison. When they did so, remarks would be passed and hostility expressed so that coming in became an ordeal for the unit staff. The screws in the main prisons were saying that it would only last three months till we got fed up with it and then we'd have a riot. When this didn't happen they started justifying this by saying that the unit staff were giving us all we wanted and were afraid to say no to anything. The hostility from the Barlinnie staff started having an effect on the families of the unit staff as nearly all of them stayed in the prison quarters. In a way this helped to bring us closer as a group.

The unit as a whole became US and the rest of the Barlinnie staff became THEM. However, it wasn't as easy as that, because it began to affect us in a practical sense. The staff who were more vulnerable to the criticism from their Barlinnie colleagues, or who had close friends amongst them, began to show signs of cracking. These signs usually took the form of them wanting a more disciplinary regime within the unit, but they were told by the group that this was not the reason for its existence. If the person couldn't come to terms with the unit he would move out back to the main prison but this happened on very few occasions.

The predictions from the main prison staff now were that come the festive season the place would erupt, that that is the time we would feel the tension. It was almost as though they were willing it to happen in order for them to say, "We told you so". They wanted us to be animals and nothing more, to prove that the cages in Inverness were the only way. One of the other problems the unit staff had was that they were now working in a regime that had no Rule Book to shield them, which meant that they were more exposed. In the old system the prison officer is always right, but in the unit this isn't the case. They had to find things to do as their time was loose, very much in the same way as ours. Before the Special Unit opened, in the pre-planning stages the department people and the professionals involved had sat on the working party and tried to predict the problem areas when the place did open. In doing so they missed out on the one side that now seemed to pose most of the problems – staff. They never predicted the hostility from the rest of the service and the pressures this would put on the staff working in the unit. Inertia was also a problem as a good number of the staff couldn't cope with having to structure their own day, but there was a great denial of this because in most institutions the staff would do anything but admit that some of their problems were the same as that of the inmates. Just like us, the staff would show, on occasions, a tendency to revert to the traditional whenever they came up against an issue where they would be seen to be wrong.

Although I had decided to have a go in helping to get the unit off the ground, it didn't mean that all my problems were solved – far from it. Accepting responsibility was the crucial one as that entailed making decisions, having to consider others, and looking at my own life in relation to others. These were things that I had to learn as I had come from a world where decision making was taken out of my hands. If I had wanted a cup of water, the toilet, soap, etc., etc., I had had to ask for it. Now I was having to cope with not only these decisions but to think in terms of other people and it was pretty frightening. In order to be able to do this and to understand others I had to find out more about myself. This is what made the Special Unit such a tough place to live in – the fact that every single one of us had to look at himself, warts and all, probably for the first time in his life. In the general penal system one could be next door to a person for years and think that one knew him, but all one really knows is the superficial "front" that that person wanted one to know. I had known Ben and Larry off and on for fifteen years in Approved School, Borstal and prisons but I was to find that they were comparative strangers to me till the point where we entered the unit. Only then was I able to get to know them in depth; and they me, I suppose. I had been in solitary in Inverness with them and it was smaller than the Special Unit, but it was the general penal system structure that existed there and this was the difference, as the unit allowed the individual to be himself. There lay the problem, as many of us, staff and inmates, began to realise we really didn't know who we were. I personally felt that the best way for me to adjust to this new way was to look on it as a rebirth; it is true to say that I was experiencing lots of things for the first time in my life.

Meanwhile the materialistic side of the unit was progressing as the mysterious "pipeline" was beginning to open up. At the meetings it was agreed that the inmates should be allowed to use metal cutlery. Until now we had been using plastic and when we were eating we would take our food in a bowl and a spoon and stand around talking to each other as we ate. One day, about six months after the unit had been going, one of the staff approached us and asked why we didn't set a table out and eat at it. My thoughts were that this was rather silly as I always ate standing up or sitting on the floor. However, he persisted and the truth was that I felt embarrassed as it had been so long since I had sat at a table and eaten a meal with others. I can remember when the first table was set I sat there feeling very self-conscious and I lifted the plate off the table onto my lap and ate it there. I had never been consciously aware of losing the ability to sit at a table to eat and it was only when confronted with it again that I was able to think about it and the very subtle way that we do become institutionalised.

It was at this time that we asked for our rations to be sent down from the main prison uncooked, so that we could prepare them for ourselves and present the food in a more tasteful way. It was a struggle, but they came round to the idea. We were still wearing the old prison uniform and so we asked for the use of our own clothing. This too was finally accepted after lots of talk and fears that it may present a security problem. When we were allowed to wear them it seemed very strange but it was nice to wear denims and casual gear. Our visitors were now allowed to bring food up so that we could eat during the visit and it was good to eat things like well-fired bread rolls, "burnt rolls" and other things that we hadn't eaten for years. It was only having experienced things like this that people on the outside see as insignificant that I was able to see that these are amongst the things that make one feel alienated.

By now I was making my own daily routine and playing a principal part in the day-to-day running of the unit. I was still doing my physical exercises, still sleeping on my hard board, and I was also doing educational courses for mental stimulation. The courses were General and Social Psychology, so that between all of this I was keeping myself very busy. Some of the staff were still resisting progress within the unit and I kept looking at this in a very subjective way, little realising the pressures they were under from their colleagues on the outside. I did know about some of the hostility from outside but was uncompromising and felt that they should have had the strength to resist it.

On the other end of the scale Ben was having serious problems and wanted out of the unit back to the old penal system. He felt he would be safer as he recognised the enemy there. Lots of us tried to work on him to get him away from this way of thinking but eventually we had to accept his wish and so after eleven months he was transferred to Saughton Prison in Edinburgh. He found the fact of being confronted by himself and having to accept the staff in the unit too much. Although he recognised it wasn't for him, he had respect for what it was doing and would never have done anything in a physical sense to damage it. He was in the prison system only weeks when he was sent back to solitary and into the way that he knew best. I was allowed to write to him, but once he got into trouble they refused to let him get in touch with me.

There is a great deal of honesty in the unit, as people are encouraged to say what they think and express themselves freely, which meant I was able to debate and criticise the penal system in a rational way with staff. There was something good about being able to discuss the earlier incidents and frustrations with the people whom I felt in many ways had been responsible. These discussions took place sometimes in the presence of the Home and Health Department officials and the mere fact that such a group could sit and discuss it was revolutionary. This direct link with the Department and the fact that the Controller, Alex Stephen, was coming down and playing an active part in meeting us and getting to know how we were developing, was very important to our survival. The then Under Secretary of State, Alick Buchanan-Smith, came to see us and it must be said that he felt the Special Unit was the model for the penal system of the future. He left us in no doubt that we had his support and he stood by this after he had gone as he was keeping a watchful eye on our progress. This sort of encouragement from the "top" was what we needed. It gave us the impetus to carry on as a group and acted as a balance to the hostility from the Prison Service staff.

In the first few months on recognising the close proximity and claustrophobic atmosphere the majority were experiencing, we felt that outside visitors should be invited in. There was also the fact that initially this was thought to be a safeguard as all of us, staff and inmates, were very suspicious of each other and so to make sure that all of us had to be straight, we thought that inviting out-siders in would act as a sort of balance. I was delighted at this as it helped all of us who were insecure about the future of the place. In the beginning it started with the two women and from there other people came to give us lectures on various subjects. Whenever one of these people came in, we would show them round the unit. We wanted this to be unlike other institutions, so an inmate was usually the one to take them round and that would usually be my task as the others were still very suspicious of it all. By now our individual cells were wallpapered, unlike those in other prisons. Whenever I took the visitors around I'd always remind them that other prisoners were staying three to this space that I had to myself and I would let them know about the conditions in long-term prisons. I wasn't being sneaky about it or anything; this was the consensus of opinion within the unit anyway. I felt duty-bound to remind people not to get carried away or complacent because the unit was a good thing. Certainly it was, but conditions elsewhere had to be remembered. I reminded them that if shown around the main penal system, they wouldn't be allowed to speak to prisoners and would get the "guided tour" treatment. It was important for me to explain these things to the people coming in as I couldn't forget what I had gone through and what others were now going through at the moment. I elected myself spokesman for everyone living under these conditions.

Being confronted with this sort of honesty certainly affected visitors and before long we found many of them coming back to see us. As time went on they grew in number and variety. We were pleased with this as all of us were proud of what we were building and felt we had nothing to hide. We believed that people should come into the penal system and get to know what it was all about and play a part in helping to improve it. By doing so they were better able to understand an ever-increasing problem in society. There was so much to gain for us all that we went out of our way to encourage them to come in.

Joyce Laing, the art therapist, was coming in from time to time and though we were very wary of art and the therapy bit, we liked her coming as she was a pretty good-looking bird. So we had to compromise and pretend to have an interest in art in order to keep her coming back. One day she brought in a 7lb bag of clay for us to mess around with and the five of us sat there humouring her and having a good laugh till such time as she had to leave. Although I had been joking along with the others I felt as though I had an affinity with the clay, almost as though I had known it before. That may sound like a cliché but it's what I felt and I did mention it to one of the others. When Joyce left, the clay was abandoned by the others but I kept on with it. The day was hot and we sat in the prison yard and I sat messing around with the material, doing a portrait of one of the guys. I liked it and that was what mattered. Then I did another straight off, without a model, and this pleased me. I felt excited, as did some of the others when they saw them. I made arrangements to get hold of more clay and I did some more pieces, so that when Joyce returned a couple of weeks later she was surprised to see the results. I felt great pleasure in creating the sculptures and knew that I had stumbled onto something within myself.

It was tremendously exciting to discover this latent talent, especially in art as this had been poofy stuff to me in the past. The nearest I had ever been to an art gallery was when we found a way of stealing empty bomb shells from the museum part of Kelvingrove Art Gallery and Museum. I soon got one or two books on sculpting techniques and read them while I worked, learning how to cast pieces of sculpture and the basic tools that were needed. I knew nothing whatsoever about it and Joyce herself knew very little, but this suited me fine as I personally felt it was all to do with this rebirth thing. I began to pour all my energies into this new means of expression and was knocked out by my depth of feeling when I completed a piece of sculpture. The only thing I could compare it to was when I'd won a victory when fighting in the past, or beating the system in some way. The difference was that I was using the energy, knowing I was just as aggressive, but creating an object that was a physical symbol, yet perfectly acceptable to society. I worked at a prolific rate with most of the work based on the expressions of my soul with pain/anger/hate/love/despair and fears embodied in it. This was very important for me as a person because it allowed me to retain all these very deep emotional feelings but also to channel them in another way – sculpture.

Meanwhile, I was still giving thought to the past and the life I had lived. All the older guys that I had looked up to when I was a kid were either dead, alcoholics or serving long prison sentences. The Gorbals had changed physically with all the new buildings and different people moving in and out but the problems were still very much the same and possibly worse. Parts of me had changed and for the first time in my life I was thinking not as a victim but as a person who had been responsible for doing things that I shouldn't have. I qualify this by pointing out that whenever I was sentenced in the past for something and came into prison, the humiliation and degradation I met with there made me think of myself as the victim. I hadn't given a shit for the person or deed I was in for, or had any sympathy, as I had been too concerned with my own miseries and misfortunes. The reason for this was that the unit was allowing me to function responsibly and in order to achieve this one had to think responsibly. As a person I was growing and developing, seeing things through new eyes, and a clear mind. The visitors coming into the unit played a big part in my becoming more socially aware, and my relationships with the unit staff were still strengthening.

By now the staff/inmate meetings were becoming something special and we dropped the old institutional tag and replaced it with Community Meetings. We had by now decided to stop censoring incoming and outgoing mail and our family visits were unsupervised. I was helping to make decisions that I would have to live by. If anyone abused the rules of the Community then they would have to be answerable to the Community. Punishment wasn't a physical thing, i.e. locked in solitary, or being beaten up. The hot seat became the ultimate weapon and this was very effective. The key to the whole thing lies in the relationships of the people within the group, and the understanding that no one person is bigger than the Community, that the commitment is to the Community and not the individual. Before experiencing this I could never have believed it, but it's true and it works. I've experienced all sorts of punishments in my life and all have been very easy in comparison with the Community hot seat. The idea of having done something that will have an effect on your friends and then having to face those friends and explain your behaviour is very heavy, especially when you have to work and live alongside them immediately afterwards still feeling as guilty as hell within yourself. There are some people that I will never get on with in my life but will still have to live with in a fashion that is tolerable to both of us. Violence is no longer my means of communication. I was becoming articulate and learning how to use it effectively. It was a whole new ball game. Small parts within me were blossoming and I was experiencing the glory of being alive. Things looked and felt differently and in a way I was gaining a form of freedom. This was freedom of the mind, a sense of awareness and the pain that goes with it. The sculpture took on a vital importance, not only in the sense that it was a medium to channel all my aggressions but a medium in which to build up and repair the damage to my inner self. I was developing with each piece and the work that I was creating was a very strong symbolic statement relevant to my past. I was purging myself of the past. I was interested in trying things with the sculpture that I would never have attempted before. I was fully aware that the barriers I was breaking through were significant. Through all these experiences I was able to see that prison staff whom I once hated were very similar to the prisoners they look after in that they too are very much victims of the system.

Rab, one of the inmates who had an alcoholic problem at fifteen years of age and had killed a kid in a drunken stupor, had been sentenced to Her Majesty's pleasure and had spent the first thirteen years of his sentence in the rigid structure of the main penal system. As he had missed all his adolescent years and his experience of being a kid at that age, he came to the unit very immature and faced tremendous problems as he developed. In the early days he would run into his cell and slam his door shut in a petulant manner. He made many mistakes along the way. The unit system was flexible in that it allowed for these inevitable mistakes. They would be discussed, sometimes at a rational level, other times not, as we too were learning and therefore could at times be very intolerant. Despite that, the problems were discussed as well as the successes.

Three years later, Rab, still in the unit, was in the position of a lodger. He matured to an extent that if the unit is to be measured as a success, then it has to be through the development of Rab. He had a full-time job and went every day to work outside. The people that he worked for have offered him full-time employment on release. He is now a very stable character who has been shown to be responsible during the year that he worked. He has built up relationships and made friends with people on the outside. Rab has been given his liberation date and told that a year from now he will be released. This is a tremendous boost to the Community within the unit. The unfortunate side to it is that Rab has had to go to an ordinary prison to finish his sentence. His visiting situation is that of an ordinary prisoner, where the glass and wire barrier separates him from them. After nine months to a year he will be allowed to get a job under the normal Training for Freedom scheme. He will be put through all of this to get to the stage which he has already reached. The Special Unit still has a lot of new ground to break.

When Ben left for another prison he was replaced by some- one else, and by this time some new staff had come in. The ones prone to the authoritarian line had moved on into what they felt were safer settings for them. Up to this point all of us had entered the unit more or less at the same time, so with the new inmates and staff we could gauge our progress. It was quite an experience for the new inmate to see me talking away and drinking coffee with staff. Afterwards one of them told me he thought they were drugging me. We had made tremendous progress and all of us knew this. I was often asked what other prisoners thought of us in the unit, and of the unit. I kept my ear to the ground and had a good idea of the feelings on the subject. It seemed to me that most of them liked the idea and felt it offered some hope for the future. Most of them knew that those of us in the unit weren't building castles for ourselves but were aiming at changing the whole decadent system. This is the only place that I know of that is offering any realistic hope for guys serving long sentences, or short ones for that matter.

Just over a year after it opened the Prisons Department asked the Community what they thought of an open day for the press. We thought this a good idea and so members of the Scottish Information Office (SIO) came along to speak to us and told us that the National press would be invited in and a date was fixed. They came in very much like other visitors and we took them round, with an SIO man trailing behind with his ear practically placed in my mouth, but after a while he left us alone. For the first time in British history the press had been allowed to sit down in a prison with staff, Prisons Department people and prisoners and have a straight talk. The SIO were in a state of near hysteria at some of the things we were saying and I was to see that there was tremendous paranoia on the official side about the press. But the Prisons Department had achieved a tremendous breakthrough in penology at a time when Attica, Parkhufst, Inverness and the Italian riots were fresh in everyone's minds. It was a bold step indeed to open and allow such a place to develop immediately after a riot, as the usual step is higher walls, more guards, more locks and other expensive security gadgets. The fact that the Special Unit was happening in the west of Scotland, where more people are being imprisoned than anywhere else in Europe, was in many ways a miracle as it is so paradoxical to the Scottish way of thinking. Scotland, with all its provincial attitudes, was for the first time leading the world by taking a bold and imaginative step in the field of penology. A friend of mine described the unit thus: "A lily in a turnip field". The press came in to see us, except for *The Scotsman*, who refused to come in under the terms that they submit their article to the SIO before publication. The others, after submitting their articles, published them and supported us tremendously. During this period I was sure that from here on we could make tremendous progress by expanding the unit's philosophy into the penal system, as all the encouragement for the Prisons Department seemed to be there.

I followed my strict routine every single day. It meant rising at 6 a.m. and going out to the small yard and running round in circles, like the mouse in the wheel, then going into the small weightlifting room to do some heavy training with weights, boxing and yoga, which would take me up to 8 a.m. I did exercises that kept me strong, full of stamina, and supple. This part was like a religion to me and I couldn't do without it. From here on my routine had to be flexible as my position within the Community was demanding.

I generally split my day between sculpting, doing a psychology course with the Open University, which by now I had entered, and writing. Prison is all about freedom or lack of it and the definition of this as far as I'm concerned isn't purely physical: it is also a state of mind. Being in prison usually means that one is left with the enormous problem of having to cope with time and keep out the boredom, so in many ways I was reversing the process which meant that instead of too much time on my hands I found too few hours in a day to allow me to get all the work done that I wanted. There were times when I was getting three or four hours' sleep a night. The fight for survival is just the same and I am determined not to vegetate or succumb to the pressures of being imprisoned. Living in this environment where one determines one's own daily routine it is simple to opt for the soft and easy like so many on the outside, but the stark reality of the past is so vivid that apathy has no place in my life.

The sculpture was playing the most prominent part in my life and was gathering interest from art circles. I had by this time thirty pieces and so Joyce Laing introduced a Mr Richard Demarco to me. He is the Director of the Richard Demarco Gallery and on seeing my work he offered me a place in his gallery to exhibit during the Edinburgh Festival. Naturally I was delighted as this was the first outside agency to have had any contact with me. Richard Demarco and I discussed the philosophy of the unit and his gallery and we found that we were working along similar lines as he was trying to open the art world to society and take it away from its elitist position. I was drawn to this idealistic principle as I was aware through my own experience of how taboo art is to those in my environment, and how barely a year ago I thought it was for "others" and not for me. I felt that I had something to offer in this direction as I realised the significance of my being labelled "Scotland's Most Violent Man" in the negative sense and turning this into the positive sense of my being a creative person. I do not remember this ever happening with any of the older criminals.

There was no dramatic change in me as basically I am still the same guy who was locked up in a cage. It's just that I am now capable of channelling all the energy and aggressions. Having said that, I am realistic enough to know that if I were thrown back into the jungle of the ordinary prison system, although I would go to great lengths to avoid violence, it's the law of the jungle there and the survival instinct is strong in me; it's not like being outside where one can walk away from it. Thinking of my past experience, the Community talked about my going to Borstal to get something going with the kids there to try to help in that area.

During these discussions it was suggested that I could also speak to prison staff at their Training College and I agreed to do this but only if I could have complete freedom to talk in a constructively critical way, if necessary. The Prisons Department people who were present agreed to this and left the matter up to the Unit Governor and the person in charge of the Borstal and Training College to arrange the details. I had made it clear to all concerned that I wasn't doing this in an evangelistic sense but in a realistic one as I felt the only way to get anywhere was to cut the crap and hypocrisy. I feel that if one can get to the level of basic honesty and straight talk with groups like prison staff, or cops for that matter, then things can grow in a positive way from there. Not like the police liaison, or community officer, or priest, or minister, who churn out complete rubbish, saying for example that the police don't do this or that, or that good and evil are anything from masturbation to always showing respect to your elders.

Around this time the Prisons Department made it clear that they would look favourably upon my being allowed out on a day parole with two escorting officers from the unit staff to visit Edinburgh and see my sculpture on exhibition. The Community discussed this and recommended it, so it was formally put to the Prisons Department, who approved. I just couldn't believe it. I had been given a date for a week hence and I lay at nights not sleeping for thinking about it. I kept thinking that they would change their minds at the last possible moment and so the days dragged on. The atmosphere within the unit was tremendous as all of us felt that we had made the first major breakthrough. Not one person in the place had any doubts or fears about my going out. When the day came, I was driven by two of the staff in one of their cars to Edinburgh and the mere fact of sitting in the back of the car alone was wonderful. The day was beautiful, with a clear blue sky and the sun shining down and all the early morning commuters making their way into Glasgow or going to Edinburgh. When we parked the car in Edinburgh, I stepped on to the street for the first time in seven years. It's not so much the seven years, but what had gone on during them. I couldn't believe it, as barely two years before I was lying in a cage with nothing, no future, nothing, yet here I was standing in a busy Edinburgh street. The whole thing was so overpowering and emotional. To feel people brush against me as they passed me by. To look at their faces. I remember stopping to look into a shop window and as I felt the glass I could see my mirrored reflection and though my face glowed, it only showed a fraction of what I felt within.

The two members of staff who were with me gave me plenty of room and didn't breathe down my neck all the time. By that I mean I could have run off at any time but the thought never entered my head. I was fascinated at the way people were taking their freedom of movement so much for granted. Out of all the things that I wanted to do, my greatest longing was to go into a shop and buy something. I went into a book shop and bought a book for Larry. Just putting my hand out to buy the book was tremendous, though I was slightly edgy about the decimalisation. I went to the Demarco Gallery, getting a tremendous welcome from the people there, and spent the day drinking in all the things that you on the outside accept without a thought. I was very much alive and walking on a cloud. The last time I had been out in Edinburgh was in a police car taking me to the appeal court when I was surrounded with a massive security guard, some of them armed, yet here I was acting responsibly a short period later. My day on parole went far beyond that of the ordinary prisoner as my whole history was against anything like this happening. All of us knew that I could have made off and nothing could have stopped me, but none of us believed this would happen. The simple basis for this belief was that we knew each other, and had built up a firm relationship over the eighteen months we had been in the unit. There was talk from our critics that we had moved "too fast too soon", but this day out was proving that we hadn't, we were sure of what we were doing.

It was obvious to me while in Edinburgh that I now had a life ahead of me. There was no way I could act irresponsibly as I was too well aware of the past and interested in investing in the future. There was this tremendous amount of responsibility placed firmly on my shoulders in that I was now in a situation where I was putting eighteen months' hard work by all of us in the unit to the ultimate test. I was concerned with helping myself and building for my own future but there was the wider issue in that I was now committed to helping the general situation on the penal and social fields. It was now that I was tasting a short spell on the outside that I realised just how committed I was to proving that people in hopeless situations like myself, who are serving very long sentences, can act responsibly and through their own experience, give something back to society. I felt that by being out I was an ambassador for the Special Unit; that I was acting on behalf of every long-term prisoner to show that change can be made; that people serving unbelievably long sentences could, if the parole system was allowed to function properly, take part in a proper re-socialising programme that would give them a realistic chance to make a future for themselves that would be acceptable to society.

I spent the day mixing with the general public. When introduced to people I wouldn't hide where I came from, as I felt it important to stress what was being done and how conditions could be improved for prisoners. I found tremendous support for the unit and what it was doing. The only near problem I had was when I entered the gallery where my sculpture was being exhibited to find a crew of BBC film men recording a show of the work and as the announcer knew me I had to hide in the toilet till they left. The reason for this was that I knew the Prisons Department abhorred publicity. Had I allowed myself to be seen by the BBC it would have been misinterpreted to look as though I was seeking publicity, and therefore it could have looked as though I was acting irresponsibly. I was also aware that if the press got hold of it then it could cause a backlash against me. It seems to be one of those paradoxical situations where in theory it is accepted that something must be done to improve the conditions of prisoners and help rehabilitate them so they become better citizens. When this is eventually tried in the only logical way possible some sections of society scream out in horror at the thought of murderers walking the streets.

One of the highlights of the day was meeting Joseph Beuys, the German sculptor, who was lecturing at the Demarco Gallery on his piece, "Documentation with a Coyote". Beuys had locked himself in a cage for some time with a coyote, one of America's most rejected animals, and after some days with the creature he learned to live with it and vice versa, though in the beginning it showed hostility towards him in a very threatening way. By doing this he proved that if we make the effort we can communicate with each other no matter how polarised. We talked and I explained to him how on many occasions I had felt very much the coyote of the human race, yet here I was by a strange coincidence standing here and speaking to him.

The glorious day came to an end and it was time for us to return to the Special Unit. All of us were filled with the success of the day as the impossible had happened. On entering the unit the others met us and questioned us about it. All of us in the Community had worked terribly hard since the beginning and realised the tremendous breakthrough that had been made this day. The place was alive. This was a positive concrete mark in its history. I had a sleepless night going over the day's events. I never thought I'd ever experience this, but more to the point I had proved to myself that my thoughts of being positive were now my deeds. I was more alive than I had ever been in my life. I was allowed out two more times in the following three weeks to visit the Festival and these two days were comparable to the first.

One morning in September, a few days after my last visit, one of the Scottish dailies reported the fact that I had been to the Edinburgh Festival on one occasion. Someone had leaked that I had been out. This shattered me as it was something I had gone to great lengths to prevent. It didn't matter who had leaked it, the fact was that it had happened. I knew that the Department dread publicity and would go on the defensive. I asked them bluntly if my paroles would now be stopped and was told they wouldn't but they said a short "cooling off" period would be better till things cooled down. The Community were against this, pointing out that the Department should be standing up and using this as an example of what they were doing not only in the Special Unit but in the penal system as a whole. We took the view that by feeding regular information and allowing more access to prisons by the media and the public the reactions which were now occurring would be reduced. The Department took the view that all the media wanted was what sold papers or raised viewing rates. We challenged the Department on their decision but at this period certain changes took place that involved the transfer of Alex Stephen, the Controller of Scottish Prisons.

The unit was now the direct responsibility of a man who was very traditional in his outlook, who had started his career as a prison officer many years ago and had worked his way through the ranks to his present position. He had come a long way and was a pioneer in his own right career-wise. There had been a change of Government some months before and the Labour Party was now in power and though we were sad to see Alick Buchanan-Smith go, all of us or most of us had more faith in the Labour Party as all our parents and friends were supporters. We finally ended up with Harry Ewing as Under Secretary, which included Prisons.

There was a complete change of thinking from the top. The first blow came in the form of refusing me permission to speak to the Borstal boys. The Scottish Prison Officers Association at the Annual Conference voted that prisoners should not be allowed to lecture to them. Understandable perhaps, but I hope that both these things will materialise in the future. The SPOA issued a statement saying that prisoners in other prisons were causing trouble to get into the Special Unit. Ken Murray, who was on the Executive Committee, disassociated himself from the statement saying it was untrue and made statements to this effect showing convincingly that what he said was true. He was removed from the SPOA executive. Shortly after this the nucleus of staff who were solidly behind the unit concept found themselves being transferred for one reason or another. Ken Murray was put on the transfer list, and all of us, outside visitors to the unit included, came together and fought this all the way. Ken appealed and won. We were fighting for our very existence and we knew it. It now became clear that I wasn't going to be allowed out on parole again. This was never said in words, but the Department were preparing us for tightening the place up, as they were saying it had got out of control, that prisoners had too much say in the running of the place.

During this very difficult period, we all went through personal crises. One morning by sheer chance I happened to look into Larry's cell: he was lying on the floor unconscious from an overdose. He was hovering between life and death. I had found him and raised the alarm and what he had done had a tremendous impact on me. I spent the day sculpting in my makeshift studio, expecting to hear any minute that he had died. We had known each other for fifteen years or so and had been through similar experiences.

Larry was born in Glasgow's Townhead district, then his parents moved out into the country and he was brought up there. I met him in St John's Approved School and Borstal, from where he had joined the army. While on leave in London he shot a barman, was convicted of manslaughter and sentenced to Life Imprisonment. He was transferred to Scotland and in Peterhead and Perth was involved in riots and convicted of stabbing prison staff, which resulted in him getting fifteen years, five years, six years and six months on top of his lifer. Larry is tall and good-looking, with shoulder-length black hair. He is extremely intelligent and over the years in the unit has become a very good poet. By now he was getting massive doses of drugs to overcome very deep depressions. He could never see himself getting released and so the drugs were an alternative way out. Over the years his tolerance level increased and with it the amount of drugs, which were seconal and nembutal barbiturates. Both of us were in similar positions but our outlooks radically differed at this point and although each of us knew this we managed to live tolerably together within this small space.

This is where one of the real problems of the penal system lies, as guys like us are being sentenced to very long terms and being kept in conditions that the general public seem to find acceptable for "criminals", although such conditions would be abhorrent to most people, even for their dogs. There was also the fact that the Parole Board and the whole parole system had become a joke to prisoners from working-class districts as they tended to select prisoners from the first-offender-type prisons. A few guys were released from the long-term prisons but just as token gestures: they would have been going out in a few weeks anyway, and it was seen as the Parole Board trying to dispel the rumours that they were discriminating, rather than as a genuine attempt to let guys see that if they wanted to change, then this facility would be there to help them. All it seemed to do was to further polarise the situation between prisoners and authorities rather than improve things. All of this was very much a part of Larry's present condition and I kept thinking of the "masked violence" of executive decision-making power that played a major part in perpetuating most of our problems. It was while working in the studio that day with all of this in my mind that

I created my first sculpture through the feeling of love. Until this period it had been motivated by feelings of anger and hatred. Later that day I was told that Larry was out of danger.

Most people, when in discussion with us, always refer to the high cost of the unit and this is an area that must be looked at. Because there is a higher ratio of staff, the cost of running the unit is higher as the wages are what makes up the bigger portion of the sum. Initially the higher ratio was justified due to our past histories and the fears that the staff had at that stage. Three out of the five of us were labelled as violent towards prison staff and there had been a Standing Order that no less than three prison officers must be present at all times when our doors were opened. With this in mind one can see that the "high cost of the unit" didn't hold much water. "A" category prisoners have a higher ratio of staff with them at all times and staff doing this duty spend their time watching prisoners. This is a far cry from the unit situation, which is giving society a great deal in return for the cash being spent. The unit was by now in the centre of an internal political struggle and we felt it was largely because of its success and the fact that it was raising some fundamental questions about the penal system.

With this traditional authoritarian attitude coming from the people now in control of the unit at Prisons Department level, a lot of the creative thought died within the place. Larry had been producing poetry and had been encouraged to write a book for publication, everything was very much in the open. Staff had been putting lots of very positive and creative ideas forward, but with this new regime many of these things were killed off. I made sculptural statements symbolising "Censorship" and "Injustice", but the main thing for me was to continue to work creatively by writing and sculpting and playing an active part in the place. By now I was writing a comprehensive daily journal of the unit and what was happening in it, the way in which it was growing and developing, the crises and the changes taking place in all of us, so this was a very sad part of what had to be documented as all of us felt that at this stage the Prisons Department were looking on us with disapproval.

We were under the microscope and had the impression that the first excuse would see our demise. Whenever we could, we would put this to the officials, who would tell us that the unit wouldn't close, but this wasn't our biggest fear. The biggest fear was that they would make life so difficult by slowly introducing more authoritarian measures, that they would effectively kill off the reason for the unit having been set up in the first place, and by putting this sort of pressure on us something would crack within. It was all very subtle but one thing was clear: the goodwill was gone from the Department and it was being turned into a "humane containment" unit. The Department people were saying one thing publicly and another internally. In spite of this we had fantastic support from the very thing that we had introduced to act as the initial balance between staff and inmates – outside visitors; people who by now had become part of the Community and who recognised the potential of the place. All of us knew that what was happening in the Special Unit had consequences wider than that of the penal system, and that some of the lessons learned here could be applicable to society in general. We had greatly expanded our policy of inviting members from the general public in, also people working in the socially deprived areas of Glasgow and the west of Scotland. We felt it was our duty to show what could be done, and is being done.

Another piece of news was giving us a considerable amount of encouragement. Ben had been released from the traditional prison and had been out for almost a year. He returned to see us and sat in at a Community Meeting and told us that a part of the unit had rubbed off on him and that he had been out of prison for the longest period of his life. He could now see its importance. Ben was particularly close to me as we had been very friendly from approved school onwards. He had come through all the institutions with me and was now a very bitter man about the treatment he had received, particularly during the last years of imprisonment. Now that he had been let out the door after seven years he felt that he owed them nothing, but his difficulties in adjusting to life on the outside were tremendous. I could feel the pressure he was under and we discussed it. The thing was that Ben had no one else to discuss them with, so it was great that he found he could come back to the unit and find some succour.

We are fortunate in that we have not had any serious problems in the first few years, although this has come as no surprise to those of us in the place. If you treat people like human beings they will act like human beings. There is no doubt that being in this line of business, crises will eventually occur; it's almost inevitable. No doubt it will give our critics a field day but by any standards we can hold our heads up. Everything has been tried from the downright brutal to the inhuman, but this is the only thing that has worked and even our critics must accept this.

During these past years I have worked tremendously hard, and am now in my third year of an Open University course. My sculpture is now in some private collections and I have had it in galleries throughout Britain. I feel I have built a strong foundation for my future in that world. I have come a long way since the days when I hated all screws and now find that I look on some of them as friends. I say this openly without fear of contradiction from guys suffering at this moment in the main penal system. The reason I say this is because the desire to change the conditions lies very deep within me. I know that to the guy lying in prison it's not so much the actual physical conditions that count but the treatment he receives from the prison staff, because within that world he is completely at the mercy of the man in control of him. Out of everything that makes up this unit, the thing that costs nothing in terms of money is staff and prisoners getting together and talking; it is the one thing that has brought about results. The emphasis is placed on seeing the individual as a person in his own right without relying on labelling or categorisation in order to identify. It is unique in the sense that two opposing factions have come together and worked towards building a Community with a remarkable degree of success. An important lesson is that no professional psychiatric or psychological experience was needed to make it so. Our basic ingredients have been some people, goodwill from all sides and with those we became the architects of a model that could be used anywhere.

As far as my past goes, I don't think that it should be forgotten about or swept under the carpet as though it doesn't exist. It does exist and is very much a part of me. My own personal experiences have taught me that mistakes made are very much a part of living. Certainly we must try to learn from them, as in this instance, and use this knowledge to let others see what can happen. I dread the thought of other kids going through my experience in order to gain the insight that I now have. Perhaps this could be used as a shortcut. What worries me in the field of human contact is that there are too many professional status seekers and not enough patients. By that I mean not enough people wanting to look at their own personal problems but quite content to diagnose the problems of others. What I have written here is not intended to be an apologetic account about what happened in my life. Certainly I have caused much suffering and have suffered, but the disease is much larger and older than me. An environment has been created that has encouraged change and that is what must be looked at.

Afterword

The Special Unit and Freedom

Fact: From the age of eleven until I received my life sentence, I had been inside institutions for all but twelve and a half months. All those years inside had taught me nothing. Up until this point I had been a dunce at school and was now a failure in life. I was aware that Barlinnie Special Unit was perceived by the prison authorities, as well as the tabloid press, to be a soft option simply because we had access to material things. Although life there was as near to normal life on the outside as possible, it didn't make imprisonment any easier. Despite everything I had come through, I can honestly say that my time in the unit was some of the hardest time I ever did.

In living the life we do as criminals, it's not just about the act of stealing or of violence – it's the mindset and lifestyle that go with it. It's a parallel universe we are immersed in, with its own slang, thought processes and behaviour, where individuals shrug off the possibility of being sent away to prison for many years. There is simply no deterrence for a great many criminals; it's a way of life. All your criminal acts are condoned by your peers. Quaintly enough, everybody inside loves a good sob story and prisons are overflowing with them. To go from what I was to who I now am was a massive shift. It was only in a place as unique as the Special Unit that such a change could take place. In order to get to where I was, I had to make great changes, hidden changes, not discernible to the human eye. My previous warped belief system that all cops, screws and authority were bastards and that we, the bad guys, were actually the good guys, ran so deep that they were truly imbedded in the way I talked, thought and acted. It has to be remembered that my fellow prisoners could be my relatives, most certainly my neighbours, so that when I went into prison they would gift me little treats such as tobacco, books, porn mags or whatever. It was similar to a working-men's club with a camaraderie echoing that. Very much a home from home.

The subtle day-to-day, free-flowing routine of the Special Unit was unknown to us at the time, gradually whittling away at our inner brick walls. For years we inmates hated prison officers and, equally, they feared and hated us. To suddenly be part of a regime where we were supposed to sit and chat to each other was incomprehensible. Some things they got badly wrong; one being that if we didn't clean our cells once a week we would be fined a shilling; two shillings if we didn't shower once a week. Contained in these rules was the ignorance and prejudice of the authorities in dealing with us. They assumed that we didn't like to wash or wanted to live in hovels. In fact, we'd have gladly showered twice a day given the chance.

Although they got some things wrong, the one thing they got absolutely right, even though we initially hated it, was the insistence that we all sit down as a community and talk things through. In those early days there would be walls of silence, and frequently some prisoners, and indeed staff, would walk out of these meetings. The thought of sitting down and talking to the enemy was anathema. The chasm of distrust between us was vast. It was, however, the acorn that was to create the oak.

Two important factors were helping us keep a tenuous grip on things. The first was that we prisoners did not want to go back to the old regime, even though we didn't know that at the time. The other was that the prison system couldn't handle us back in the old regime.

One of the principle characters amongst the staff playing their part in all this was Ken Murray, a senior prison officer who grasped the concept of the unit and its potential. He was a man of vision. We hit it off and in a sense both of us became the leading personalities in the place. Although Ken and I thought alike we were still surrounded by the old traditional attitudes that could easily explode. Nevertheless, we had to find an acceptable gel that would hold everything together, and it came from the group as a community. Together we made a decision to invite outsiders in as neutral observers.

One of the first people to come in was art therapist Joyce Laing. We were a bit wary of the therapist bit, but she did bring in art materials and just left them. One evening I worked with 7lb of clay and miraculously did a reasonable portrait of one of the guys. It was like opening a creative dam inside me. It was about the first positive thing I'd done in my life. The gushing waterfall of energy inside me was now being redirected in a positive way. I managed to get hold of an old Olivetti typewriter and began writing diaries. All through my life I had scribbled things down on scraps of paper, and doing so somehow made me feel better. Those were heady days indeed.

Initially when Joyce came in, prison staff would stand close to her imagining we would hurt or sexually assault her. This would have been abhorrent to us, totally unthinkable. Obviously they couldn't take the chance but, again, it was about how prisoners and staff perceived each other. As a result of these misperceptions we were occasionally brought to the edge of the abyss. These would always be defused through community meetings that were raw to the bone. Happily, the successful introduction of Joyce gave us the confidence to expand this experiment.

We invited members of the internationally acclaimed Citizens Theatre to visit us. Giles Havergal, the director, and David Hayman, who was later to play me in the movie of this book, were the first to come inside during opening hours. Before long, the Citizens group had become as familiar as the prison bars. They made an immense contribution to the changing atmosphere inside the place. Another visitor, Kay Carmichael, who had been in Harold Wilson's kitchen cabinet, was also very influential.

The introduction of outside visitors now seen as successful, the idea was expanded to include other groups and individuals. They could come in during the day or for two hours in the evening. Daily exposure to this sort of social exchange was, in effect, breaking up the narrow criminal mindset endemic within traditional prison regimes. In the unit, I could handle money, make my own meals, buy my own clothes, which I therefore had to budget for. I could, if I wanted, play snooker all day, watch TV or whatever. Instead, I would write, study, sculpt, create a physical fitness regime and, in general, live a productive life. In making myself socially literate everyone was benefiting. I was learning how to use my leadership skills in a positive way. Isn't that the purpose, expected by the public, of the prison system?

My interests were taking me more into the art world, something I could never previously have imagined. As well as Joyce, another art pioneer who visited us was Richard Demarco, of the Demarco Art Gallery in Edinburgh. He is one of the most remarkable people I have ever met, truly international in his vision. Richard gave me my first sculpture exhibition in 1974. By then I was carving stone and wood and casting pieces for bronze sculpture.

In 1976, I wrote *A Sense of Freedom* in six weeks, though it took a lot longer to edit. It was the most amazing time for me in terms of personal growth and discovery, and yet alongside this was the constant reminder that when the visit was over that person walked through the prison gates to freedom. In this sense, our relationships were always bittersweet. Each of us had to find our own mechanism for coping with it. I did so by throwing myself into this new way of life. Instead of reading *Scarface*, I was reading Giacometti. Richard brought along many international artists to the unit, amongst them the German artist Joseph Beuys and performance artist Marina Abramović Beuys, and I hit it off immediately, as he had just performed a piece in New York in 1974, where he was locked in a cage with a Coyote for a week. I truly identified with this, as both he and the Coyote learned to co-exist and communicate during that period. When I met him, I introduced myself as "The Coyote". In that one performance piece with an animal he was enacting what we in the Special Unit were now living. I understood immediately; I got it.

An important narrator of Beuys' work was the art critic and filmmaker Caroline Tisdall, who always accompanied him. It was as a result of this that we collaborated on a few projects together. In 1975, I created an installation titled "In Defence of the Innocent" but the prison authorities wouldn't allow me to attend the opening, so Joseph flew in from Germany especially: JB stood in for JB. One of his big ideas was the Free International University, where he invited international artists to look at society and devise or suggest alternative ways of dealing with particular issues. An example being him suggesting I should consider presenting a Paper on crime and punishment. He was a man with a huge complex personality, as all great artists must be. He was interested in human energy and how it equates with behaviour, and on this topic he created some of his famous, and most important, blackboard pieces, titled "Jimmy Boyle Days", which are currently in the Museum Abteiberg in Mönchengladbach. His curiosity was constant. My relationship and collaborations with Beuys were documented in various books of his work, written and published by Caroline Tisdall. We stayed in communication after my release through to his death in the mid-eighties. His view was that everyone is an artist. In believing this, he was trying to demystify the art world, trying to make it less elitist. He was a truly remarkable artist and human being. It was no coincidence that the meeting of minds and energy of Joseph and Richard Demarco came together, as it was a force meant to be.

It has to be said that, by associating himself with me and the special unit in such a public way, Richard Demarco and his art gallery incurred the wrath of the Scottish establishment, including the Scottish Arts Council. The whole attitude of "let's keep things as they are" or "let's not rock the boat" was so much a part of their DNA, and here was a man who was pushing back the barriers, be it in Barlinnie Prison, the Bosnian war, or for avant-garde artists anywhere else in the world. He was a creative force in a land of philistines. I'm glad to say that we have remained friends and supported each other through the years into our now twilight ages.

During this quite revolutionary period I had some girlfriends, mostly from the art world. The fact that they were meant they were very distant from my old way of life. These women thought differently, spoke differently and had a broader view of life. Trying to maintain a relationship in prison is difficult, which is natural given the circumstances. But, in a positive sense, I was engaging at a sensitive and intimate level with members of the opposite sex while in a confined space. On this matter, we ran a tight ship, as it was a taboo subject, and the tabloids and their antennae were never far away. It is a great testament to all of these women that during these years not one of them talked to the media. I was certainly very grateful for what each of them gave me in our relationships, and, indeed, many continue to do so as friends.

One such visitor was to become my future wife: Sarah Trevelyan. Prior to meeting her in late 1979, I had seen Sarah on TV discussing prisoners' rights and was impressed with her views and courage. A mutual friend had told her to come and see me. Sarah was a doctor doing psychiatry in a hospital in the Borders area of Scotland. She visited and we sort of bonded; we had a great deal in common, both in our interests and views, politically and socially. This relationship was more substantial than my previous ones. The situation, however, was problematic due to my circumstances and the fact I didn't have a release date. However, by now I was feeling positive about my future, all due to the fact that I felt I was in the land of the living rather than the land of the dead. We decided to commit to each other and got married in January 1980. Due to media interest – someone had leaked it – the event was very much a media circus. However, that's the price one pays. Nowadays, journalists quote that Sarah was my psychiatrist when we met, which was nonsense.

The Parole Board, on giving me a release date for November 1982, deemed that I be tested in the old system for what remained of my time inside. Returning to this was an experience I wasn't looking forward to but there was nothing I could do about it. It was quite clear that the hardliners in the prison department, who perceived the Special Unit as being a soft option, had won the argument. In putting me back, I would not have access to art or writing materials. There followed a public outcry, which led to Joseph Beuys and other artists trying to get the High Court in Edinburgh to reverse the decision, to no avail.

Having deemed that I return to prison proper, I was transferred to what was known as Saughton Prison, Edinburgh in early 1980.

Having known this system inside out, I was determined to use all my new inner resources to withstand the negative aspects of this regime over the next twenty months. It wouldn't be without its trials, but I just had to get on with it. My visits with Sarah would be once a month, and one letter per week. It left her rather isolated and I knew it wasn't easy being the wife of Jimmy Boyle. Not ideal encouragement for maintaining a marriage.

Another difficulty facing me on the near horizon was that the movie rights for *A Sense of Freedom* had been sold to UK television. In a way this was creative revenge, as my story and that of prison brutality and police corruption would be going into every household in the UK. I knew the prison guards would not take to it kindly, being portrayed in this light, and so I had to prepare myself for a tough time ahead. As expected, the forthcoming film generated lots of pre-publicity, and then it was shown. Next morning, the guards would open the cell doors around 6 a.m. The only reaction I got when my door was unlocked was the guard whispering, "It was brilliant", and then he hurried on. That was it, much ado about nothing.

As my time went on, I was eventually allowed to participate in a Training for Freedom scheme. I was allowed outside to work on a housing-estate project near the prison. My role was to work with borderline youths on the verge of getting involved in crime. It was an ideal situation for me and the local people were brilliant in accepting me into their community. During this period I made many lasting friends, and felt that at long last I could use all my past negative experiences to shy young people away from a life of crime. Even though I was working outside, the prison department decided that Sarah could not see me in my working environment. She had to abide by the rules and visit me in prison once a month. The absurdity of this flew in the face of everything else, and indeed provoked the local community to defy the rule and invite her along to events. This Calvinistic, grudging attitude crammed with petty restrictions from the authorities was pretty pathetic. They were afraid of success, which speaks volumes when placed against the abominable prison failure rate.

• • •

It was 6 a.m., 1st November 1982 when I stepped through the front gate to freedom, after fifteen years. It was a day that for many years I thought would never come. Now it had. It is so difficult to express how one feels on such a momentous occasion. It is something that has to be experienced to be understood. Sarah was there to meet me and we drove home for breakfast followed by a posse of journalists. Now, on this day of freedom, I knew for certain that my previous way of life was gone, finished. I left prison confident that I could build a new life for myself, and that failure was no longer a part of my vocabulary.

Sarah and I decided to set up a community project in Edinburgh. This city was beginning to see a large influx of heroin coming onto the streets. Many of the young people from the housing project I had previously worked on were now serious addicts. Our centre, the Gateway Exchange project, was voluntary in that young people could walk in from the streets, a self-referral centre. The central theme of the project was creativity. There was a sculpting and painting department, a dark room for photography, a cafe and art gallery, and eventually, the 200-seater Mandela Theatre. Sarah and I ran the centre for almost ten years and during that period it was a hive of human activity. During our years there we had two children, Suzi and Kydd. Throughout their childhood, they had the wonderful experience of mixing with all the amazing characters that came through the doorway of the Gateway.

In the early nineties HIV/AIDS became a horrendous scourge on Edinburgh as a city. Indeed, many of the young people using the Gateway, and who successfully beat addiction, suddenly found they had HIV. During those early years, HIV carried such a stigma that whenever the local government tried to open a centre to deal with the victims, local outrage would prevent them succeeding. Over the years of the Gateway's existence, we had won over the local community. As a result, we were approached by a local government representative and asked if we would make the Gateway Exchange Trust available for the treatment of HIV/AIDS. We agreed and so became the first HIV/AIDS Resource Centre in Scotland. Seeing this as a great victory for the HIV community, the downside was that many of the participants in this new centre had frequented the Gateway for years, amongst them three brothers, Graham, Slimey and Minger, in their early twenties. Sarah and I saw them through to their deaths as a result of AIDS. It was a cruel and harrowing experience.

Although Sarah and I were elected onto the board of the new centre, I wanted to take a step back from the front-line of community work, which I had been doing by then for ten years. Doing so, allowed us to focus on giving more time to Suzi and Kydd. Sarah set up a private practice counselling individuals, while I concentrated on my sculpture and written work. We retained the Gateway Exchange name and turned it into a trust fund, making cash contributions to community groups involved in self-help. In this endeavour we met some amazing people, amongst them Davy Bryce from Glasgow.

Dave's group, Calton Athletic Football Club, was probably the most successful project we ever funded. The team was made up of dozens of young ex-addicts, men and women, from the streets of Glasgow. Their collective spirit was something to behold. No one in authority would fund them as they were quite a renegade group – let's say rough around the edges. They would cram into small tenement flats to hold meetings and would set up events to raise money for football kit and gym time. Seeing their potential, we at the Gateway Trust gave them a substantial donation to rent office space big enough for meetings and, most importantly, a phone line as this was in the days before mobile phones. This office space and much-needed funds were the catalyst they craved in order to expand the already successful work they were doing. In fact they were consultants to the director Danny Boyle prior to filming Irvine Welsh's book, *Trainspotting*. Also the comedian/actor Lenny Henry, a great admirer of Davy and his team, met with them and did a TV drama based on Calton Athletics' experiences. Sadly, Davy passed away in 2011.

After twenty years of life together, in 2000 Sarah and I decided to split up. We had drifted apart; no other person was involved. I suppose it would be described by others as an amicable divorce and, given our special circumstances, I'm sure people were surprised it lasted so long. They couldn't be further from the truth;

what we had was a very deep love that those circumstances brought about. We decided to separate in a dignified manner. I would go to our house in the south of France to avoid the attention of the tabloid newspapers, as we didn't want Suzi and Kydd being troubled during what were important points in their schooling. But despite the lovely surroundings, my time there was hell. I felt an utter despair, believing that I had failed my children. Having been given this second chance in life, I had wanted what we had to be for ever. I truly didn't see it coming, and by that I don't mean to imply fault on Sarah's side. No one was to blame. We just took two different paths without realising it, until it hit us. Both of us knew that Suzi and Kydd should come first, and as responsible parents that's what happened.

My life had by now been transformed into something that I could never have imagined. Gone were the days of actively campaigning for prison and drug reform. I felt I had given many years to helping others and I guess it was my way of trying to give something back. Although it may well be the case, I didn't want my whole life to be defined as an ex-prisoner or former murderer. Instead, I now put all my time into my creative work. I published a book of my prison diaries, and wrote and published my first novel, as well as co-authoring two plays for theatre. Alongside this, I spent most of my time sculpting in my studio, exhibiting my work nationally and internationally. My work is now in many private collections. Since leaving prison ten years previously, this was the first time I was able to live my life away from the public eye and concentrate on what I was good at, my art. All of this made possible by lifting that 7lb of clay and doing something with it.

As for my murder conviction, the truth is that Babs Rooney, the man I was convicted of murdering, was killed by my co-accused, William Wilson. The whole dynamics of this sum up the world where I once lived. I kept strictly to the "no grassing" rule. I put myself away for fifteen years for the gangster badge of honour that I wasn't a grass. My co-accused was found in the flat with the dead body, covered in blood and a knife nearby. That same knife was found in my tenement flat. At our trial Nicholas Fairbairn Q. C., who defended William Wilson, turned to him and whispered,

"Think yourself lucky that the person you're in the dock with is Jimmy Boyle."

Nowadays, with the massive level of police corruption uncovered in the Hillsborough football disaster or the Stephen Lawrence case, we find it all par for the course. Back then it was unthinkable. I don't hold any anger or bitterness about this because that isn't who I am. The fact is that I was out of control and if it hadn't been this particular crime it would have been something else. In a strange sort of way, despite everything I went through, it made me who I am today: a good person who is deeply sorry for anyone I may have hurt in my life. Now, at seventy-one years old, I ask myself, what was all of that about? All that violence, theft, anger and hatred for territorial or material gain, when in fact none of us own anything. In life we are passing through, guardians of what we have, certainly not owners.

I have remarried, to Kate Fenwick, whom coincidentally I first met in 1986 when she rented the Mandela Theatre (in the old Gateway) with a group of actors from Oxford University during the Edinburgh International Festival. I hadn't seen her since then and suddenly in 1999 she appeared at a book reading I was doing at the Brighton Book Festival and the rest, as they say, is history. Kate is a wonderful partner and we've been together for fifteen magical years.

I do confess to having mixed feelings about this book being re-published, despite having given permission. In living between the south of France and Morocco I have made myself and my past "invisible" to the media for fifteen years. Please don't misinterpret this, as the truth is my past is an important part of who I now am. I suppose the most sensitive issue regarding publication relates to Suzi and Kydd, who are now adults. I do waver between have I, have I not made the right decision? I suppose my reason for giving permission to publish is my view that no lessons have been learned. If anything, things have got worse. The prison system seems to be a lost cause. No one cares. Drug intake, in my day, was not the dominant factor it is today. It is a dereliction of duty by the authorities when a prisoner's only chance of getting off drugs is when they are released. It makes no economic sense that politicians accept the failure rate of the prison system. Every single failure results in another victim in the community, as well as the cost of keeping that person in prison. Rehabilitation shouldn't be a dirty word; it should be one of civic pride. Most prisoners are looking for a way out of a lifestyle in which they feel trapped. It is only right that we should equip them with the tools to do so.

If republishing this book can, again, raise the debate on what prisons are for, then maybe, just maybe, I've made the right decision. Only time will tell.